NO LONGER PROPERTY OF
DENVER PUBLIC LIBRARY

DATE DUE

Also by John Updike

POEMS

The Carpentered Hen (1958) · *Telephone Poles* (1963) · *Midpoint* (1969) · *Tossing and Turning* (1977) · *Facing Nature* (1985)

NOVELS

The Poorhouse Fair (1959) · *Rabbit, Run* (1960) · *The Centaur* (1963) · *Of the Farm* (1965) · *Couples* (1968) · *Rabbit Redux* (1971) · *A Month of Sundays* (1975) · *Marry Me* (1976) · *The Coup* (1978) · *Rabbit Is Rich* (1981) · *The Witches of Eastwick* (1984) · *Roger's Version* (1986) · *S.* (1988) · *Rabbit at Rest* (1990) · *Memories of the Ford Administration* (1992)

SHORT STORIES

The Same Door (1959) · *Pigeon Feathers* (1962) · *Olinger Stories* (a selection, 1964) · *The Music School* (1966) · *Bech: A Book* (1970) · *Museums and Women* (1972) · *Too Far to Go* (a selection, 1979) · *Problems* (1979) · *Bech Is Back* (1982) · *Trust Me* (1987)

ESSAYS AND CRITICISM

Assorted Prose (1965) · *Picked-Up Pieces* (1975) · *Hugging the Shore* (1983) · *Just Looking* (1989) · *Odd Jobs* (1991)

PLAY

Buchanan Dying (1974)

MEMOIRS

Self-Consciousness (1989)

CHILDREN'S BOOKS

The Magic Flute (1962) · *The Ring* (1964) · *A Child's Calendar* (1965) · *Bottom's Dream* (1969)

COLLECTED POEMS

John Updike

COLLECTED
POEMS
1953-1993

Alfred A. Knopf   New York

1993

THIS IS A BORZOI BOOK
PUBLISHED BY ALFRED A. KNOPF, INC.

Copyright © 1993 by John Updike

All rights reserved under International and Pan-American Copyright Conventions. Published in the United States by Alfred A. Knopf, Inc., New York, and simultaneously in Canada by Random House of Canada Limited, Toronto. Distributed by Random House, Inc., New York.

Most of the poems in this work are from the following Alfred A. Knopf, Inc., collections: *The Carpentered Hen*, copyright © 1954, 1955, 1956, 1957, 1958, 1982 by John Updike, copyright renewed 1982 by John Updike; *Telephone Poles*, copyright © 1958, 1959, 1960, 1961, 1962, 1963 by John Updike; *Midpoint*, copyright © 1963, 1964, 1965, 1966, 1967, 1968, 1969 by John Updike; *Tossing and Turning*, copyright © 1968, 1969, 1970, 1971, 1972, 1973, 1974, 1975, 1976, 1977 by John Updike; *Facing Nature*, copyright © 1985 by John Updike.

Library of Congress Cataloging-in-Publication Data

Updike, John.
  [Poems. Selections]
  Collected poems, 1953–1993 / John Updike. — 1st ed.
    p. cm.
  Includes bibliographical references.
  ISBN 0-679-42221-8
  I. Title.
PS3571.P4A6   1993
811'.54—dc20   92-28957
                                                    CIP

Manufactured in the United States of America
First Edition

Acknowledgments

The following publications first printed certain of these poems: *Agni, The American Poetry Review, The American Scholar, American Way, Antaeus, The Atlantic Monthly, The Bennington Review, Bits, Boston Magazine, The Boston Review of the Arts, Boston University Journal, Boulevard, The Christian Century, Commonweal, The Connecticut Poetry Review, Crazy Horse, The Formalist, Grand Street, Harper's, Harvard Advocate, The Harvard Bulletin, The Harvard Lampoon, Ladies' Home Journal, Life, Look, Mānoa, Michigan Quarterly Review, Modern Poetry: East and West, The Nation, Negative Capability, New England Monthly, The New Republic, The New Yorker, New York Quarterly, The New York Times, The Ontario Review, The Oxford American, Parabola, The Paris Review, Plum, Poetry, Poetry Review, Poets and Writers Celebration Program, Polemic, Polymus, Première, Punch, Quest Magazine, River City, The Saturday Review, Scientific American, Shenandoah, South Beach, The Southern California Anthology, South Shore, Sycamore Review, Syracuse 10, The Transatlantic Review, What's New.*

And the following presses and publishers issued broadsides and limited editions of various poems: The Adams and Lowell House Printers, Albondocani Press, Bits Press, Country Squires Books, Eurographica, Frank Hallman, Halty Ferguson, Lord John Press, Mummy Mountain Press, Palaemon Press, Press-22, Rook Broadsides, Santa Susana Press, Waves Press, and Wind River Press.

for all of my families
from John Franklin Hoyer,
born in 1863,
to Wesley Doudi Githiora Updike
born in 1989

Contents

Light Verse

xix

Preface

As a boy I wanted to be a cartoonist. Light verse (and the verse that came my way was generally light) seemed a kind of cartooning with words, and through light verse I first found my way into print. The older I have grown, the less of it I have written, but the idea of verse, of poetry, has always, during forty years spent working primarily in prose, stood at my elbow, as a standing invitation to the highest kind of verbal exercise—the most satisfying, the most archaic, the most elusive of critical control. In hotel rooms and airplanes, on beaches and Sundays, at junctures of personal happiness or its opposite, poetry has comforted me with its hope of permanence, its packaging of flux.

In making this collection, I wanted to distinguish my poems from my light verse. My principle of segregation has been that a poem derives from the real (the given, the substantial) world and light verse from the man-made world of information—books, newspapers, words, signs. If a set of lines brought back to me something I actually saw or felt, it was not light verse. If it took its spark from language and stylized signifiers, it was. A number of entries wavered back and forth across the border; the distinction becomes a subjective one of tone. You will find in the light category a game of solitaire, a pair of glasses, and a shaving mirror that were all real to me. Artificial in essence, light verse usually employs the artifices of rhyme and strict form, but not always. Nor are rhyming poems always light; those reporting from specific places ("Azores," "Antigua") seemed to me earnest enough, in delivering up a piece of our planet, to be considered poems. The very first poem here, bearing a comically long title, yet conveyed, with a compression unprecedented in my brief writing career, the mythogenetic truth of telephone wires and poles marching across a stretch of Pennsylvania farmland. I still remember the shudder, the triumphant sense of capture, with which I got these lines down, not long after my twenty-first birthday.

But every set of lines herein gave me the excited sensation of being a maker, a *poiētēs*. Almost all of the poems in my five previous volumes of verse have been included, along with some seventy more. I have sought out their dates of composition—given in the index of titles—and arranged them, within the two broad categories, in the order in which they were written. They form thus, with their sites and occasions, the thready backside of my life's fading tapestry. Not included are verse translations, rhyming salutes for the birthdays and weddings of children and stepchildren, the lyrics of a children's opera called *The Fisherman and His Wife,* a set of seasonal poems titled *A Child's Calendar,* and a "cheerful alphabet" of "pleasant objects" composed with my infant first son in mind. An appendix lists the titles previously collected but dropped from this conclusive gathering. The stanza breaks, I trust, are all clear. *Sic stat.* My poems are my oeuvre's beloved waifs, and I feared that if I did not perform the elementary bibliographical decencies for them no one would.

J.U.

COLLECTED POEMS

Why the Telephone Wires Dip
and the Poles Are Cracked and Crooked

The old men say
young men in gray
hung this thread across our plains
acres and acres ago.

But we, the enlightened, know
in point of fact it's what remains
of the flight of a marvellous crow
no one saw:
each pole, a caw.

Cloud Shadows

I

That white coconut, the sun,
    is hidden by his blue leaves,
piratical great galleons.

Our sky their spanking sea,
    they thrust us to an ocean floor,
withal with certain courtesy.

II

These courtly cotton-bellies rub
    around the jewel we live within
and down to the muddled hub

drop complements.
   Down shafts of violet fall
counterweights of shadow, hence

brown, blue, and gray occur
   upon the chipmunk-colored
earth's fur.

III

Pine islands in a broken lake.
   Beyond Laconia the hills,
islanded by shadows, take

in cooling middle distance
   a motion from above, and lo!
grave mountains belly dance.

Ex–Basketball Player

Pearl Avenue runs past the high-school lot,
Bends with the trolley tracks, and stops, cut off
Before it has a chance to go two blocks,
At Colonel McComsky Plaza. Berth's Garage
Is on the corner facing west, and there,
Most days, you'll find Flick Webb, who helps Berth out.

Flick stands tall among the idiot pumps—
Five on a side, the old bubble-head style,
Their rubber elbows hanging loose and low.
One's nostrils are two S's, and his eyes
An E and O. And one is squat, without
A head at all—more of a football type.

Once Flick played for the high-school team, the Wizards.
He was good: in fact, the best. In '46
He bucketed three hundred ninety points,
A county record still. The ball loved Flick.
I saw him rack up thirty-eight or forty
In one home game. His hands were like wild birds.

He never learned a trade, he just sells gas,
Checks oil, and changes flats. Once in a while,
As a gag, he dribbles an inner tube,
But most of us remember anyway.
His hands are fine and nervous on the lug wrench.
It makes no difference to the lug wrench, though.

Off work, he hangs around Mae's Luncheonette.
Grease-gray and kind of coiled, he plays pinball,
Smokes those thin cigars, nurses lemon phosphates.
Flick seldom says a word to Mae, just nods
Beyond her face toward bright applauding tiers
Of Necco Wafers, Nibs, and Juju Beads.

A Modest Mound of Bones

That short-sleeved man, our
   uncle, owns
the farm next our farm, south
   and west of us, and
he butchers for a living, hand-to-mouth.
   Once, walking on his land,
we found a hill, topped by a flower,
   a hill of bones.

They were rain-scrubbed clean—
   lovely things.

Depending how the white
    sun struck, chips of color
(green, yellow, dove-blue, a light
    bay) flew off the sullen
stilled turning there. To have seen
    those clickless rings,

those prisonerless
    ribs, complex
beyond the lathe's loose jaws,
    convolute compounds
of knobs, rods, hooks, moons, absurd paws,
    subtle flats and rounds:
no man could conceive such finesse,
    concave or -vex.

Some curve like umbrella
    handles, keys
to mammoth locks. Some bend
    like equations hunting
infinity, toward which to tend.
    How it sags!—what bunting
is flesh to be hung from such ele-
    gant balconies?

Sunflower

Sunflower, of flowers
the most lonely,
yardstick of hours,
long-term stander
in empty spaces,
shunner of bowers,
indolent bender

seldom, in only
the sharpest of showers:
tell us, why
is it your face is
a snarl of jet swirls
and gold arrows, a burning
old lion face high
in a cornflower sky,
yet by turning
your head we find
you wear a girl's
bonnet behind?

March: A Birthday Poem

My child as yet unborn, the doctors nod,
Agreeing that your first month shall be March,
A time of year I know by heart and like
To talk about—I, too, was born in March.

March, like November a month largely unloved,
Parades before April, who steals all shows
With his harlequinade of things renewed.
Impatient for that pastel fool's approach,
Our fathers taunted March, called him *Hlyd-monath*,
Though the month is mild, and a murmurer.
Indeed, after the Titan's fall and shatter
Of February, March seems a silence.
The Romans, finding February's ruins
At the feet of March, heard his wind as boasting
And hailed his guilt with a war-god's name.

As above some street in a cobbled sea-town
From opposing walls two huge boards thrust

To advertise two inns, so do the signs
Of Pisces the Fish and Aries the Ram
Overhang March. Depending on the day,
Your fortunate gem shall be the bloodstone
Or the diamond, your lucky color crimson
Or silver-gray. You shall prove affable,
Impulsive, lucky in your friends, or not,
According to the counterpoint of stars.
So press your business ventures, wear cravats,
And swear not by the moon. If planting wheat,
Do it at dawn. At dusk for barley. Let
The tide transplant kohlrabi, leeks, and beans.
Toward the month's end, sow hardy annuals.

It was this month when Caesar fell, Stalin died,
And Beethoven. In this month snowflakes melt—
Those last dry crusts that huddle by the barn.
Now kites and crocuses are hoisted up.
Doors slap open. Dogs snuffle soggy leaves,
Rehearsing rusty repertoires of smells.
The color of March is the one that lies
On the shadow side of young tree trunks.

March is no land of extremes. Dull as life,
It offers small flowers and minor holidays.
Clouds stride sentry and hold our vision down,
While underfoot the agony of roots
Is hidden by earth. Much, much is opaque.
The thunder bluffs, wind cannot be gripped,
And kites and crocuses are what they are.
Still, child, it is far from a bad month,
For all its weight of compromise and hope.
As modest as a monk, March shall be there
When on that day without a yesterday
You, red and blind and blank, gulp the air.

Burning Trash

At night—the light turned off, the filament
Unburdened of its atom-eating charge,
His wife asleep, her breathing dipping low
To touch a swampy source—he thought of death.
Her father's hilltop home allowed him time
To sense the nothing standing like a sheet
Of speckless glass behind his human future.
He had two comforts he could see, just two.

One was the cheerful fullness of most things:
Plump stones and clouds, expectant pods, the soil
Offering up pressure to his knees and hands.
The other was burning the trash each day.
He liked the heat, the imitation danger,
And the way, as he tossed in used-up news,
String, napkins, envelopes, and paper cups,
Hypnotic tongues of order intervened.

English Train Compartment

These faces make a chapel where worship comes easy:
Homo enim naturaliter est animal sociale.

The flutter of a *Guardian*, the riveted image
of Combe-in-Teignhead, faded by decades of eyes,
the sting of smoke, the coughs, the whispering
lend flavor to piety's honest bone.

Half-sick, we suck our teeth, consult our thumbs,
through brown-stained glass confront the barbered hills

and tailored trees of a tame and castrate land.
Sheep elegant enough for any eclogue
browse under Constable clouds. The unnatural
darkness swells, and passengers stir
at the sound of tapping fingernails. Rain,
beginning, hyphenates our racing windows.

And hands and smiles are freed by the benediction.
The lights, always on, now tell. One man talks,
and the water, sluicing sideways, teases our direction.
Indeed, we are lively, smug, and brave
as adventurers safe after some great hazard,
while beside our shoulders the landscape streams
as across the eye of a bathysphere surfacing.

Tao in the Yankee Stadium Bleachers

Distance brings proportion. From here
the populated tiers
as much as players seem part of the show:
a constructed stage beast, three folds of Dante's rose,
or a Chinese military hat
cunningly chased with bodies.
"Falling from his chariot, a drunk man is unhurt
because his soul is intact. Not knowing his fall,
he is unastonished, he is invulnerable."
So, too, the "pure man"—"pure"
in the sense of undisturbed water.

"It is not necessary to seek out
a wasteland, swamp, or thicket."
The opposing pitcher's pertinent hesitations,
the sky, this meadow, Mantle's thick baked neck,

the old men who in the changing rosters see
a personal mutability,
green slats, wet stone are all to me
as when an emperor commands
a performance with a gesture of his eyes.

"No king on his throne has the joy of the dead,"
the skull told Chuang-tzu.
The thought of death is peppermint to you
when games begin with patriotic song
and a democratic sun beats broadly down.
The Inner Journey seems unjudgeably long
when small boys purchase cups of ice
and, distant as a paradise,
experts, passionate and deft,
hold motionless while Berra flies to left.

How to Be Uncle Sam

My father knew
    how to be
        Uncle Sam.

Six feet two,
    he led the
        parade

the year
    the boys came back
        from war.

Splendidly
    spatted, his legs
        like canes,

his dandy coat
  like a
    bluebird's back,

he led the parade,
  and then
    a man

(I've never been sure
  he was honestly
    canned—

he might have been
  consciously
    after a laugh)

popped
  from the crowd,
    swinging his hands,

and screamed,
  "You're the s.o.b.
    who takes

all my money!"
  and took
    a poke at

my own father!
  He missed
    by half

an inch; he felt
  the wind, my father
    later said.

When the cops
   grabbed that one,
      another man

shouted from the
   crowd in a
      voice like brass:

"I don't care if
   you take a poke at
      Updike,

but keep your
   mitts off
      Uncle Sam!"

3 A.M.

By the brilliant ramp
of a ceaseless garage

the eye like a piece of newspaper
staring from a collage

records on a yellowing
gridwork of nerve

"policemen move on feet of glue,
sailors stick to the curb."

Mobile of Birds

There is something
in their planetary weave that is comforting.

The polycentric orbits, elliptical
with mutual motion,
random as nature, and yet, above all,
calculable, recall
those old Ptolemaic heavens small
enough for the Byzantine Trinity,
    Plato's Ideals,
    formal devotion,
seven levels of bliss, and numberless wheels
of omen, balanced occultly.

                         A small bird
at an arc's extremity
adequately weights
his larger mates'
compounded mass: absurd
but actual—there he floats!

Persisting through a doorway, shadow-casting light
    dissolves on the wall
    the mobile's threads
and turns its spatial conversation
dialectical. Silhouettes,
projections of identities,
merge and part and reunite
in shapely syntheses—
                  an illusion,
for the birds on their perches of fine wire avoid collusion
and are twirled
alone in their suspenseful world.

Shillington

The vacant lots are occupied, the woods
Diminish, Slate Hill sinks beneath its crown
Of solvent homes, and marketable goods
On all sides crowd the good remembered town.

Returning, we find our snapshots inexact.
Perhaps a condition of being alive
Is that the clothes which, setting out, we packed
With love no longer fit when we arrive.

Yet sights that limited our truth were strange
To older eyes; the town that we have lost
Is being found by hands that still arrange
Horse-chestnut heaps and fingerpaint on frost.

Time shades these alleys; every pavement crack
Is mapped somewhere. A solemn concrete ball,
On the gatepost of a sold house, brings back
A waist leaning against a buckling wall.

The gutter-fires smoke, their burning done
Except for, fanned within, an orange feather;
We have one home, the first, and leave that one.
The having and leaving go on together.

Suburban Madrigal

Sitting here in my house,
looking through my windows
diagonally at my neighbor's house,
I see his sun-porch windows;

they are filled with blue-green,
the blue-green of my car,
which I parked in front of my house,
more or less, up the street,
where I can't directly see it.

How promiscuous is
the world of appearances!
How frail are property laws!
To him his window is filled with his
things: his lamps, his plants, his radio.
How annoyed he would be to know
that my car, legally parked,
yet violates his windows,
paints them full
(to me) of myself, my car,
my well-insured '55 Fordor Ford
a gorgeous green sunset streaking his panes.

Telephone Poles

They have been with us a long time.
They will outlast the elms.
Our eyes, like the eyes of a savage sieving the trees
In his search for game,
Run through them. They blend along small-town streets
Like a race of giants that have faded into mere mythology.
Our eyes, washed clean of belief,
Lift incredulous to their fearsome crowns of bolts, trusses,
    struts, nuts, insulators, and such
Barnacles as compose
These weathered encrustations of electrical debris—
Each a Gorgon's head, which, seized right,
Could stun us to stone.

Yet they are ours. We made them.
See here, where the cleats of linemen
Have roughened a second bark
Onto the bald trunk. And these spikes
Have been driven sideways at intervals handy for human legs.
The Nature of our construction is in every way
A better fit than the Nature it displaces.
What other tree can you climb where the birds' twitter,
Unscrambled, is English? True, their thin shade is negligible,
But then again there is not that tragic autumnal
Casting-off of leaves to outface annually.
These giants are more constant than evergreens
By being never green.

Mosquito

On the fine wire of his whine he walked,
Unseen in the ominous bedroom dark.
A traitor to his camouflage, he talked
A thirsty blue streak distinct as a spark.

I was to him a fragrant lake of blood
From which he had to sip a drop or die.
A reservoir, a lavish field of food,
I lay awake, unconscious of my size.

We seemed fair-matched opponents. Soft he dropped
Down like an anchor on his thread of song.
His nose sank thankfully in; then I slapped
At the sting on my arm, cunning and strong.

A cunning, strong Gargantua, I struck
This lover pinned in the feast of my flesh,

Lulled by my blood, relaxed, half-sated, stuck,
Engrossed in the gross rivers of myself.

Success! Without a cry the creature died,
Became a fleck of fluff upon the sheet.
The small welt of remorse subsides as side
By side we, murderer and murdered, sleep.

Trees Eat Sunshine

It's the fact:
their broad leaves lap it up like milk
and turn it into twigs.

Fish eat fish.
Lamps eat light
and when their feast has starved their filament
go out.

So do we,
and all sweet creatures—
cats eating horses, horses grass, grass earth, earth water—
except for the distant Man

who inhales the savor of souls—
let us all strive to resemble this giant!

Winter Ocean

Many-maned scud-thumper, tub
of male whales, maker of worn wood, shrub-
ruster, sky-mocker, rave!
portly pusher of waves, wind-slave.

Modigliani's Death Mask

Fogg Museum, Cambridge

The shell of a doll's head,
It stares askew, lopsided in death,
With nervous lips, a dirty tan,
And no bigger than my hand.
Could the man have been that small?
Or is life, like rapid motion,
An enlarging illusion?
Ringed, Italianly, with ivy,
The mask makes an effect of litter,
Preserved inside its glass case like
An oddly favored grapefruit rind.

Seagulls

A gull, up close,
looks surprisingly stuffed.
His fluffy chest seems filled
with an inexpensive taxidermist's material
rather lumpily inserted. The legs,
unbent, are childish crayon strokes—
too simple to be workable.
And even the feather-markings,
whose intricate symmetry is the usual glory of birds,
are in the gull slovenly,
as if God makes too many
to make them very well.

Are they intelligent?
We imagine so, because they are ugly.
The sardonic one-eyed profile, slightly cross,

the narrow, ectomorphic head, badly combed,
the wide and nervous and well-muscled rump
all suggest deskwork: shipping rates
by day, Schopenhauer
by night, and endless coffee.

At that hour on the beach
when the flies begin biting in the renewed coolness
and the backsliding skin of the after-surf
reflects a pink shimmer before being blotted,
the gulls stand around in the dimpled sand
like those melancholy European crowds
that gather in cobbled public squares in the wake
of assassinations and invasions,
heads cocked to hear the latest radio reports.

It is also this hour when plump young couples
walk down to the water, bumping together,
and stand thigh-deep in the rhythmic glass.
Then they walk back toward the car,
tugging as if at a secret between them,
but which neither quite knows—
walk capricious paths through the scattering gulls,
as in some mythologies
beautiful gods stroll unconcerned
among our mortal apprehensions.

Seven Stanzas at Easter

Make no mistake: if He rose at all
it was as His body;
if the cells' dissolution did not reverse, the molecules reknit,
    the amino acids rekindle,
the Church will fall.

It was not as the flowers,
each soft spring recurrent;
it was not as His Spirit in the mouths and fuddled eyes of the
    eleven apostles;
it was as His flesh: ours.

The same hinged thumbs and toes,
the same valved heart
that—pierced—died, withered, paused, and then regathered
    out of enduring Might
new strength to enclose.

Let us not mock God with metaphor,
analogy, sidestepping, transcendence,
making of the event a parable, a sign painted in the faded
    credulity of earlier ages:
let us walk through the door.

The stone is rolled back, not papier-mâché,
not a stone in a story,
but the vast rock of materiality that in the slow grinding of
    time will eclipse for each of us
the wide light of day.

And if we will have an angel at the tomb,
make it a real angel,
weighty with Max Planck's quanta, vivid with hair, opaque in
    the dawn light, robed in real linen
spun on a definite loom.

Let us not seek to make it less monstrous,
for our own convenience, our own sense of beauty,
lest, awakened in one unthinkable hour, we are embarrassed
    by the miracle,
and crushed by remonstrance.

B.W.I.

Under a priceless sun,
   Shanties and guava.
Beside an emerald sea,
   Coral and lava.

On the white dirt road,
   A blind man tapping.
On dark Edwardian sofas,
   White men napping.

In half-caste twilight, heartfelt
   Songs to Jesus.
Across the arid land,
   Ocean breezes.
The sibilance of sadness
   Never ceases.

The empty cistern.
   The broken Victrola.
The rusted praise of
   Coca-Cola.

Old yellow tablecloths,
   And tea, and hairy
Goats, and airmail
   Stationery.

Copies of *Punch* and *Ebony*.
   Few flowers.
Just the many-petalled sun above
   The endless hours.

February 22

Three boys, American, in dungarees,
walk at a slant across the street
against the mild slant of the winter sun,
moseying out this small, still holiday.

The back of the cold is broken; later snows
will follow, mixed with rain, but today
the macadam is bare, the sun loops high,
and the trees are bathed in sweet grayness.

He was a perfect hero: a man of stone,
as colorless as a monument,
anonymous as Shakespeare. We know him
only as the author of his deeds.

There may have been a man: a surveyor,
a wencher, a temper, a stubborn farmer's mind;
but our legends seem impertinent
graffiti scratched upon his polished granite.

He gazes at us from our dollar bills
reproachfully, a strange green lady,
heavy-lidded, niggle-lipped, and wigged,
who served us better than we have deserved.

More than great successes, we love great failures.
Lincoln is Messiah; he, merely Caesar.
He suffered greatness like a curse.
He fathered our country, we feel, without great joy.

But let us love him now, for he crossed the famous ice,
brought us out of winter, stood, and surveyed
the breadth of our land exulting in the sun:
looked forward to the summer that is past.

Summer: West Side

When on the coral-red steps of old brownstones
Puerto Rican boys, their white shirts luminous,
gather, and their laughter
conveys menace as far as Central Park West,

When the cheesecake shops on Broadway
keep open long into the dark,
and the Chinaman down in his hole of seven steps
leaves the door of his laundry ajar,
releasing a blue smell of starch,

When the curbside lines of parked cars
appear embedded in the tar,
and the swish of the cars on the Drive
seems urgently loud—

Then even the lapping of wavelets
on the boards of a barge on the Hudson
is audible,
and Downtown's foggy glow
fills your windows right up to the top.

And you walk in the mornings with your cool suit
sheathing the fresh tingle of your shower,
and the gratings idly steam,
and the damp path of the street-sweeper evaporates,

And—an oddly joyful sight—
the dentists' and chiropractors' white signs low
in the windows of the great ochre buildings on Eighty-sixth
    Street
seem slightly darkened
by one more night's deposit of vigil.

Wash

For seven days it rained that June;
A storm half out to sea kept turning around like a dog trying
    to settle himself on a rug;
We were the fleas that complained in his hair.

On the eighth day, before I had risen,
My neighbors' clothes had rushed into all the back yards
And lifted up their arms in praise.

From an upstairs window it seemed prehistorical:
Amongst the sheds and fences and vegetable gardens,
Workshirts and nightgowns, long-soaked in the cellar,

Underpants, striped towels, diapers, child's overalls,
Bibs and black bras were thronging the sunshine
With hosannas of cotton and halleluiahs of wool.

Maples in a Spruce Forest

    They live by attenuation,
    Straining, vine-thin,
Up to gaps their gold leaves crowd
    Like drowning faces surfacing.

    Wherever dappled sun persists,
    Shy leaves work photosynthesis;
Until I saw these slender doomed,
    I did not know what a maple is.

    The life that plumps the oval
    In the open meadow full

Is beggared here, distended toward
The dying light available.

Maturity of sullen spruce
Will murder these deciduous;
A little while, the fretted gloom
Is dappled with chartreuse.

Vermont

Here green is king again,
Usurping honest men.
Like Brazilian cathedrals gone under to creepers,
Gray silos mourn their keepers.

Here ski tows
And shy cows
Alone pin the ragged slopes to the earth
Of profitable worth.

Hawks, professors,
And summering ministers
Roost on the mountainsides of poverty
And sniff the poetry,

And every year
The big black bear,
Slavering through the woods with scrolling mouth,
Comes further south.

The Solitary Pond

The fall we moved to the farm, I was thirteen;
the half-wild grapes on the dilapidated arbor
could not be eaten, and the forests and brown fields
also seemed to have no purpose. I grew accustomed,

that winter before the first spring, to hike alone,
ducking first under our barbed wire, then our neighbor's,
through thorny and hurricane-hit woods to a store
selling candy and soft drinks and gas by Route 11.

Returning one afternoon along an old wall,
I came to a shallow, solitary pond, frozen,
not more than fifteen feet across, and lined with stalks
and briar-strands that left the center scarcely open.

Recalling the rink in the town we had moved from,
I fetched my dull skates from the attic chest and blundered
back through sharp thickets while the cold grew and a frown
from the sky deepened the ominous area under

the black branches. My fingers were numb at the laces,
and the ice was riddled with twigs, and my intent
to glide back to childhood absurd. I fell, unstable
on the clutter of wood and water bubbled and bent
like earth itself, and thrashed home through the trees hating
the very scratches left by my experiment.

Flirt

The flirt is an antelope of flame,
igniting the plain
wherever she hesitates.
She kisses my wrist, waits,
and watches the flush of pride
absurdly kindle my eyes.
She talks in riddles,
exposes her middle,
is hard and strange in my arms:
I love her. Her charms
are those of a fine old book with half-cut pages,
bound in warm plush at her white neck's nape.

Fever

I have brought back a good message from the land of 102°:
God exists.
I had seriously doubted it before;
but the bedposts spoke of it with utmost confidence,
the threads in my blanket took it for granted,
the tree outside the window dismissed all complaints,
and I have not slept so justly for years.
It is hard, now, to convey
how emblematically appearances sat
upon the membranes of my consciousness;
but it is a truth long known,
that some secrets are hidden from health.

Earthworm

We pattern our Heaven
on bright butterflies,
but it must be that even
in earth Heaven lies.

The worm we uproot
in turning a spade
returns, careful brute,
to the peace he has made.

God blesses him; he
gives praise with his toil,
lends comfort to me,
and aerates the soil.

Immersed in the facts,
one must worship there;
claustrophobia attacks
us even in air.

Old-Fashioned Lightning Rod

Green upright rope
of copper, sprouting
(from my perspective) from
an amber ball—jaundiced amber,
the belly-bulb
of an old grasshopper—
braced between three
sturdy curlicues of wrought
iron (like elegancies

of logical thought)
and culminating—the rod,
the slender wand of spiral
copper weathered pistachio-pale—
in a crown, a star
of five radiating thorns
honed fine on the fine-grained
grinding blue wheel of sky:
flared fingers, a torch,
a gesture, crying,
"I dare you!"

Sunshine on Sandstone

Golden photon white on granulated red
  makes brown,
wall-broad in this instance,
  house-high:
splendiferous surface, the stucco
  worn bare
here and there, stones nicked, cracked,
  flecked, marked,
scored warmly, worn considerably, having
  wept rust,
borne whitewash, mortar, known weather,
  these spots
seem meditating irregularities:
  Lord's thoughts.

The Stunt Flier

I come into my dim bedroom
innocently and my baby
is lying in her crib face-down;
just a hemisphere of the half-bald head
shows, and the bare feet, uncovered,
the small feet crossed at the ankles
like a dancer doing easily
a difficult step—or,
more exactly, like a cherub
planing through Heaven,
cruising at a middle altitude
through the cumulus of the tumbled covers,
which disclose the feet crossed
at the ankles *à la* small boys who,
exulting in their mastery of bicycles,
lift their hands from the handlebars
to demonstrate how easy gliding is.

Calendar

Toward August's end,
a hard night rain;
and the lawn is littered
with leaves again.

How the seasons blend!
So seeming still,
summer is fettered
to a solar will

which never rests.
The slanting ray
ignites migration
within the jay

and plans for nests
are hatching when
the northern nation
looks white to men.

The Short Days

I like the way, in winter, cars
Ignite beneath the lingering stars
And, with a cough or two, unpark,
And roar to work still in the dark.

Like some great father, slugabed,
Whose children crack the dawn with play,
The sun retains a heavy head
Behind the hill, and stalls the day.

Then red rims gild the gutter-spouts;
The streetlamp pales; the milk-truck fades;
And housewives—husbands gone—wash doubts
Down sinks and raise the glowing shades.

The cars are gone, they will return
When headlights in a new night burn;
Between long drinks of Acheron
The thirst of broad day has begun.

Boil

In the night the white skin
cries aloud to be broken,
but finds itself a cruel prison;
so it is with reason,
which holds the terror in,
undoubted though the infection.

Widener Library, Reading Room

Eight years removed from them, I sit among
The weary faces of the hopeful young.
All self-reflectively, my gaze is bent
To where the mirror proves recalcitrant.

The frosted glass of vanished time before
My eyes suggests the firm-locked office door
Of some august professor who has sent
For me and then forgot our appointment.

Mater, behold your son, not prodigal
But having, eager pen in hand, done all
Your discipline implied; the feat feels meant
Ill, here in the vault of its vague intent.

Movie House

View it, by day, from the back,
from the parking lot in the rear,
for from this angle only

the beautiful brick blankness can be grasped.
Monumentality
wears one face in all ages.

No windows intrude real light
into this temple of shades,
and the size of it,
the size of the great rear wall measures
the breadth of the dreams we have had here.
It dwarfs the village bank,
outlooms the town hall,
and even in its decline
makes the bright-ceilinged supermarket seem mean.

Stark closet of stealthy rapture,
vast introspective camera
wherein our most daring self-projections
were given familiar names:
stand, stand by your macadam lake
and tell the aeons of our extinction
that we, too, could house our gods,
could secrete a pyramid
to sight the stars by.

Vibration

The world vibrates, my sleepless nights
discovered. The air conditioner hummed;
I turned it off. The plumbing
in the next apartment sang;
I moved away, and found a town
whose factories shuddered as they worked
all night. The wires on the poles
outside my windows quivered in an ecstasy

stretched thin between horizons.
I went to where no wires were; and there,
as I lay still, a dragon tremor
seized my darkened body, gnawed
my heart, and murmured, *I am you.*

The Blessing

The room darkened, darkened until
our nakedness became a form of gray;
then the rain came bursting,
and we were sheltered, blessed,
upheld in a world of elements
that held us justified.
In all the love I had felt for you before,
in all that love,
there was no love
like that I felt when the rain began:
dim room, enveloping rush,
the slenderness of your throat,
the blessèd slenderness.

My Children at the Dump

The day before divorce, I take my children
on this excursion;
they are enchanted by
a wonderland of discard where
each complicated star cries out
to be a momentary toy.

. . .

To me, too, the waste seems wonderful.
Sheer hills of television tubes, pale lakes
of excelsior, landslides
of perfectly carved carpentry-scraps,
sparkplugs like nuggets, cans iridescent
as peacock plumes, an entire lawnmower
all pluck at my instinct to conserve.

I cannot. These things
were considered, and dismissed
for a reason. But my children
wander wondering among tummocks of junk
like stunted starvelings cruelly set free
at a heaped banquet of food too rich to eat.
I shout, "Don't touch the broken glass!"

The distant metal delicately rusts.
The net effect is floral: a seaward wind
makes flags of cellophane and upright weeds.
The seagulls weep; my boys bring back
bent tractors, hoping what some other child
once played to death can be revived by them.

No. I say, "No." I came to add
my fragments to this universe of loss,
purging my house, ridding a life
no longer shared of remnants.
My daughter brings a naked armless doll,
still hopeful in its dirty weathered eyes,
and I can only tell her, "Love it now.
Love it now, but we can't take it home."

The Great Scarf of Birds

Ripe apples were caught like red fish in the nets
of their branches. The maples
were colored like apples,
part orange and red, part green.
The elms, already transparent trees,
seemed swaying vases full of sky. The sky
was dramatic with great straggling V's
of geese streaming south, mare's-tails above them;
their trumpeting made us look up from golf.
The course sloped into salt marshes,
and this seemed to cause the abundance of birds.

As if out of the Bible
or science fiction,
a cloud appeared, a cloud of dots
like iron filings which a magnet
underneath the paper undulates.
It dartingly darkened in spots,
paled, pulsed, compressed, distended, yet
held an identity firm: a flock
of starlings, as much one thing as a rock.
One will moved above the trees
the liquid and hesitant drift.

Come nearer, it became less marvellous,
more legible, and merely huge.
"I never saw so many birds!" my friend exclaimed;
we returned our eyes to the game.
Later, as Lot's wife must have done,
in a pause of walking, not thinking
of calling down a consequence,
I shifted my bag and looked back.

. . .

The rise of the fairway behind us was tinted,
so evenly tinted I might not have noticed
but that at the rim of the delicate shadow
the starlings were thicker and outlined the flock
as an inkstain in drying pronounces its edges.
The gradual rise of green was vastly covered;
I had thought nothing in nature could be so broad but grass.

And as
I watched, one bird,
prompted by accident or will to lead,
ceased resting; and, lifting in a casual billow,
the flock ascended as a lady's scarf,
transparent, of gray, might be twitched
by one corner, drawn upward, and then,
decided against, negligently tossed toward a chair:
dissolving all anxiety,
the southward cloud withdrew into the air.

Azores

Great green ships
    themselves, they ride
at anchor forever;
    beneath the tide

huge roots of lava
    hold them fast
in mid-Atlantic
    to the past.

The tourists, thrilling
    from the deck,

hail shrilly pretty
　　hillsides flecked

with cottages
　　(confetti) and
sweet lozenges
　　of chocolate (land).

They marvel at
　　the dainty fields
and terraces
　　hand-tilled to yield

the modest fruits
　　of vines and trees
imported by
　　the Portuguese:

a rural landscape
　　set adrift
from centuries ago.
　　The rift

enlarges.
　　The ship proceeds.
Again the constant
　　music feeds

an emptiness astern,
　　Azores gone.
The void behind, the void
　　ahead are one.

Erotic Epigrams

I

The landscape of love
can only be seen
through a slim windowpane
one's own breath fogs.

II

Iseult, to Tristan
(condemned to die),
is like a letter of reprieve
which is never delivered
but he knows has been dispatched.

III

Hoping to fashion a mirror, the lover
doth polish the face of his beloved
until he produces a skull.

Hoeing

I sometimes fear the younger generation will be deprived
  of the pleasures of hoeing;
    there is no knowing
how many souls have been formed by this simple exercise.

The dry earth like a great scab breaks, revealing
  moist-dark loam—
    the pea-root's home,
a fertile wound perpetually healing.

How neatly the green weeds go under!
   The blade chops the earth new.
   Ignorant the wise boy who
has never rendered thus the world fecunder.

Report of Health

I

I am alone tonight.
The wrong I have done you
sits like a sore beneath my thumb,
burns like a boil on my heart's left side.
I am unwell.

My viscera, long clenched in love of you,
have undergone a detested relaxation.

There is, within, a ghostly maze
of phantom tubes and nodules where
those citizens, our passions, flit; and here,
like sunlight passing from a pattern of streets,
I feel your bright love leaving.

II

Another night. Today I am told,
dear friend, by another,
you seem happy and well.
Nothing could hurt me more.

How dare you be happy, you,
shaped so precisely for me,
my cup and my mirror—

how dare you disdain to betray,
by some disarray of your hair,
my being torn from you?

I would rather believe
that you knew your friend would come to me,
and so seemed well—
"not a hair / out of place"—
like an actress blindly hurling a pose
into the fascinated darkness.

As for me, you are still the eyes of the air.
I travel from point to point in your presence.
Each unattended gesture hopes to catch your eye.

III

I may not write again. My voice
goes nowhere. Dear friend,
don't let me heal. Don't
worry, I am well.
I am happy
to dwell in a world whose Hell I will:

the doorway hints at your ghost
and a tiger pounces on my heart;
the lilac bush is a devil
inviting me into your hair.

Fireworks

These spasms and chrysanthemums of light
are like emotions

exploding under a curved night that corresponds
to the dark firmament within.

See, now, the libidinous flare,
spinning on its stick in vain resistance
to the upright ego and mortality's gravity;
behold, above, the sudden bloom,
turquoise, each tip a comet,
of pride—followed, after an empty bang,
by an ebbing amber galaxy, despair.

We feel our secrets bodied forth like flags
as wide as half the sky. Now
passions, polychrome and coruscating, crowd
one upon the other in a final fit,
a terminal display
that tilts the children's faces back in bleached dismay
and sparks an infant's crying in the grass.

They do not understand, the younger ones,
what thunderheads and nebulae,
what waterfalls and momentary roses fill
the world's one aging skull,
and are relieved when in a falling veil
the last awed outburst crumbles to reveal
the pattern on the playroom wall
of tame and stable stars.

Lamplight

Sent straight from suns
on slender stems
whose fangèd tendrils
leech the walls,

it sadly falls
on tabletops
and barren floors
where rugs lie flat
as sunburnt crops.

Yet by this glow,
while daylight leans
outside the door
like an idle ax,
green voices wax,
red tongues thrust seeds
deep in the soil
of our harrowed needs,
and conversations grow.

Nuda Natens

Anthea, your shy flanks in starlight
sank into the surf like thumbs into my heart.
Your untanned skin,
shaped like a bathing suit,
lifted me thick from my thighs,
old Adam in air
above the cool ribs of sand.
My lust was a phosphor in a wide black wash,
and your quick neck the stem of a vase,
and your shoulders a crescent perilously balanced
where darkness was sliding on darkness.
You led me up, frightened with love,
up from the wet to where warm wind
bathed us in dust, and your embarrassed beauty
bent silver about your pudenda.

Postcards from Soviet Cities

Moscow

Gold onions rooted in the sky
Grow downward into sullen, damp
Museums where, with leaden eye,
Siberian tourists dumbly tramp.

The streets are wide as silences.
The cobblestones between the GUM
And Kremlin echo—an abyss
Lies sealed within a giant room.

The marble box where Lenin sleeps
Receives the Tartar gaze of those
Who come from where Far Russia keeps
Her counsels wrapped in deadening snows.

St. Basil's, near at hand, erects
The swirlings that so charmed the czar
He blinded both the architects
To keep such beauty singular.

Leningrad

"To build a window on the west"
Great Peter came to Neva's mouth
And found a swamp, which he oppressed
With stones imported from the south.

The city, subtly polychrome
(Old ochre, green, and dull maroon),

Can make Italians feel at home
Beneath the tilted arctic noon.

The Palace holds, pistachio,
A wilderness of treasure where
The ghosts of plump czarinas go
On dragging diamonds up the stair.

Suburban acres of the dead
Memorialize the Siege, a hell
Of blackened snow and watered bread.
Some couples Twist in our hotel.

Kiev

Clutching his cross, St. Vladimir
Gazes with eyes that seem to grieve
Across the sandy Dnieper, where
He baptized godforsaken Kiev.

Now deconverted trolleys turn
Around the square, emitting sparks.
The churches, cold as attics, burn
With gilt above the poplar parks.

Beneath the earth, in catacombs,
Dried patriarchs lie mummified;
Brocaded silk enmeshed with bones
Offends our trim, mascaraed guide,

Who, driving homeward, gestures toward
The ruins of Moussorgsky's Gate—
Like some old altar, unrestored,
Where peasant women supplicate.

Tbilisi

Rich Georgian farmers send their sons
(Black-haired, with pointed stares and feet)
To town for educations—
They loiter laughing on the street.

A "working" church: its inside smells
Of tallow, mold, incense, and chrism.
The long-haired priest, wax-pallid, sells
His candles with a shopgirl's grimace.

The poets, overhonored, toast
Themselves with liquid syllables;
The alphabet is strange. They boast
Their tongue is older than their hills.

Instead of Stalin, who indulged
His native land with privilege,
A blank steel woman, undivulged
By name, surmounts the once-walled ridge.

Yerevan

Armenia, Asia's waif, has here
At last constructed shelter proof
Against all Turkish massacre.
A soft volcanic rock called tuff

Carves easily and serves to be
The basis of the boulevards
That lead from slums of history
Into a future stripped of swords.

· · ·

The crescent-shaped hotel is rose
And looks toward Lenin Square and tan
Dry mountains down which power flows
From turbines lodged in Lake Sevan.

Mount Ararat, a conscience, floats
Cloudlike, in sight but unpossessed,
For there, where Noah docked his boat,
Begins the brutal, ancient West.

Camera

Let me gaze, gaze forever
into that single, vaguely violet eye:
my fingertips dilate
the veiled pupil circumscribed
by crescent leaves of metal
overlapping, fine as foil, and oiled.

Let me walk, walk with its weight
as telling as gold, declaring
precious works packed tight:
the air is light,
all light, pure light alive
with the possibility of capture.

Let all, all be still until
the cleaver falls: I become female,
having sealed secure
in the quick clicked womb of utter black, bright semen
of a summer day, coiled fruit
of my eyes' axed rapture.

Roman Portrait Busts

Others in museums pass them by,
but I, I
am drawn like a maggot to meat
by their pupilless eyes
and their putrefying individuality.

They are, these Livias and Marcuses,
these pouting dead Octavias,
no two alike: never has art
so whorishly submitted
to the importunities of the real.

In good conscience one must admire
the drab lack of exaggeration,
the way each head,
crone's, consul's, or child's,
is neither bigger nor smaller than life.

Their eyes taste awful.
It is vile,
deliciously, to see selves so
unsoftened by history, such
indigestible gristle.

Fellatio

How beautiful to think
that each of these clean secretaries
at night, to please her lover, takes
a fountain into her mouth
and lets her insides, drenched in seed,

flower into landscapes:
meadows sprinkled with baby's breath,
hoarse twiggy woods, birds dipping, a multitude
of skies containing clouds, plowed earth stinking
of its upturned humus, and small farms each
with a silver silo.

Décor

Brown dominates this bar
where men come to age:
the waiters Negro,
the whiskey unwatered,
the overheard voices from Texas,
the cigars and varnished wood.

Brown, the implication is,
is a shade of the soul,
the color of a man:
well-tanned and stained
to the innermost vein
as if life is a long curing.

Poem for a Far Land

Russia, most feminine of lands,
    Breeder of stupid masculinity,
Only Jesus understands
    Your interminable virginity.

Raped, and raped, and raped again,
    You rise snow-white, the utter same,

With tender birches and ox-eyed men
   Willing to perish for your name.

Though astronauts distress the sky
   That mothers your low, sad villages,
Your vastness yearns in sympathy
   Between what was and that which is.

Late January

The elms' silhouettes
again relent,
leafless but furred

with the promise of leaves,
dull red in a sky dull yellow
with the threat of snow.

That blur, verging on growth:
Time's sharp edge is slitting
another envelope.

Dog's Death

She must have been kicked unseen or brushed by a car.
Too young to know much, she was beginning to learn
To use the newspapers spread on the kitchen floor
And to win, wetting there, the words, "Good dog! Good dog!"

We thought her shy malaise was a shot reaction.
The autopsy disclosed a rupture in her liver.
As we teased her with play, blood was filling her skin
And her heart was learning to lie down forever.

Monday morning, as the children were noisily fed
And sent to school, she crawled beneath the youngest's bed.
We found her twisted and limp but still alive.
In the car to the vet's, on my lap, she tried

To bite my hand and died. I stroked her warm fur
And my wife called in a voice imperious with tears.
Though surrounded by love that would have upheld her,
Nevertheless she sank and, stiffening, disappeared.

Back home, we found that in the night her frame,
Drawing near to dissolution, had endured the shame
Of diarrhoea and had dragged across the floor
To a newspaper carelessly left there. *Good dog.*

Home Movies

How the children have changed! Rapt, we stare
    At flickering lost Edens where
    Pale infants, squinting, seem to hark
To their older selves laughing in the dark.

And then, by the trellis of some old spring—
    The seasons are unaltering—
    We gather, smoother and less bald,
Innocently clowning, having been called

To pose by the off-screen cameraman.
    How strangely silently time ran!
    We cannot climb back, nor can our friends,
To that calm light. The brief film ends.

Antigua

The wind, transparent, cannot displace
　The vertical search of sun for skin.
The colonel's fine-veined florid face
　Has bloomed though sheltered deep within
His shining hat's mauve shade. His eyes
　Glare bluer than the coral-bleached
　Soft sea that feebly nags the beach
And hones its scimitar with sighs.

His wife, in modest half-undress,
　Swings thighs pinched red between the sea
　And sky, and smiles, serenely free
Of subcutaneous distress.
Above, sere cliffs attend their hike,
　And colored scraps give tattered hints
Of native life, and, higher, like
　A flaw in glass, an airplane glints.

Amoeba

Mindless, meaning no harm,
it ingested me.
It moved on silent pseudopods
to where I was born, inert, and I
was inside.

Digestive acids burned my skin.
Enzymes nuzzled knees and eyes.
My ego like a conjugated verb
retained its root, a narrow fear
of being qualified;

alas, suffixes swarmed.
I lost my mother's arms, my teeth,
my laugh, my protruding faith.
Reduced to the O of a final sigh,
in time I died.

Elm

My thousand-thousand-leaved,
with what a graceful straining
you greet the year's gray turning
and put forth green.

Sleepless, at two this morning,
above the lakelike street,
I saw your far fronds hanging
like long hands trailed in water;

I saw your ferny curtains
translucent like distant fields,
your crown's impassive dreaming
powdered with uneclipsed stars.

Great shape, most godly thing
I know, don't die. The blight
is a cliff's edge each year you skirt,
returning to dye the night.

Daughter

I was awakened from a dream,
a dream entwined with cats,

by a cat's close presence.
In the darkness by my bedside there
had loomed a form with shining hair—
squarish, immense-eyed, still.
Its whiskers pricked my lips:
I screamed.
           My daughter cried,
in just proportion terrified.
I realized that,
though only four, all skin and smiles,
my daughter is a lioness, taken as a cat.

Eurydice

Negress serene though underground,
what weddings in northward Harlem
impressed upon you this cameo
stamp of stoic repose?
Beauty should never be bored
with being beautiful.

Bright lights are shattered by our speed.
The couplings cluck, the darkness yells.
The child beside you sidles in
and out of sleep, and I,
poor sooty white man scarcely visible,
try not to stare.

O loveliness blind to itself:
sockets thumbed from clay wherein
eyelids are petals of shadow,
cheekbones and jawbone whose carriage
is of a proud rider in velvet,
lips where eleven curves live.

Eurydice, come follow me,
my song is silent, listen:
I'll hold your name in love so high
oceans of years will leave it dry;
mountains of time will not begin
to move a moment of your skin.

The doors gape wide at Fifty-ninth.
The kiosk steps are black with blood.
I turn and find,
rebuked by light,
you gone, Negress serene,
tugged northward into night.

Seal in Nature

Observed from down the beach, the seal
seemed a polished piece of the rock he was on.
Closer approached, he became distinct
from the boat-shaped barnacled mineral mass,
twenty yards safe from shore, he had chosen
to be his pedestal—a living sculpture,
a Noguchi, an Arp, a Brancusi smoothed
from a flexible wood whose grain was hair,
whose gray was white in the abstract glisten,
and black where his curve demanded a shadow.

The sea his amphitheatre, the mammal,
both water and stone, performed aloof tricks:
he wound the line of horizon on his nose
and scratched his back with the top of his head
and, twisting like a Möbius strip, addressed
the sky with a hollowing desolate howl
echoing empty epochs when,

in acres of basalt sown thick with steam,
beneath dull skies, life's circus performed
for the silent Observer Supreme.

Air Show

(Hanscom Field, Bedford, Mass.)

In shapes that grow organic and bizarre
Our Air Force ramifies the forms of war.
The stubby bomber, dartlike fighter yield
To weirder beasts caught browsing on this field,
With wry truncated wings, anteater snouts,
And burnished bellies full of ins and outs.
  Caressing curves of wind, the metal smiles
And beds the pilot down in sheets of dials.
Eggheaded, strapped, and sucking gas, he roars
To frozen heights all other life abhors,
Where, having left his dirty sound behind,
In pure blue he becomes pure will and mind.
  These planes, articulate in every part,
Outdo the armor-forger's Tuscan art—
The rivets as unsparingly displayed
As pearls upon a chasuble's brocade,
The wiring bundled thick, like chordate brains,
The posing turbine balanced grain by grain,
The silver skin so stencilled it amounts
To an encyclical of do's and don't's.
  Our dollars! Dumb, like muzhiks come from far
To gaze upon the trappings of a czar,
Their sweat turned into gems and cold faïence,
We marvel at our own extravagance:
No mogul's wasteful lust was half so wide
And deep as this democracy's quick pride.

Omega

This little lightweight manacle whereby
My wrist is linked to flux and feels time fly,
This constant bracelet with so meek a jewel,
Shall prove at last implacable and cruel
And like a noose jerk taut, and hold me still,
And add me to the unseen trapper's kill.

The Angels

They are above us all the time,
the good gentlemen, Mozart and Bach,
Scarlatti and Handel and Brahms,
lavishing measures of light down upon us,
telling us, over and over, there is a realm
above this plane of silent compromise.
They are around us everywhere, the old seers,
Matisse and Vermeer, Cézanne and Piero,
greeting us echoing in subway tunnels,
springing like winter flowers from postcards
Scotch-taped to white kitchen walls,
waiting larger than life in shadowy galleries
to whisper that edges of color
lie all about us innocent as grass.
They are behind us, beneath us,
the abysmal books, Shakespeare and Tolstoy,
the Bible and Proust and Cervantes,
burning in memory like leaky furnace doors,
minepits of honesty from which we escaped
with dilated suspicions. Love us, dead thrones:
sing us to sleep, awaken our eyes,
comfort with terror our mortal afternoons.

Bath After Sailing

From ten to five we whacked the waves,
the hostile, mobile black
that lurched beneath the leeward winch
as helplessly we heeled.

Now, after six, I lie at ease,
at ease in a saltless sea my size,
my fingertips shrivelled as if dead,
the sway of the sloop still haunting the tub.

I can't stop seeing the heartless waves
the mirthless color of green tar
sliding on themselves like ball-bearings,
deep and opaque and not me,

not me: I was afraid,
afraid of heeling over in the wind
and inhaling bubbling lead
and sinking, opaque as stone.

Lord, how light my feet,
wed to their salt-soaked sneakers,
felt on the dock, amid the mysterious
steadiness of trees and air.

I did not want, I had not wanted
to die. I saw death's face
in that mass absorbed
in shrugging off its timeless weight,

the same dull mass blond Vikings scanned,
impervious to all the sailor love

thrust onto it. My shredded hand
ached on the jib-sheet line.

The boat would clumsily, broken
wings flapping, come about,
and the slickered skipper search
the sea-face and find me gone,

his surprise not total,
and one wave much like the rest,
a toppling ton, a rib of time,
an urgent message from nothing to nothing.

I thank you, God of trees and air,
whose steeples testify
to something steady slipped by chance
upon Your tar-green sliding face,

for this my mock survival.
My children's voices plumb my death.
My rippling legs are hydra limbs.
My penis, my representative,

my emissary to darkness, survivor
of many a plunge, flipflops
sideways, alive and small
and pallid in reprieve.

Black sea, deep sea, you dangle
beneath my bliss like a dreadful gamble.
Mute, white as a swimming-pool cork,
I float on the skin

of sleepiness, of my sleep,
of all sleep. . . . How much I prefer

this microcosmic version
of flirting with immersion.

Topsfield Fair

Animals seem so sad to be themselves—
the turkey a turkey even to his wattle,
the rabbit with his pink, distinctly, eyes,
the prize steer humble in his stall.
What are they thinking, the pouter pigeons,
shaped like opulent ladies' hats,
jerking and staring in aisles of cages;
what does the mute meek monkey say?

Our hearts go out to them, then stop:
our fellows in mortality, like us
stiff-thrust into marvellous machines
tight-packed with chemical commands
to breathe, blink, feed, sniff, mate,
and, stuck like stamps in species, go out of date.

Pompeii

They lived, Pompeiians,
as installments of flesh in slots of stone;
they died in postures preserved,
by a ghoulish casting process, in the dank museum here.
Outside the gates, living Pompeiian men
peddle antique pornography.

One feels this place
was cursed before that noon in 79
when lunching gluttons found

their sturgeon mouths hot-stuffed with screaming ash.
   There's not much to admire but the fact
      of preservation, and the plumbing.

      The plumbing lingers
   like a sour aftertaste—the loving conduits,
      the phallic fountains, the three degrees,
so technically astute, of public bath. These Romans
   enslaved their liquids well; pornography
      became their monument.

Sand Dollar

This disc, stelliferous,
survived the tide
to tell us some small creature
lived and died;
its convex delicacy
defies the void
that crushed a vanished
echinoid.

Stoop down, delighted;
hoard in your hand
this sand-colored coin
redeemed from the sand
and know, my young sudden
archaeologist,
that other modes of being
do exist.

Behold the horizon.
Vastness acts
the wastrel with

its artifacts.
The sea holds lives
as a dream holds clues;
what one realm spends
another can use.

Washington

Diagonal white city dreamed by a Frenchman—
the *nouveau* republic's Senecan pretension
populated by a grid of blacks—
after midnight your taxi-laced streets
entertain noncommittal streetlight shadows
and the scurry of leaves that fall still green.

Site, for me, of a secret parliament
of which both sides agreed to concede
and left the issue suspended in brandy,
I think of you longingly, as a Yankee
longs for Lee, sorry to have won,
or as Ho Chi Minh mourns for Johnson.

My capital, my alabaster Pandemonium,
I rode your stunned streets with a groin
as light and docile as a baby's wrist,
guilt's senators laughing in my skull's cloakroom,
my hurried heart corrupt with peace,
with love of my country, of cunt, and of sleep.

Dream Objects

Strangest is their reality,
their three-dimensional workmanship:

veined pebbles that have an underside,
maps one could have studied for minutes longer,
books we seem to read page after page.

If these are symbols cheaply coined
to buy the mind a momentary pardon,
whence this extravagance? Fine
as dandelion polls, they surface and explode
in the wind of the speed of our dreaming,

so that we awake with the sense
of having missed everything, tourists
hustled by bus through a land whose history
is our rich history, whose artifacts
were filed to perfection by beggars we fear.

Midpoint

I. Introduction

ARGUMENT: The poet begins, and describes his beginnings. Early
intimations of wonder and dread. His family on the Hill of Life in 1939,
and his own present uncomfortable maturity. Refusing to take good advice,
he insists on the endurance of the irreducible.

Of nothing but me, me
—all wrong, all wrong—
as I cringe in the face of glory

I sing, lacking another song.
Proud mouths around me clack
that the livelong day is long

but the nip of night tugs back
my would-be celebrant brain
to the bricks of the moss-touched walk,

the sweet cold grass that had no name,
the arbor, and the wicker chair
turned cavernous beneath the tapping rain.

Plain wood and paint pressed back my stare.
Stiff cardboard apples crayoned to sell
(for nickels minted out of air)

from orange crates with still a citrus smell:
the thermometer: the broom:
this code of things contrived to tell

a timid God of a continuum
wherein he was delimited.
Vengeful, he applied his sense of doom

with tricycle tires to coppery-red
anthills and, dizzy in his Heaven, grieved
above his crushed Inferno of the dead.

A screen of color said, *You are alive.*
A skin of horror floated at my feet.
The corpses, comma-shaped, indicted, *If*

a wheel from far above (in summer heat,
loose thunders roamed the sky like untongued wagons)
would turn, you'd lie squashed on the street.

That bright side porch in Shillington:
under the sun, beneath grape leaves,
I feared myself an epiphenomenon.

The crucial question was, *Why am I me?*
In China boys were born as cherishing
of their small selves; in buried Greece

their swallowed spirits wink
like mica lost in marble.
Sickened by Space's waste, I tried to cling

to the thought of the indissoluble:
a point infinitely hard
was luminous in me, and cried *I will.*

I sought in middling textures particles of iridescence, scintillae
in dullish surfaces; and pictured art

as my descending, via pencil, into dry
exactitude. Behind the beaded curtain
of Matter lurked an understanding Eye.

Clint Shilling's drawing lessons: in
the sun he posed an egg on paper, and said
a rainbow ran along the shadow's rim—

the rainbow at the edge of the shadow of the egg.
My kindergarten eyes were sorely strained
to see it there. My still-soft head

began to ache, but docilely I feigned
the purple ghosts of green in clumsy wax:
thus was I early trained

and wonder, now, if Clint were orthodox.
He lived above a spikestone-studded wall
and honed his mustache like a tiny ax

and walked a brace of collies down our alley
in Pennsylvania dusk
beside his melodic wife, white-haired and tall.

O Philadelphia Avenue! My eyes lift up
from the furtive pencilled paper
and drown, are glad to drown, in a flood

of light, of trees and houses: our neighbors
live higher than we, in gaunt
two-family houses glaring toward our arbor.

Five-fingered leaves hold horse chestnuts.
The gutter runs with golden water
from Flickinger's ice plant. Telephone wires hunt

through the tree crowns under orders
to find the wider world
the daily *Eagle* and the passing autos

keep hinting the existence of. And girls
stroll toward Lancaster Avenue and school
in the smoke of burning leaves, in the swirl

of snow, in the cruel
brilliance that follows, in the storm of buds that marries
earth to the iron sky and brings renewal

to the town so wide and fair from quarry
to trolley tracks, from Kenhorst to Mohnton,
from farmers' market to cemetery,

that a boy might feel himself point N
in optics, where plane ABCD—
a visual phenomenon—

converges and passes through to be
(inverted on the other side,
where film or retina receives it)

a kind of afterlife,
knife-lifted out of flux
and developed out of time:

the night sky, with a little luck,
was a camera back, the constellations
faint silver salts, and I the crux

of radii, the tip of two huge cones,
called Empyrean and Earth,
that took their slant and spin from me alone.

I was that N, that white-hot nothing, yet
my hands, my penis, came also into view,
and as I grew I half unwilling learned

to seem a creature, to subdue
my giant solipsism to a common scale.
Reader, it is pure bliss to share with you

the plight of love, the fate
of death, the need for food,
the privileges of ignorance, the ways

of traffic, competition, and remorse.
I look upon my wife, and marvel that
a woman, competent and good,

has shared these years; my children, protein-fat,
echo my eyes and my laugh: I am disarmed
to think that my body has mattered,

has been enrolled like a red-faced farm-
boy in the beautiful country club
of mankind's copulating swarm.

I did not expect it; humble
as a glow-worm, my boneless ego asked
only to witness, to serve as the hub

of a wheeling spectacle that would not pass.
My parents, my impression was,
had acted out all parts on my behalf;

their shouting and their silences
in the hissing bedroom dark
scorched the shadows; a ring of ashes

expanded with each smoldering remark
and left no underbrush of fuel
of passion for my intimidated spark.

My mother's father squeezed his Bible
sighing, and smoked five-cent cigars
behind the chickenhouse, exiling the smell.

His wife, bespectacled Granma,
beheaded the chickens
in their gritty wire yard

and had a style of choking during dinner;
she'd run to the porch, where one of us
would pound her on the back until her inner

conflict had resolved. Like me, she was nervous;
I had sympathetic stomach cramps.
We were, perhaps, too close,

the five of us. Our lamps
were dim, our carpets worn, the furniture
hodgepodge and venerable and damp.

And yet I never felt that we were poor.
Our property included several stray
cats, one walnut tree, a hundred feet or more

of privet hedge, and fresh ice every other day.
The brothers pressing to be born
were kept, despite their screams, offstage.

The fifth point of a star, I warmed
to my onliness, threw tantrums,
and, for my elders' benison, performed.

Seven I was when to amuse them
I drew the Hill of Life.
My grandfather, a lusty sixty-some,

is near the bottom, beside
the Tree to God, though twice twelve years
in fact would pass before he, ninety, died,

of eating an unwashed peach.
His wife, crippled but chipper, stepped
above him downward and, true, did not precede

him up that Tree, but snored and slept
six seasons more before her speechless spirit
into unresisted silence crept.

A gap, and then my father, Mr.
Downdike of high-school hilarity,
strides manful down the dry, unslippery

pencil line. My mother is at the peak—
eleven days short of thirty-five—
and starting up the lonely slope is me,

dear Chonny. Now on the downward side
behold me: my breath is short,
though my parents are still alive.

For conscientious climbing, God gave me these rewards:
fame with its bucket of unanswerable letters,
wealth with its worrisome market report,

rancid advice from my critical betters,
a drafty house, a voluptuous spouse,
and *quatre enfants*—none of them bed-wetters.

From *Time*'s grim cover, my fretful face peers out.
Ten thousand soggy mornings have warped my lids
and minced a crafty pulp of this my mouth;

and yet, incapable of being dimmed,
there harbors still inside me like the light
an anchored ketch displays, among my ribs,

a hopeful burning riding out the tide
that this strange universe employs
to strip itself of wreckage in the night.

"Take stock. Repent. The motion that destroys
creates elsewhere; the looping sun
sees no world twice." False truths! I vouch for boys

impatient, inartistically, to get things done,
armored in speckled cardboard
and an untoward faith in the eye/I pun.

71

II. The Photographs

ARGUMENT: The pictures speak for themselves. A cycle of growth, mating, and birth. The coarse dots, calligraphic and abstract, become faces, with troubled expressions. Distance improves vision. Lost time sifts through these immutable old screens.

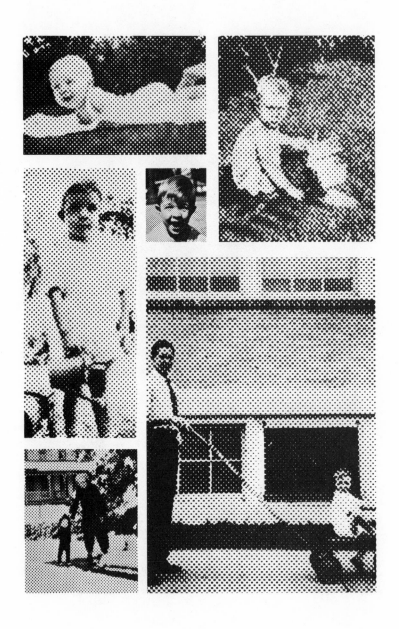

74

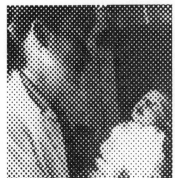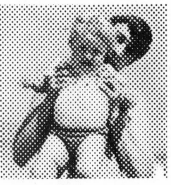

III. The Dance of the Solids

ARGUMENT: In stanzas associated with allegory the actual atomic structure of solids unfolds. Metals, Ceramics, and Polymers. The conduction of heat, electricity, and light; nonsymmetry and magnetism. Solidity emerges as intricate and giddy.

All things are Atoms: Earth and Water, Air
    And Fire, all, *Democritus* foretold.
    Swiss *Paracelsus,* in's alchemic lair,
    Saw Sulphur, Salt, and Mercury unfold
    Amid Millennial hopes of faking Gold.
    Lavoisier dethroned Phlogiston; then
    Molecular Analysis made bold
    Forays into the gases: Hydrogen
Stood naked in the dazzled sight of Learned Men.

The Solid State, however, kept its grains
    Of Microstructure coarsely veiled until
    X-ray diffraction pierced the Crystal Planes
    That roofed the giddy Dance, the taut Quadrille
    Where Silicon and Carbon Atoms will
    Link Valencies, four-figured, hand in hand
    With common Ions and Rare Earths to fill
    The lattices of Matter, Salt or Sand,
With tiny Excitations, quantitively grand.

The *Metals,* lustrous Monarchs of the Cave,
    Are ductile and conductive and opaque
    Because each Atom generously gave
    Its own Electrons to a mutual Stake,
    A Pool that acts as Bond. The Ions take
    The stacking shape of Spheres, and slip and flow
    When pressed or dented; thusly *Metals* make

A better Paper Clip than a Window,
Are vulnerable to Shear, and, heated, brightly glow.

Ceramic, muddy Queen of Human Arts,
   First served as simple Stone. Feldspar supplied
   Crude Clay; and Rubies, Porcelain, and Quartz
   Came each to light. Aluminum Oxide
   Is typical—a *Metal* close-allied
   With Oxygen ionically; no free
   Electrons form a lubricating tide,
   Hence, Empresslike, *Ceramics* tend to be
Resistant, porous, brittle, and refractory.

Prince *Glass, Ceramic*'s son, though crystal-clear,
   Is no wise crystalline. The fond Voyeur
   And Narcissist alike devoutly peer
   Into Disorder, the Disorderer
   Being Covalent Bondings that prefer
   Prolonged Viscosity and spread loose nets
   Photons slip through. The average *Polymer*
   Enjoys a Glassy state, but cools, forgets
To slump, and clouds in closely patterned Minuets.

The *Polymers,* those giant Molecules,
   Like Starch and Polyoxymethylene,
   Flesh out, as protein Serfs and plastic Fools,
   This Kingdom with Life's Stuff. Our time has seen
   The synthesis of Polyisoprene
   And many cross-linked Helixes unknown
   To *Robert Hooke;* but each primordial Bean
   Knew Cellulose by heart. *Nature* alone
Of Collagen and Apatite compounded Bone.

What happens in these Lattices when *Heat*
   Transports Vibrations through a solid mass?

$T = 3Nk$ is much too neat;
A rigid Crystal's not a fluid Gas.
Debye in 1912 proposed Elas-
Tic Waves called *phonons* that obey *Max Planck's*
$E = hv$. Though amorphous *Glass*,
Umklapp Switchbacks, and Isotopes play Pranks
Upon his Formulae, *Debye* deserves warm Thanks.

Electroconductivity depends
    On Free Electrons: in Germanium
    A touch of Arsenic liberates; in blends
    Like Nickel Oxide, *Ohms* thwart Current. From
    Pure Copper threads to wads of Chewing Gum
    Resistance varies hugely. Cold and Light
    As well as "doping" modify the sum
    Of *Fermi* levels, Ion scatter, site
Proximity, and other Factors recondite.

Textbooks and Heaven only are Ideal;
    Solidity is an imperfect state.
    Within the cracked and dislocated Real
    Nonstoichiometric Crystals dominate.
    Stray Atoms sully and precipitate;
    Strange holes, *excitons,* wander loose; because
    Of Dangling Bonds, a chemical Substrate
    Corrodes and catalyzes—surface Flaws
Help Epitaxial Growth to fix adsorptive claws.

White Sunlight, *Newton* saw, is not so pure;
    A Spectrum bared the Rainbow to his view.
    Each Element absorbs its signature:
    Go add a negative Electron to
    Potassium Chloride; it turns deep blue,
    As Chromium incarnadines Sapphire.
    Wavelengths, absorbed, are reëmitted through

Fluorescence, Phosphorescence, and the higher
Intensities that deadly *Laser Beams* require.

Magnetic Atoms, such as Iron, keep
    Unpaired Electrons in their middle shell,
    Each one a spinning Magnet that would leap
    The *Bloch Walls* whereat antiparallel
    Domains converge. Diffuse Material
    Becomes *Magnetic* when another Field
    Aligns domains, like Seaweed in a swell.
    How nicely Microscopic Forces yield,
In Units growing visible, the World we wield!

IV. The Play of Memory

ARGUMENT: The poet remembers and addresses those he has loved.
Certain equations emerge from the welter, in which Walt Whitman swims.
Arrows urge us on. Imagery from Canto II returns, enlarged. Sonnet to
his father. Conception as climax of pointillism theme.

At the foot of the playground slide

                FEET,

                          striking the dust,
                          had worn a trough
                          that after a rain
                          became a puddle.

Last night
        lying listening to rain
                    myriads of points of sound
                              myriads
memory of girl—worker for McCarthy—came to our door—zaf-
tig—lent her my wife's bathing suit—she pinned it—she was

smaller than my wife—pinned it to fit—the house upstairs
hushed—velvety sense of summer dust—she came down—we
went to beach—talked politics lying on pebbles—her skin so
pale—bra too big so the curve of her breast was revealed nearly
to the nipple—"If he ever got any real power it'd ruin him for
me"—pebbles hurt her young skin—we came home—she took
shower—should have offered to wash her back—passing me
on the way to the bathroom—skin—dawn-colored skin—eyes
avoided—eye/I—I should have offered to wash her back—
dressed in her own cool clothes, she handed me back the bathing
suit, unpinned again—lovely skin of her arms untanned from a
summer of campaigning by telephone—strange cool nerve taking a shower in married man's wifeless home—the velvety summer dust waiting to be stirred, to be loved, by the fan—left her
by South Green—"You'll be all right"—"Oh sure"—girls hitch-
hike now—a silk-skinned harem drifting through this con-
science-stricken nation

CLEAN GENE

                              and empty arms
I made a note for this poem
                    in the dark
                         Where am I?
                                   ALL
wrong, all wrong
               myriads
                    window mullions
                                   dust motes
Sense of Many Things
                    what was being said through them?

S o m e t h i n g

              "huh?"

also we
used to
play hop-
scotch
with a
rubber heel ⟶ **1**

2

3

4 5

6 7

8

9↓**10**   *"Hey!"*

You who used to swing on the pavilion rafters
        showing me your underpants
you with whom I came six times in one night
                    back from St. Thomas sunburned
in my haste to return
        my skin peeling from my chest like steamed wallpaper
my prick toward morning a battered miracle
            of response
and your good mouth wetter than any warm washrag
        and the walk afterwards toward the Park
            past Doubleday's packed with my books
your fucked-out insides airy in your smile
        and my manner a proud boy's
                    after some stunt
did you know you were showing me your underpants?
        did you know they said you laid
            beneath the pines by the poorhouse dam?

and in the Algonquin you
    in the persimmon nightie just down to your pussy
and your air of distraction
    your profile harassed against the anonymous wall
        that sudden stooping kiss
a butterfly on my glans
your head beat like a wing on the pillow
    your whimper in the car
you wiped blood from me with a Kleenex
    by the big abandoned barn I never drive past
        without suffering
you who outran me at fox-in-the-morning
    whom I caught on the steps of the Fogg
        the late games of Botticelli
you in your bed Ann in hers
    and the way we would walk to the window
        overlooking the bird sanctuary
our hands cool on each other's genitals
    have you forgotten?
we always exuded better sex than we had
    should I have offered to wash your back?
  you whose breast I soaped
        and you my cock, and your cunt
indivisible from the lather and huge as a purse and the mirror
    giving us back ourselves
        I said look because we were so beautiful and
you said "we're very ordinary"
    and in the Caribbean the night you knelt
to be taken from behind and we were entangled
    with the mosquito netting
and in the woods you let me hold your breasts
    your lipstick all flecked
the twigs dissolved in the sky above and I jerked off
    driving home alone one-handed
singing of you
        you

who demurely clenched
your thighs and came and might have snapped my neck
you who nursed me
and fed me dreams of Manhattan in the cloudy living room
and rubbed my sore chest with VapoRub
     and betrayed me with my father
         and laughed it off
and betrayed me with your husband
         and laughed it off
and betrayed me beneath the pines
         and never knew I thought I knew
your underpants were ghostly gray and now
     you wear them beneath your nightie
              and shy from my hug
      pubescent
      my daughter
who when I twirled you and would not stop bit my leg
     on West Thirteenth Street
you who lowered your bathing suit in the dunes
     your profile distracted against the sand
        your hips a table
     holding a single treat
your breasts hors d'oeuvres
you fed me tomatoes until I vomited
     because you wanted me to grow and you
said my writing was "a waste" about "terrible people"
    and tried to call me down from the tree
       for fear I'd fall
and sat outside nodding while I did toidy
     because I was afraid of ghosts
and said to me "the great thing about us is
     you're sure of the things I'm unsure about and
     I'm sure of the things you're unsure about"
       and you blamed yourself for my colds
    and my skin and my gnawing panic to excel, you
    walked with me on Penn Street

the day I tried to sell cartoons to Pomeroy's
and they took our picture **LOANS**
Oh Mother above
our heads it said

LOANS

I think of you and mirrors:
the one that hung in the front hall
murky and flyspecked and sideways
and the little round one with which you
conducted arcane examinations by the bedside
I lying on the bed and not daring
look over the edge
I was a child and as an infant
I had cracked this mirror in a tantrum
it had a crack
it was a crack
O
↘
MIRRORS ARE VAGINAS
and everywhere I go I plunge my gaze
into this lustrous openness
to see if I have grown
❝ Prodigal, you have given me love!
Therefore I to you give love!"
"O I am wonderful!
I cannot tell how my ankles bend"
"The smallest sprout shows
there is really no death"
"And the pismire is equally perfect,
and a grain of sand,
and the egg of the wren"

"What is commonest, cheapest,
            nearest, easiest, is Me"

   .   .   .   .   ⌣   ⌣

                            .   .

                                                  ▼

Given **M** = **V**
and sex as a "knowing";
      "knowing" = "seeing"
                                        ↘
            ∴ **PENISES ARE EYES**
"his eyes shut and a bird flying below us he was shy all the same
I liked him like that moaning I made him blush a little when I
got over him that way when I unbuttoned him and took his out
and drew back the skin it had a kind of eye in it"
                                        Q.E.D.

and you who sat
            and so beautifully listened
your gray hair limpid and tense like a forest pool
"nor whence the cause of my faintest wish"
            listened as I too effortlessly talked
                  after putting on my glasses
                  (you called them my "magic eyes")
shielding my genitals (remember
                  the Cocteau movie where he slashes an egg?
not to mention poor Gloucester's
            "vile jelly")
talked but never explicit anent sex
            "shy all the same"
trying to wheedle your love
            and after months and years

you pronounced at last:

> "are demonstrations of flying ability to this ugly earth-
> mother figure, successively incarnated in the husbands,
> rather than true relationships with the women"

"Oh,"

o o o͡ o o o͜o͡o͡ o o o ● ● ● ➡

I said, "how sad if true"
       staggering out past the next patient
             in that room of old *Newsweek*s
                cured
sing   *oh*
    "adulterous offers made, acceptances,
                  rejections with convex lips"
"Copulation is no more rank
              to me than death is"
"And mossy scabs of the worm fence,
            and heap'd stones, elder,
                   mullen and poke-weed"
and Mother those three-way mirrors
       in Croll & Keck's you
             buying me my year's jacket
my Joseph's coat
       I saw my appalling profile
and the bulge at the back of my head
       as if my brain were pregnant
"apart from the pulling and hauling stands what I am"
       I felt you saw me as a fountain spouting
gray pool unruffled as you listened to me
       telling cleverly how I loved the mail
how on Philadelphia Avenue I would lie
       in the hall with the flecked mirror
waiting for Mr. Miller
       to plop the mail through the slot
           spilling over me

MALE/MAIL

letter-slots are vaginas
  and stamps are semen swimming in the dark
    engraved with DNA
    "vile jelly"
  and mailboxes wait capaciously to be fucked
  throughout the town as I insomniac
    you pet
"To touch my person to some one else's
     is about as much as I can stand"
"And I know I am solid and sound"
      "The well-taken photographs—
but your wife or friend close and solid in your arms?"

"I tighten her all night to my thighs and lips"
the bed of two beds in the cabin
    whose levels did not meet
the pine needles myriad about us
and the double-decker bunk
    so that mounting me you bumped your
            head
and the sleeping bag spread   ↓
on the lawn by the saltwater inlet   *ow*
    mosquitoes
    myriads

  · · · · · · · · · · · ·
 · · · · · · · · · · · · · · · ·
  · · · · · · · · · · · · · · ·

. . . .
  . . . .
        scintillations of grass
        conversation of distant water
"The play of shine and shade
        on the trees as the supple boughs wag"
    What is pressing through?
        take me
"For every atom belonging to me,
        as good belongs to you"
rien
"And nothing, not God,
        is greater to one than one's self is"
à trente et six ans
"Behavior lawless as snow-flakes"
    having waited out numerous dead nights with listening
        and with prayer
    having brought myself back from the dead with extra-
        vagant motions of the mind
the slide
    the puddle
        the clack of box hockey
           the pavilion
many years later you
    sat on my lap at a class reunion
  your fanny was girdled and hard
a mother of four and I the father of four
    your body metallic with sex
  and I was so happy I stuttered
perhaps Creation is a stutter of the Void
    (I could revise the universe if I just knew math)
  I think it may all turn out to be an illusion
    the red shift merely travel fatigue
  and distance losing its value like inflated currency
    (physicists are always so comfortably talking

about infinite flashlight beams
and men on frictionless roller skates)
and the atom a wrinkle that imagines itself
and mass a factor of our own feebleness
"And to die is different from what any one supposed,
and luckier"
and if my body is history
then my ego is Christ
and no inversion is too great for me
no fate too special
a drowning man cannot pull
himself out by his own hair (Barth)
and you above me in the bunk
coming and crying, "Fuck, John!"
all our broken veins displayed
the honey of your coming a hummingbird's tongue
an involuntary coo

"the
ant's a
centaur
in his
dragon
world"

you pulled

j'ai pensé que
having inwardly revolved numerous Protestant elements—
screen doors, worn Bibles, rubber condoms that snap and
hurt, playground grass that feet have beaten into a dusty
fuzz, certain Popsicle pleasures and hours of real reading,
dental pain, the sociable rasp of Sunday drinks, the roses
dozing, the children bored—
where you were always present
whose shampooed groin
held all I wished to know—
(dance, words!)
I deduced
a late bloomer but an early comer
my works both green and overripe
(Proust spurred me to imitation,
the cars a-swish on Riverside Drive,
and Kierkegaard held back the dark waters, but)

je suis arrivé à la pensée que

$$ASS = \frac{1}{ANGST}$$

you pulled me up
    I did fly
joy pulled a laugh from me
    your hands, voice fluttered
"Is that funny? Is it?"
    your nerves, voice tumbling
a two-body circus

thank you

the taint of performance

forgive me

your
face

your
tense
hand

your
good
sad
shoes

"In vain the mastodon retreats
                    beneath its own powder'd bones"
these dreadful nights of dust
      of discrete and cretin thoughts
            the mind searching for a virtue
      whereon to pillow and be oblivious
"The palpable is in its place,
                    and the impalpable is in its place"
rummaging amid old ecstasies
                    "your poetry began to go to pot
when you took up fucking housewives"
      a hitching post for the heart
            the devil rides in circles

1 2 3 4 6 7 9 8 01

all wrong

wherever we turn we find a curved steel wall
                        of previous speculation
and the water leaking from the main conduits
and the gauges rising
                    the needles shivering like whipped bitches
"The nearest gnat is an explanation,
                    and a drop or motion of waves a key"
"I effuse my flesh in eddies,
                    and drift in lacy jags"

try again

FATHER, as old as you when I was four,
I feel the restlessness of nearing death

But lack your manic passion to endure,
Your Stoic fortitude and Christian faith.
Remember, at the blackboard, factoring?
My life at midpoint seems a string of terms
In which an error clamps the hidden spring
Of resolution cancelling confirms.
Topheavy Dutchmen sundered from the sea,
Bewitched by money, believing in riddles
Syrian vagrants propagated, we
Incline to live by what the world belittles.
    God screws the lukewarm, slays the heart that faints,
    And saves His deepest silence for His saints.

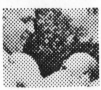

I am a paper bag
                I am trying to punch my way out of
"Out of the dimness opposite equals advance—
                always substance and increase,
                                always sex"

                                                    let's go

"Always a knit of identity—
                always distinction—
                                always a breed of life"
you who breathe beside me
                on Sparks Street spilled your cool nudity
across my eyes

above the summer dust
        body of ivory I have marred, silk I have stretched
you came against me kneeling
                while a truck passed rumbling below
        and in Vermont
the only souls in a square mile of mountain
                the mantle lamps
                the deck of cards
                the Unitarian paperbacks
                the spinning wheel gnawed by a porcupine
we, too, had our violence
"The butcher-boy puts off his killing clothes"
        beside me like a sacrifice
mildly curious as to the knife
        we did conceive
                in that square mile of wooded loneliness
a twinned point began to ravel
        you took me in
                "the fish-eggs are in their place"
most gracious   *merci*

V. Conclusion

ARGUMENT: The poet strives to conclude, but his aesthetic of dots prevents him. His heroes are catalogued. World politics: a long view. Intelligent hedonistic advice. Chilmark Pond in August. He appears to accept, reluctantly, the advice.

An easy Humanism plagues the land;
I choose to take an otherworldly stand.
The Archimedean point, however small,
Will serve to lift the whole terrestrial Ball.
Reality transcends itself within;
Atomically all pundits must begin.
The Truth arrives as if by telegraph:
One dot; two dots; a silence; then a laugh.
The rules inhere, and will not be imposed
Ab alto, as most Liberals have supposed.
Praise *Kierkegaard,* who splintered *Hegel*'s creed
Upon the rock of Existential need;
Praise *Barth,* who told how saving Faith can flow
From Terror's oscillating Yes and No;
Praise *Henry Green,* who showed how lifetimes sift
Through gestures, glances, silly talk, and drift.
Praise *Disney,* for dissolving *Goofy*'s stride
Into successive stills our eyes elide,
And *Jan Vermeer,* for salting humble bread
With dabs of light, as well as bricks and thread.
Praise IBM, which boiled the brain's rich stores
Down to a few electric either/ors;
Praise Pointillism, Calculus, and all
That turn the world infinitesimal:
The midget of the alphabet is I;
The Infinite is littleness heaped high.
All wrong, all wrong—throughout phenomena
There gleams the sword of Universal Law;

Elegant formulations sever Chance
From Cause, and clumsy Matter learns to dance.
A magnet subdivides into Domains
Till ratios are reached where Stasis reigns.
An insect's structure limits it: an Ant
Can never swell to be an Elephant.
The Demiurge expands up to a rim
Where calculable cold collapses Him.
   In human matters, too, Inductions act,
Cleave circumstance, and bare the general Fact.
Karl Marx and *Sigmund Freud* together show
Oppression alternates with Overthrow.
The proletarian Id combines its mass
With Superego's castellated class
To pinch the bourgeois Ego out of power.
The flag of Anarchy besports a flower;
The telescopic cock and winking cunt
Emblazon Urban Youth's united front.
   The world boils over; Ho and Mao and Che
Blood-red inaugurate a brighter day.
Apocalypse is in; mad Eros drives
The continents upon a shoal of lives.
Awash with wealth, the fair Republic creaks,
While boilermen below enlarge the leaks;
What child is this, who gathers up still more
Confetti from the tilting ballroom floor?

   Well, times are always desperate; our strange
Earth greets the old catastrophe of Change.
In bins of textbooks, holocausts lie stacked:
"No life was spared when Genghis Khan attacked."
It little counts in History's jaded eye
Just how we copulate, or how we die.
Six million Jews will join the Congolese
King Leopold of Belgium cleared like trees,

And Hiroshima's epoch-making flash
Will fade as did the hosts of *Gilgamesh*.
The Judgment Day seems nigh to every age;
But History yawns, and turns another page.
Our lovely green-clad mother spreads her legs—
Corrosive, hairy, rank—and, shameless, begs
For Pestilence to fuck her if he can,
For War to come, and come again, again.
   The meanwhile, let us live as islanders
Who pluck what fruit the lowered branch proffers.
Each passing moment masks a tender face;
Nothing has had to be, but is by Grace.
Attend to every sunset; greet the dawn
That combs with spears of shade the glistening lawn.
Enjoy the risen morning, upright noon,
Declining day, and swollen leprous moon.
Observe the trees, those clouds of breathing leaf;
Their mass transcends the insect's strident grief.
The forest holds a thousand deaths, yet lives;
The lawn accepts its coat of bone and gives
Next spring a sweeter, graver tone of green.
Gladly the maple seed spins down, between
Two roots extends a tendril, grips beneath
The soil, and suffers the mower's spinning teeth.
Nothing is poorly made; nothing is dull:
The Crabgrass thinks itself adorable.
   Cherish your work; take profit in the task:
Doing's the one reward a Man dare ask.
The Wood confides its secrets to the plane;
The Dovetail fits, and reconfirms the Grain.
The white-hot writhing Steel is tonged and plunged,
A-sizzle, into Form, all flecks expunged.
The Linotyper leans above his keys,
And feathers down a ton of journalese;
Engraver and Apprentice, in their room

Of acid baths and photophobic gloom,
Transform to metal dots ten shades of gray,
And herald Everyman's beginning day.
   The Clergyman, beside the sighing bed,
Strains for a sign of Credence from the dead.
The Lawyer eagle-eyed for Falsehood's glint,
The Doctor bent on Hardening's murmured hint,
The Biochemist analyzing sera,
The Astrophysicist alone with Lyra,
The Archaeologist with pick and brush,
The Nature-walker having heard a thrush—
Attentiveness! The pinpoint is the locus
Of Excellence in lands of softened focus.
   Applaud your Neighbor; admire his style
That grates upon you like a bastard file.
His trespasses resemble yours in kind;
He, too, is being crowded from behind.
Don't kill; or, if you must, while killing, grieve.
Doubt not; that is, until you can't believe.
Don't covet Mrs. X; or if you do,
Make sure, before you leap, she covets you.
   Like meat upon the table, we will spoil:
Time is the troubled water; Faith, the oil.
The curse of Tempo regulates the dance;
To move necessitates Impermanence.
So flow, flow outward; *Heraclitus* saw,
In Nature's crystalline, the fluid flaw:
Our Guilt inheres in sheer Existing, so
Forgive yourself your death, and freely flow.
   Transcendent Goodness makes elastic claims;
The merciful Creator hid His Aims.
Beware false Gods: the Infallible Man,
The flawless formula, the Five-Year Plan.
Abjure bandwagons; be shy of machines,
Charisma, Ends that justify the Means,
And oaths that bind the postulant to kill

99

His own Self-love and independent Will.
A Mussolini leads to Hitler; hate
Apostles of the all-inclusive State.
   Half-measures are most human; Compromise,
Inglorious and gray, placates the Wise.
By messianic hopes is Mankind vexed;
The Book of Life shows margin more than text.
Ecclesiastes and our glands agree:
A time for love, for work, for sleep, for tea.
Organic drumbeats score our ancient nerves:
Hark to their rhythms, conform to their curves.

   All wrong? Advice, however sound, depends
Upon a meliorism Truth upends;
A certain Sinkingness resides in things.
The restless heart rejects what Fortune brings;
The Ego, too athletic, grows perverse
And muscle-builds by choosing worse and worse.
Our bones are prison-bars, our flesh is cells:
Where Suicide invites, Death-wish impels.
Earthquake, Diseases, Floods, Eruptions, Drought,
Black Comets, Starry Landslides, Wreck and Rout—
Beneath a cliff of vast Indifference
We light our frail fires, peg our poor tents.
The sleepless mouse-gray hours gnaw and stress:
"The Wisdom of the Earth is Foolishness."
   Yet morning here, by Chilmark Pond, is fair.
The water scintillates against the air,
The grassy Earth spins seed from solar rage,
And patiently denies its awful age.
   I am another world, no doubt; no doubt
We come into this World from well without.
The seasons lessen; Summer's touch betrays
A tired haste, a cool Autumnal trace.
The playground dust was richer, once, than loam,
And green, green as Eden, the slow path home.

No snows have been as deep as those my sled
Caressed to ice before I went to bed.
Perhaps Senility will give me back
The primitive rapport I lately lack.
   Adulthood has its comforts: these entail
Sermons and sex and receipt of the mail,
Elimination's homely paean, dreams'
Mad gaiety, avoidance of extremes,
The friendship of children, the trust of banks,
Thoracic pangs, a stiffness in the shanks,
Foretastes of death, the aftertaste of sin,
In Winter, Whiskey, and in Summer, Gin.
   The marsh gives way to Pond, to Dunes, to Sea;
Cicadas call it good, and I agree.
At midpoint, center of a Hemisphere
Too blue for words, I've grown to love it here.
Earth wants me, it shall have me, yet not yet;
Some task remains, whose weight I can't forget,
Some package, anciently addressed, of praise,
That keeps me knocking on the doors of days.
   The time is gone, when *Pope* could ladle Wit
In couplet droplets, and decanter it.
Wordsworth's sweet brooding, *Milton*'s pride,
And *Tennyson*'s unease have all been tried;
Fin-de-siècle sickliness became
High-stepping Modernism, then went lame.
Art offers now, not cunning and exile,
But blank explosions and a hostile smile.
   Deepest in the thicket, thorns spell a word.
Born laughing, I've believed in the Absurd,
Which brought me this far; henceforth, if I can,
I must impersonate a serious man.

April–August 1968

Chloë's Poem

When Chloë flies on silken wings
   She pulls the sky itself along,
And every tugging moment brings
   The butterfly's request: "Be strong."
Her several mouths are graciousness;
   Her many hands, discovery:
A hurricane in each caress
   Is Chloë's way of treating me.

Minority Report

My beloved land,
here I sit in London
   overlooking Regent's Park ⎫
   overlooking my new Citroën ⎭ both green,
exiled by success of sorts.
I listen to Mozart
   in my English suit and weep,
      remembering a Swedish film.
But it is you,
   really you I think of:
      your nothing streetcorners
      your ugly eateries
      your dear barbarities
      and vacant lots
(Brer Rabbit demonstrated:
      freedom is made of brambles).
They say over here you are choking
   to death on your cities and slaves,
      but they have never smelled dry turf,

smoked Kools in a drugstore,
or pronounced a flat "a," an honest "r."
Don't read your reviews,
A ☆ M ☆ E ☆ R ☆ I ☆ C ☆ A:
you are the only land.

Living with a Wife

At the Piano

Barefoot in purple pants
and my ski sweater you
play the piano most seriously
Mozart fumbled with a grimace
the lamplight fumbling unfelt
in the down of your neck

Kind field from which my progeny
have fled to grow voices and fangs
you are an arena where art
like a badly killed bull swerves again

Your bare foot lifts
the lamplight pedals on
my house is half music
my wife holds no harm

In the Tub

You are a pond mirroring
pink clouds there is moss

where your white roots meet
when you lift your arm to shave
you are a younger kind of tree

Silver you rise from the lead
your swan arm seeks a towel
magic has taken place because
my Excalibur razor is dull
and the water would boil a man

Under the Sunlamp

Neuter your hair tugged back
harshly your face a shield
of greased copper less sexy
than a boy by Donatello
too bright to look at long
eyelids sealed in *Urfreude*
metal locked in blinding earth

During Menstruation

My house is on fire red
pain flickers on the walls wet
flame runs downstairs eggs
are hurled unripe from the furnace
and a frown hurts like smoke

Help I am sliding my cry
stands helpless as Galileo
at the side of moons revolving
of unwinding novae burning
flinging Tampax tubes of ash

All the While

Upstairs to my downstairs
echo to my silence
you walk through my veins shopping
and spin food from my sleep

I hear your small noises
you hide in closets without handles
you surprise me from the cellar
your foot-soles bright black

You slip in and out of beauty
and imply that nothing is wrong
Who sent you?
What is your assignment?

Though years sneak by like children
you stay as unaccountable
as the underwear set to soak
in the bowl where I brush my teeth

À l'École Berlitz

Mademoiselle Printemps, my sometimes instructress,
with whom I slowly form pained sentences
(*Je n'y en ai pas vu,*
par exemple, ou
À quelle heure vous êtes-vous couchée hier soir?),
at the end of one lesson
let down her French, and we faced
each other naked, I stripped

of the strange tongue that stiffly cloaks
each cretin utterance in dignity,
and she exposed in all her English vowels,
as luminous and slow as skin,
her consonants curling like bits of fleece,
the sense of her sentence as stunning and clear
as a tear-filled surrender.
"I am interested in doing translation,"
she said, and I couldn't think of a word. Not one.

South of the Alps

Signorina Angeli, veteran of *Vogue*
and a New York marriage, had a heavy foot
between Milan and Como.
                              The speedometer swung
to 160 kilometers per hour,
pressed through, trembling, and clung
like a locust husk that cannot let go.

        Presto, troppo presto!
the sides of our Alfa Romeo hissed
at aquavita trucks we narrowly missed.
Less fluidly, in middle distance, villages
in red hats slowly turned to gaze
like groups of streetcorner pensioners
who had seen worse ruins than ours.
Green Alps, bearing aqueducts,
        drew dreamily near—
        a *quattrocento* paradise
extending its wings to bear us away.

Her chatting lover occupied the death seat. As
I cringed behind him, I felt my face

on the edge of explosion, my tender teeth
strewn in a stew of glass, my spine
a row of dominoes, my ghostless flesh
an interval of metal; and I saw her eyes
suspended in the rearview mirror,
immaculately calm:
                                fringed jewels flattered
by the velvet hypnosis of her task.

        She was an icon nailed
to the blank wall of our blinding speed:
her nose stiletto-straight, her nostrils
nice as a skull's, her lips downdrawn
upon the candy of her pout—
reversed details that linked
in clever foldout to the real:
to the empress oval of her tight-pulled hair,
her ear's pearl curve, her hands
at rest, with tips of nacre, on the wheel.

Beauty, deep in hock to time,
is reckless with its assets; I,
a cowardly word-hoarder, hugged my wish
to smudge more proofs with dubious
corrections. She was clean copy,
        her future a back issue.
Of course I adored her, though my fate
was a midge on her wrist she could twitch away;
the Old Testament said truly: fear
is love and love is rigid-making fear.

A traffic circle. The lake. We slowed.
Acknowledging my *grazie*, Signorina showed
on her smiling jaw a small mole *Vogue*
had airbrushed out.
                        Her mother—

who calls the Pope "Montini" and considers
him a Communist—had had the marriage annulled.
Hence, she is still "Signorina."

We ate, she, I, and her beau,
        above Lake Como
        in green air so
soft we were not dizzy though
the lake was a little sky below,
the motorboats blunt comets.

        The wine
was Piedmontese and suave; the breeze
like a nerved-up gambler fidgeted with chips
of sunlight on the faded tablecloth.
        Bella, troppo bella.
Her hand fell heavy on my arm and grasped.
"Tell me—why doesn't anything last?"

A Bicycle Chain

Left lying in the grass,
                unconnected to anything,
rusted and disjunct,
                it becomes itself.
Dangled, it will stiffly dance,
                parodying legs,
or curl upon itself in balky knots
                nothing like string's.

Neither liquid nor rigid,
                it returns its metal
to organic semi-looseness: consult
                a snake's skeleton

in a museum case, or watch
                              a python's differential curve
parabolize in oozy increments
                              behind safe glass.

Think of Insecta
                    rigged and riveted together,
of protein atoms
                    lightninged into viral chains,
of language's linked lines.
                              The thing is weighty
with its ancient seedtime secret,
                                        articulation.

Tossing and Turning

The spirit has infinite facets, but the body
confiningly few sides.
                              There is the left,
the right, the back, the belly, and tempting
in-betweens, northeasts and northwests,
that tip the heart and soon pinch circulation
in one or another arm.
                              Yet we turn each time
with fresh hope, believing that sleep
will visit us here, descending like an angel
down the angle our flesh's sextant sets,
tilted toward that unreachable star
hung in the night between our eyebrows, whence
dreams and good luck flow.
                              Uncross
your ankles. Unclench your philosophy.
This bed was invented by others; know we go
to sleep less to rest than to participate

in the twists of another world.
This churning is our journey.
                              It ends,
can only end, around a corner
we do not know
                    we are turning.

On an Island

Islanded, my wife turned on the radio for news of home.
Instead she heard that near us a plane had crashed into the
    sea.

She told me after dinner she couldn't face the flight home:
"What would I tell the children as we go down?"

I pooh-poohed her of course, said the odds were against it;
we made love with a desperate undercurrent, and fell asleep.

Then I awoke in the dark, and her fears appeared real.
The blinds were tilted black, my sunburn hurt, I was thirsty.

The tranquil ocean was yet enormous in its noise;
its hissing pursued me into each of the rooms.

My children were asleep, each small mouth darkly open;
"The radio said that a couple with a ten-year-old child

was found in the water, their bodies still clutching him."
Moonlight, pale as a moth, chasmed the front room with
    shadow

and lay white on the water, white on the sliding,
the huge-shushing sliding from island to island—

sleepless, inanimate, bottomless, prayer-denying,
the soughing of matter cast off by the sun, blind sun

among suns, massed liquid of atoms that conceives
and consumes, that communes with itself only,

soulless and mighty; our planes, our islands sink:
a still moon plates the sealed spot where they were.

Sunday Rain

The window screen
is trying to do
its crossword puzzle
but appears to know
only vertical words.

Marching Through a Novel

Each morning my characters
    greet me with misty faces
willing, though chilled, to muster
    for another day's progress
through the dazzling quicksand,
    the marsh of blank paper.
With instant obedience
    they change clothes and mannerisms,
drop a speech impediment,
    develop a motive backwards
to suit the deed that's done.
    They extend skeletal arms
for the handcuffs of contrivance,

slog through docilely
maneuvers of coincidence,
    look toward me hopefully,
their general and quartermaster,
    for a clearer face, a bigger heart.
I do what I can for them,
    but it is not enough.
Forward is my order,
    though their bandages unravel
and some have no backbones
    and some turn traitor
like heads with two faces
    and some fall forgotten
in the trenchwork of loose threads,
    poor puffs of cartoon flak.
Forward. Believe me, I love them
    though I march them to finish them off.

Night Flight, over Ocean

Sweet fish tinned in the innocence of sleep,
we passengers together navigate
the firmament's subconscious-colored deep,
streaming aligned toward a landlocked gate.
Schooled (in customs, in foreign coin), from zone
to zone we slip, each clutching at the prize
(a camera, a seduction) torn from some lone
shore lost in our brains like the backs of our eyes.
Nationless, nowhere, we dream the ocean
we motionless plummet above, fuel roaring,
and stewardesses padding, and stray yen
or shillings jingling in the sky of our snoring.
Incipient, we stir; we burgeon, blank
dim swimmers borne toward the touchdown spank.

Phenomena

The tide goes up and down in the creek.
I wake each morning to witness
the black-clay banks bared like senile gums
or the marsh eclipsed by a second sky.

My furnace went out.
The man who fixed it let me look
at the rejuvenated flame;
it was astonishing.
In a cave of asbestos a vivid elf
went *dancy, dancy, dancy;*
his fingers and feet were uncountable;
he was all hot eye
and merry, so merry he roared.

I handle stones.
They like, perhaps, being handled.
In the earth, at the shovel's first strike,
they are mysterious—one might be
the tip of a China-sized cathedral.
But grubbing and cunning and cursing
bring them one by one to light,
disappointing when dried in the sun,
yet *there,* waterproof, fireproof,
dull veins disclosing a logic of form
and formation, but endurance the foremost quality.
I pile them; I alter their position in the universe.
By a tissue's-width difference, it matters.
Their surfaces say something to my hands.

At night, lying down, I cannot breathe.
A tree inside me clenches and I sweat.
There are reasons, there is medicine;

the frost of death
has found a chink in me, is all.
I breathe easier and, breathing, sleep.
The tide sighs and rises in my sleep.
The flame is furious in its cell below.
Under the moon the cold stones wait.

Wind

If God has any voice it is the wind.

How women hate
this seeking of a vacuum;
it gets their edges up,
they cannot sleep, they think
of Boreas impregnating primeval Night,
of skirts rudely lifted in funhouses.

It is death made loud:
nowhereness bellowing,
now reedy along the copper eaves,
now ballooned to a manifold softness by a tree,
now scraping like flint on the surface of water,
making arrowhead wrinkles,
seeking somewhere to stop and be.

I lie here listening.
God is crying, *for-*
giiiive, demanding, *for-*
go-ooo, proclaiming, *no-*
wheerrre, and begging,
let go-oo-ohhh.

In His mouth my body tastes like stale milk.

Sunday

This day that would tell us what we are
        if we would but listen
this day that is all gray sea
    with no bell buoys to ring the changes
        or turn us toward an appointed shore

into our boredom break
    (a wedding: flecks of rice) flecks
        on windowpanes where
    a branchlet taps (a witch's claw)
        rust-red in rain now
        O lovely failing of the light
that opens our pupils as sunlight never does
        admitting

pale sun   brown lawn   blurred hills   dull sky
    this the necessary palette
        bare bones of our time here
        where all days are Sundays
    disguised as work days

Touch of Spring

Thin wind winds off the water,
earth lies locked in dead snow,
but sun slants in under the yew hedge,
and the ground there is bare,
with some green blades there,
and my cat knows,
sharpening her claws on the flesh-pink wood.

The House Growing

April 1972

The old house grows, adding rooms of silence.
My grandfather coughing as if to uproot
burdock from his lungs,
my grandmother tapping a ragged path
from duty to duty, and now
my father, prancing and whinnying
to dramatize his battle for the dollar,
pricking himself with pens to start each day—
all silent. The house grows vast.
Its windows take bites of the sky
to feed its flight toward emptiness. The mantel
restates its curve of molding undismayed;
the hearthstones fatten on the vanished.

Cunts

*(Upon Receiving a Solicitation for Membership
in The Swingers Life Club)*

The Venus de Milo didn't have one, at least no pussy
that left its shadow in the marble, but Botticelli's Venus,
though we cannot see it for her sea-anemone hand,
did, no doubt—an amber-furred dear mouth we would kiss
could we enter the Arcadian plane of the painting.
We must assimilate cunts to our creed of beauty.
September Morn held her thighs tight shut, and the dolls

we grew up undressing had nothing much there, not even
      MADE IN USA,
but the beauties we must learn to worship now all
have spread legs, splayed in bedspreaded motel beds,
and the snowflakes that burst forth are no two alike:
convolute snapdragons, portals and tears
and T-bones of hair, lips lurid as slices of salmon,
whirlpooly wisps more ticklish than skin, black brooms
a witch could ride cackling through the spatter of stars,
assholes a-stare like monocles tiny as dimes.

"I adore french culture and can really blow your mind"
"half of an ultra-sophisticated couple who prefers"
"love modelling with guys or gals and groovy parties"
"affectionate young housewife would like to meet"
"attractive broadminded funloving exotic tastes"
glory Gloria fellatio Felicia Connie your cunt
is Platonism upside down and really opens innocence
the last inch wider: I bite and I believe.

"Who put this mouse between my legs if not the Lord?
Who knocks to enter? Pigs of many stripes.
My cunt is me, it lathers and it loves
because its emptiness knows nothing else to do.
Here comes the stalwart cock, numb-headed hater,
assassin dragging behind him in a wrinkled sack
reproduction's two stooges; refrigerated in blood,
the salt sperm thrashes to mix with my lipstick.
Nibble my nipples, you fish. My eyelashes tickle your glans
while my cunt like a shark gone senile yawns for its meal.
In my prison your head will lean against the wet red wall
and beg for a pardon and my blood will beat back No.
Here is my being, my jewel, simpler than a diamond,
finer-spun than Assyrian gold and the Book of Kells,
nobler than a theorem by Euler, more darling than a dimple

in a Steuben-glass Shirley Temple—flesh-flower, riddle
of more levels than a Pyramid passageway greased with balm.
Adore!"

      A woman once upon a bed with me
to kiss my soul went down but in addition thrust
her ass up to my face and trembled all her length
so I knew something rare was being served; of course
the lapping was an ecstasy, but such an ecstasy
I prayed her distant face grow still so I could drink
the deeper of this widening self that only lacked
the prick of stars to be a firmament.

                        "Adore
this hole that bleeds with the moon so you can be born!"
Stretched like a howl between the feet pushing the stirrups
the poor slit yields up the bubble of a skull.
Glad tunnel of life, foretaste of resurrection,
slick applicant of appropriate friction
springing loose the critical honey from the delirious bee.

*"You can meet these swinging gals" "you
can be in direct contact with these free-thinking modern people"
"if you are a polaroid photography enthusiast"
"you can rest assured your membership"
"you will discover the most exquisite, intimate"
"you"*   and the clitoris
like a little hurt girl turns its face to the corner.

Well, how were we to know that all you fat sweethearts
were as much the vagina's victim as the poor satyr who sells
his mother's IBM preferred to procure three whores
to have three ways at once—by land, by sea, by air?
"It was all a sacred mush of little pips to me."
Now you tell us, tell us and tell us, of a magical doorbell
crocheted of swollen nerves beneath the fur

and all the pallid moon from scalp to toes decuple
not quite this molehill of a mountain is
the Mare of Disenchantment, the Plain of No Response.
Who could have known, when you are edible all over?
So edible we gobble even your political views
as they untwist in lamplight, like lemon peel from a knife.

Tell us O tell us why is it why
the hairs on the nape of your neck say cunt
and the swirl in your laugh says cunt
and your fingernails flanking your cigarette
and the red of the roof of your mouth and your mischief
and your passion for sleeping dogs and the way
you shape hamburgers naked-handed and the way
you squat to a crying child so the labia stain
your underpants cry cunt CUNT there is almost
CUNT too much of a CUNT good thing CUNT

"And howzabout
that split banana second when
(a clouded tear in its single eye,
stiff angel stuffed with ichor)
the semen in good faith leaps
(no shadows live on marble
like these that coat my helpless hands)
and your [unmentionable]
enhouses the cosmic stranger with a pinch?"

☞ It is true, something vital ebbs from the process
once the female is considered not a monstrous emissary
from the natural darkness but as possessing personhood
with its attendant rights, and wit.

I pulled a Tampax with my teeth and found it, darling,
not so bloody. I loved the death between your toes.
I gazed my sallow fill in motel light until

your cunt became my own, and I a girl. I lost
my hard-on quite; my consciousness stayed raised.
Your mouth became a fumble at my groin.
You would not let me buck away. I came,
and sobbed, triumphantly repentant. You said
with a smile of surprise it was warm,
warm on the back of your throat, hitting,
and not salty, but sweet.
We want to fill your cunt but are unmanned.
My sobbing felt like coming. Fond monster,
you swallowed my tears. We were plighted.
I was afraid. I adore your cunt. But why
is there only one? Is one enough? You *cunt.*

*"I'm available . . . and so are hundreds of other
eager young girls who are ready to pose FOR YOU!"*
Corinna, even your shit has something to be said for it
"avant garde of a new era of freedom" (Coronet)
"dawn of a cultural phenomenon" (Playboy)
"Dr. Gilbert Bartell, the renowned cultural anthropologist"
*"page after page of totally rewarding sexual knowledge
that will be an invaluable asset in your search for greater
sexual understanding Only through complete understanding
can man hope" "Discretion is our middle name!"*
Daphne, your fortune moistens. Stand. Bend down. Smile.

Apologies to Harvard

The Phi Beta Kappa Poem, 1973

Fair, square Harvard, crib of the pilgrim mind;
Home of the hermit scholar, who pursues
His variorums undistracted by

All riots, sensual or for a cause;
Vast village where the wise enjoy the young;
Refuge of the misshapen and unformed;
Stylistic medley (Richardson's stout brown,
Colonial scumble, Puseyite cement,
And robber-baron Gothic pile their slates
In floating soot, beneath house-tower domes
The playtime polychrome of M & Ms);
Fostering mother: time, that doth dissolve
Granite like soap and dries to bone all tears,
Devoured my quartet of student years
And, stranger still, the twenty minus one
Since I was hatched and certified your son.

A generation steeped in speed and song,
In Doctor Spock, TV, and denim *chic*
Has come and gone since, Harvard, we swapped vows
And kept them—mine, to grease the bursar's palm,
To double-space submitted work, to fill
All bluebooks set before me (spilling ink
As avidly as puppies lap a bowl
Till empty of the blankness of the milk),
To wear a tie and jacket to my meals,
To drop no water bags from windows, nor
Myself (though *Werther*, Kierkegaard, and *Lear*
All sang the blues, the deans did not, and warned
That suicide would constitute a blot
Upon one's record), to obey the rules
Yclept "parietal" (as if the walls, not I,
Were guilty if a girl were pinched between
Them after ten); in short, to strive, to bear,
To memorize my notes, to graduate:
These were my vows. Yours were, in gourmet terms,
To take me in, raw as I was, and chew
And chew and chew for one quadrennium,
And spit me out, by God, a gentleman.

We did our bits. All square, and no regrets.
On my side, little gratitude; but why?
So many other men—the founding race
Of farmer-divines, the budding Brahmins
Of Longfellow's time, the fragile sprats
Of fortunes spun on sweatshop spindles
Along the Merrimack, the golden crew
Of raccoon-coated hip-flask-swiggers and
Ritz-tea-dance goers, the continual tribe
Of the studious, the smart, and the shy—
Had left their love like mortar 'twixt your bricks,
Like sunlight synthesized within your leaves,
Had made your morning high noon of their days
And clung, there seemed no need for me to stay.
I came and paid, a trick, and stole away.

The Fifties—Cold-War years *par excellence*—
Loom in memory's mists as an iceberg, slow
In motion and sullenly radiant.
I think, those years, it often snowed because
My freshman melancholy took the print
Of a tread-marked boot in slush, crossing to Latin
With Cerberean Dr. Havelock
In Sever 2, or to Lamont's Math 1
With some tall nameless blameless section man
To whom the elegant was obvious,
Who hung Greek letters on his blackboard curves
Like trinkets on a Christmas tree and who
I hope is happy in Schenectady,
Tending toward zero, with children my age then
To squint confused into his lucent mind.
There was a taste of coffee and of cold.
My parents' house had been a hothouse world
Of complicating, inward-feeding jokes.
Here, wit belonged to the dead; the wintry smiles
Of snowmen named Descartes and Marx and Milton

Hung moonlit in the blizzards of our brains.
Homesick, I walked to class with eyes downcast
On heelprints numberless as days to go.

And when bliss came, as it must to sophomores,
Snow toppled still, but evening-tinted mauve,
Exploding on the windows of the Fogg
Like implorations of a god locked out
While we were sealed secure inside, in love,
Or coolly close—but close enough, we felt,
To make a life or not, as chances willed.
Meanwhile there were cathedral fronts to know
And cigarettes to share—our breaths straight smoke—
And your bicycle, snickering, to wheel
Along the wet diagonal of the walk
That led Radcliffewards through the snowy Yard.
Kiss, kiss, the flakes surprised our faces; *oh,*
The arching branches overhead exclaimed,
Gray lost in gray like limestone ribs at Rheims;
Wow-ow!—as in a comic-strip balloon
A siren overstated its alarm,
Bent red around a corner hurtling toward
Extragalactic woe, and left behind
Our blue deserted world of silent storm.
Tick, tick-a, tick-a, tick, your bike spokes spake
Well-manneredly, not wishing to impose
Their half-demented repetitious thoughts
Upon your voice, or mine: what *did* we say?
Your voice was like your skin, an immanence,
A latent tangency that swelled my cells,
Young giant deafened by my whirling size.
And in your room—brave girl, you had a room,
You were a woman, with inner space to fill,
Leased above Sparks Street, higher than a cloud—
Water whistled itself to tea, cups clicked,
Your flaxen flat-mate's quick Chicago voice

Incited us to word games, someone typed,
The telephone and radio checked in
With bulletins, and, nicest noise of all,
All noises died, the snow kept silent watch,
The slanting back room private as a tent
Resounded with the rustle of our blood,
The susurration of surrendered clothes.

We took the world as given. Cigarettes
Were twenty-several cents a pack, and gas
As much per gallon. Sex came wrapped in rubber
And veiled in supernatural scruples—call
Them chivalry. A certain breathlessness
Was felt; perhaps the Bomb, which after all
Went *mu*SHROOM! as we entered puberty,
Waking us from the newspaper-nightmare
Our childhoods had napped through, was realer then;
Our lives, at least, were not assumed to be
Our right; we lived, by shifts, on sufferance.
The world contained policemen, true, and these
Should be avoided. Governments were bunk,
But well-intentioned. Blacks were beautiful
But seldom met. The poor were with ye always.
We thought one war as moral as the next,
Believed that life was tragic and absurd,
And were absurdly cheerful, just like Sartre.
We loved John Donne and Hopkins, Yeats and Pound,
Plus all things convolute and dry and pure.
Medieval history was rather swank;
Psychology was in the mind; abstract
Things grabbed us where we lived; the only life
Worth living was the private life; and—last,
Worst scandal in this characterization—
We did not know we were a generation.

Forgive us, Harvard; Royce and William James

Could not construe a Heaven we could reach.
We went forth, married young, and bred like mink.
We seized what jobs the System offered, raked
Our front yards, stayed together for the kids,
And chalked up meekly as a rail-stock-holder
Each year's depreciation of our teeth,
Our skin-tone, hair, and confidence. The white
Of Truman's smile and Eisenhower's brow
Like mildew furs our hearts. The possible
Is but a suburb, Harvard, of your city.
Seniors, come forth; we crave your wrath and pity.

Commencement, Pingree School

Among these North Shore tennis tans I sit,
In seersucker dressed, in small things fit;
Within a lovely tent of white I wait
To see my lovely daughter graduate.

Slim boughs of blossom tap the tent and stamp
    Their shadows like a bower on the cloth.
The brides in twos glide down the grassy ramp
    To graduation's candle, moth and moth.

The Master makes his harrumphs. Music. Prayer.
    Demure and close in rows, the seniors sway.
Class loyalty solidifies the air.
    At every name, a body wends her way

Through greenhouse shade and rustle to receive
A paper of divorce and endless leave.
As each accepts her scroll of rhetoric,
Up pops a Daddy with a Nikon. *Click.*

Conversation

My little girl keeps talking to me.
"Why do you look so sad?" she asks,
and, "Isn't Mommy beautiful?"

As if she knows next summer she
will be too near a woman's state
to be so bold, she propositions,
"Let's run along the beach!"
So, hand in hand, we feel to fly
until as if with grains of sand
our skin turns gritty where we touch.
We flirt and giggle, driving back.

With nervous overkill of love
she comes to see me hammer
at the barn, and renders praise:
"You must be the carefullest shingler
in all the world." Indeed, I snap
the blue-chalked line
like a ringmaster's whip, and stare
in aligning the cedar butts
as if into a microscope whose slides
have sectioned the worms of my mind.

At night, guarding her treasure,
watching me frown and read, she falls
asleep, her morning-brushed hair
gone stiff like straw, her braces
a slender cage upon her humid face.
Too heavy to lift, slumped helpless
beneath the power of my paternal gaze,
her half-formed body begs,
"Don't leave. Don't leave me yet."

Melting

Airily ice congeals on high
from Earth's calm breath and slantwise falls
and six-armed holds its crystal faith until
Sun, remembering his lordly duty, burns.

Commences then this vast collection:
gutters, sewers, rivulets
relieve the finned drift's weight
and the pace-packed pavement unsheathe.

It glistens, drips, purls—the World:
brightness steaming, elixir sifting
by gravity's simplicity from all that will silt.

The round-mouthed drains, the square-mouthed grates
take, and they take; down tunnels runs
the dead storm's soul to the unmoved sea.

Query

Pear tree, why blossom?
Why push this hard glitter
of life from your corpse?

Headless and hollow,
each major limb broken
by old storm or snowfall,
you startle the spring.

Doesn't it hurt?
Your petals say not,

froth from your shell
like laughter, like breath.

But (your branchlets spew up
in an agony's
spoutings) it must.

Heading for Nandi

Out of Honolulu
heading for Nandi
I ask them, "Where's Nandi?"
The man tells me, "Fiji."

The airport is open
the night sky black panels
between cement pillars.
I wish I had a woman.

Around me Australians
are holding hands matily
as back in Waikiki
the honeymooners strolled.

By daylight bikinis
strolled bare on the pavement
the honeymoon brides
with waists white as milk

and the Japanese couples
posed each for the other
the women as dainty
as self-painted dolls

and the watching Polynesians
laughed quick as Fayaway
dark as cooking chocolate
that always tasted bitter

and the haunted Americans
with flatland accents
in plastic leis wandered
the blue streets of love.

From the taxi I witnessed
two men embracing
embracing and crying.
I assumed they were sailors.

Nandi? I'll see it
or die in these hours
that face me like panels
in a chapel by Rothko.

I wish I had a woman
to touch me or tell me
she is frightened to go there
or would be, but for me.

Sleepless in Scarsdale

Prosperity has stolen stupor from me.
The terraced lawn beneath my window
has drained off fatigue; the alertness
of the happy seizes me like rage.

Downstairs, the furniture matches.
The husband and wife are in love.

One son at Yale, another in law,
a third bowls them over in high school.

I rejoice. The bed is narrow.
I long for squalor's relaxation,
fantasizing a dirty scene
and mopping the sheet with a hanky.

There is a tension here. The books
look arranged. The bathroom
has towels of too many sizes.
I weigh myself on the scales.

Somewhere, a step. Muffled.
The stairs are carpeted.
A burglar has found us. A son
is drunk. The wife desires me.

But nothing happens, not even
oblivion. Life can be too clean.
Success like a screeching of brakes
pollutes the tunnel of silence.

Mock-Tudor, the houses are dark.
Even these decent trees sleep.
I await the hours guiltily,
hoping for one with whom I can make a deal.

Note to the Previous Tenants

Thank you for leaving the bar of soap,
the roll of paper towels,
the sponge mop, the bucket.

. . .

I tried to scrub the white floor clean,
discovered it impossible,
and realized you had tried, too.

Often, no doubt. The long hair in the sink
was a clue to what? Were you
boys or girls or what?

How often did you dance on the floor?
The place was broom clean. Your lives
were a great wind that had swept by.

Thank you; even the dirt
seemed a gift, a continuity
underlying the breaking of leases.

And the soap, green in veins
like meltable marble, and curved
like a bit of an ideal woman.

Lone, I took a bath with your soap
and had no towel not paper ones
and dried in the air like the floor.

Pale Bliss

Splitting a bottle of white wine
with a naked woman
in the middle of the day.

Mime

on the black stage he
was in an imaginary box
mime mime mime mime mi

its inner surface stopped his
hand. the audience gasped
amazing amazing amazing ama

he climbed stairs that were
not there, walked and went
nowhere nowhere nowhere no

the real world was what his
head told his hands to delimit
in air in air in air in a

chill certain as glass. the
other world was fuzzy and
treacherous treacherous trea

he took a plane, it began
to fall, the passengers shrieked
help o God o help help he

the mime imagined a box.
his feet hit glass, the plane's
fall halted. up, up. praise be
mimesis mimesis mimesis mime

Golfers

One-gloved beasts in cleats, they come clattering
down to the locker room in bogus triumph, bulls
with the *pics* of their pars still noisy in them,
breathing false fire of stride, strike, stride, and putt.
We dread them, their brown arms and rasp of money,
their slacks the colors of ice cream, their shoes,
whiter than bones, that stipple the downtrodden green
and take an open stance on the backs of the poor.

Breathing of bourbon, crowing, they strip:
the hair of their chests is grizzled, their genitals
hang dead as practice balls, their blue legs twist;
where, now, are their pars and their furor?
Emerging from the shower shrunken, they are men,
mere men, old boys, lost, the last hole a horror.

Poisoned in Nassau

By the fourth (or is it the fifth?)
day, one feels poisoned—by
last night's rum, this morning's sun,
the tireless pressure of leisure.

The sea's pale green seems evil.
The shells seem pellets, the meals
forced doses, Bahamian cooking
as bitterly obsequious as
the resentful wraiths that serve it.

Vertigo is reading at the beach
words a thousand miles away,

is tasting Coppertone again,
is closing one's eyes once more against
the mismatch of poverty and beauty.

The beautiful sea is pale, it is
sick, its fish sting like regrets.
Perhaps it was the conch salad, or is
the something too rich in Creation.

You Who Swim

You who in water move as one
long rounded to this use, a stone
that gently fails to sink, you tint
as wind tints air this element.

Androgynous, your round face shorn
by bathing cap, you feign to drown.
"The dead man's float," you say and smile,
your lashes wet and animal.

Soft teacher, otter, other, moth
to the sunk sun, you play at death;
the surface glitter slips, and air
slices your throat with shards of glare.

At night you rise beside me, face
wet with the dark, your dim lips spaced
to hold the bubble love. Your eyes
are shut. We swim our dead men's lives.

Sunday in Boston

The fags and their gay dogs are patrolling
the Garden; on Boylston the blacks,
hollow-backed, demonstrate styles of meander
in this hearttown theirs by default.

The winos on Commonwealth, wiser than wisdom,
blink eyes pale as bottle bottoms;
sun-pickled and lined fine as maps, their faces
beam from within this particular nowhere.

Pistachio George sits high. July beds bloom.
The Ritz's doorman sports his worn maroon.
Above us like a nearer sky great Pei's
glass sheet, cerulean, clasps clouds to its chest.

And, unapologetic in their pallor, girls
in jigging halters and sordid shorts parade
festive colorless flesh regathered from
its Saturday spill, the bearded lover split.

Brick Boston, city of students and drunks!
In Godless, doggy righteousness we bask.
The suburbs send us their stifling cars, and we
in turn give back the hollow sound of bells.

Raining in Magens Bay

The sky, paid to be blue,
yields at most patches of silver
and then, salted with sun, rain
(we can't quite believe it)

135

so heavy the branches of sea-grape
afford no shelter. Run!

The towel, the book, the sunglasses:
save them, and save our fair skins
from the pelting,
bitter and chill, that dyes the arms
of the bay the color of smoke
and erases Outer Brass Island.

Wait, there is a way,
a way not to panic. The picnic
by the cabaña has not stopped cackling;
its voices ricochet louder,
wind-whipped, from lips
an inch above the skin of water.

They have gone swimming,
and the lovers up the beach
persist in embracing submerged.
Come, the calm green is alive
with drops, and soft; one's shadow
no longer lurks below like a shark.

The way to get out of the rain
is to get into the water.
The way for rain to fall
is mixed with sun, like salt.
The way for man to be is mixed
with sun and salt and sea and shadow.

Leaving Church Early

What, I wonder, were we hurrying to,
my grandfather, father, mother, myself,
as the last anthem was commencing? Were
we avoiding the minister's hand at the door?
My mother shied, in summer, from being touched.
Or was it my father, who thought life was grim
and music superfluous, dodging the final hymn?
Or could, I wonder now, the impetus
that moved the small procession of us up
and out, apologizing, from the pew
have come from the ancient man, mysterious
to me as an ancestor turned to ash,
who held some thunders though, a tavern bully
in his time and still a steadfast disliker
of other people's voices? Whatever the cause,
we moved, *bump* and whisper, down
the side aisle, while the organ mulled Stanza One,
a quadruped herd, branded as kin, I
the last of the line, adolescent, a-blush,
out through the odor of piety and the scents
(some purchased at Kresge's, some given by God)
my buxom country cousins harbored in
their cotton dresses, to the sighing exit
which opened on the upbeat as the choir
in love of the Lord and imperfect unison
flung its best self over the balcony.

The lifted voices drifted behind us, spurned.
Loose pebbles acknowledged our shoes.
Our Buick, black and '36, was parked
in a hickory picnic grove where a quoit stake,
invisible as Satan in the grass
of Eden, might spear a tire "of the unwary,"

as my grandfather put it. The interior
of the auto hit us with an hour's heat.
We got in gear, our good clothes mussed,
and, exonerated for the week, bounced home.

Home: the fields, red, with acid rows of corn
and sandstone corner-markers. The undertone
of insect-hum, the birds too full to sing.
A Sunday haze in Pennsylvania.
My unchurched grandma stoops in the foursquare house,
as we prattle in the door, like a burglar
trapped in mid-theft, half-paralyzed, her frame
hung in my memory between two tasks,
about to do something, but what? A cream
jug droops in her hand, empty or it would spill—
or is it a potato-masher, or
a wooden spoon? White-haired, stricken, she stares
and to welcome us back searches for a word.

What had we hurried back to? There could be
no work: a mock-Genesiac rest reigned
in the bewitched farmland. Our strawberries
rotted in their rows unrummaged-for;
no snorting, distant tractor underlined
the rasp of my father's pencil as he marked,
with his disappointed grimace, math exams.
The dogs smelled boredom, and collapsed their bones.
The colors of the Sunday comics jangled,
printed off-key, and my grandfather's feet,
settling in for a soliloquy, kicked up fuzz.
My father stood to promenade his wounds.
I lay down, feeling weak, and pulled a book
across my eyes the way a Bedouin
in waiting out a sandstorm drapes his sheet.
The women clucked and quarrelled with the pots

over who was cook. A foody fog
arose. The dogs rose with it, and the day
looked as if it might survive to noon.

What is wrong with this picture? What is strange?
Each figure tends its own direction, keeps
the axis of its own theatric chore,
scattered, anarchic, kept home by poverty,
with nowhere else to go. A modern tribe
would be aligned around "the television,"
the family show-off, the sparkling prodigy
that needs a constant watching lest it sulk and cease
to lift into celebrity the arc
of interlocked anonymous: we were not such.
We spurned all entertainment but our misery.
"Jesus," my father cried, "I hate the world!"
"Mother," my mother called, "you're in the way!"
"Be grateful for your blessings," Grandpa advised,
shifting his feet and showing a hairless shin.
"*Ach,*" Grandma brought out in self-defense,
the syllable a gem of German indignation,
its guttural edge unchipped, while I,
still in the sabbath shirt and necktie, bent
my hopes into the latest Nero Wolfe, imagining
myself orchidaceous in Manhattan and
mentally constructing, not Whodunit,
but How to Get Out of Here: my dastardly plot.

The rug, my closest friend, ignored
my jabbing elbows. Geraniums raged on the sills.
The furniture formed a living dismal history
of heritage, abandonment, and purchase,
pretension, compromise, and wear: the books
tried to believe in a better world but failed.
An incongruous painting told of dunes

and a dab of unattainable sea.
Outside, a lone car passed; the mailbox held
no hope of visitation—no peacock magazine,
wrapped in brown paper, rife with ads, would come
to unremind us of what we were, poor souls
who had left church early to be about
the business of soaking ourselves in Time,
dunking doughnuts let fall into the cup.
Hot Pennsylvania, hazy, hugged the walls
of sandstone two feet thick as other cells
enfold the carcinomic hyperactive one; we were
diseased, unneighborly, five times alone, and quick.

What was our hurry? Sunday afternoon
beckoned with radioed ball games, soft ice cream,
furtive trips in the creaking auto, naps
for the elderly, daydreams for the young,
while blind growth steamed to the horizon of hills,
the Lord ignoring His own injunction to rest.
My book grew faint. My grandfather lifted his head,
attentive to what he alone divined;
his glasses caught the light, his nose
reclaimed an ancient handsomeness.
His wife, wordless, came and sat beside.
My father swished his hips within his bath of humor
and called his latest recognition to the other
co-captain of dissatisfaction; my mother
came to the living-room doorway, and told us off.
She is the captive, we are the clumsy princes
who jammed the casket with our bitter kisses.
She is our prison, the rampart of her forehead
a fiery red. We shake our chains, amused.
Her myths and our enactment tickle better
the underside of facts than Bible fables;
here to this house, this mythy *then*, we hurried,

dodging the benediction to bestow,
ourselves upon ourselves, the final word.

Envoi

My mother, only you remember with me—
you alone still populate that room.
You write me cheerful letters mentioning Cher
and Barbara Walters as if they were there with you,
realer than the dead. We left church early
why? To talk? To love? To eat? To be free
of the world's crass consensus? Now you read,
you write me, Aristotle and Tolstoy
and claim to be amazed, how much they knew.
I send you this poem as my piece of the puzzle.
We know the truth of it, the past, how strange,
how many corners wouldn't bear describing,
the angles of it, how busy we were forgiving—
we had no time, of course, we *have* no time
to do all the forgiving that we must do.

Another Dog's Death

For days the good old bitch had been dying, her back
pinched down to the spine and arched to ease the pain,
    her kidneys dry, her muzzle white. At last
I took a shovel into the woods and dug her grave

in preparation for the certain. She came along,
which I had not expected. Still, the children gone,
    such expeditions were rare, and the dog,
spayed early, knew no nonhuman word for love.

.   .   .

She made her stiff legs trot and let her bent tail wag.
We found a spot we liked, where the pines met the field.
    The sun warmed her fur as she dozed and I dug;
I carved her a safe place while she protected me.

I measured her length with the shovel's long handle;
she perked in amusement, and sniffed the heaped-up earth.
    Back down at the house, she seemed friskier,
but gagged, eating. We called the vet a few days later.

They were old friends. She held up a paw, and he
injected a violet fluid. She swooned on the lawn;
    we watched her breathing quickly slow and cease.
In the wheelbarrow up to the hole, her warm fur shone.

Dream and Reality

I am in a room.
Everything is white, the walls
are white, there are no windows.
There is a door.
I open it, and neatly
as a shadow a coating of snow
falls door-shaped into the room.
I think, *Snow,* not surprised
it is inside and outside both,
as with an igloo.
I move through the open door
into the next room; this, too, is
white and windowless and perfect.
I think, *There must be more than this.*
This is a dream.

.   .   .

My daughter finds bones
on the marshes. I examine them:
deer heads with sockets round as
cartoon eyes, slender jaws broken.
There are tiny things, too,
no bigger than a pulled tooth,
and just that white—burrs of bone,
intricate, with pricking flanges
where miniature muscles attached.
She says, *Those are mouse jaws.*
Indeed: I see teeth like rows
of the letter "i" in diamond type.
She tells me, *I find them
in the cough balls of owls.*
And this is reality.

Dutch Cleanser

My grandmother used it, Dutch Cleanser,
in the dark Shillington house,
in the kitchen darkened by the grape arbor,
and I was frightened of the lady on the can.
Why was she carrying a stick?
Why couldn't we see her face?

Now I, an aging modern man,
estranged, alone, and medium gray,
I tip Dutch Cleanser onto a sponge,
here in this narrow bathroom,
where the ventilator fan has to rumble
when all I want to switch on is light.

. . .

The years have spilled since Shillington,
the daily *Eagles* stacked in the closet
have burst the roof! Look up,
Deutsche Grossmutter—I am here!
You have changed, I have changed,
Dutch Cleanser has changed not at all.

The lady is still upholding the stick
chasing dirt, and her face
is so angry we dare not see it.
The dirt she is chasing is ahead of her,
around the can, like a minute hand
the hour hand pushes around.

Rats

A house has rotten places: cellar walls
where mud replaces mortar every rain,
the loosening board that begged for nails in vain,
the sawed-off stairs, and smelly nether halls
the rare repairman never looks behind
and if he did would, disconcerted, find
long spaces, lathed, where dead air grows a scum
of fuzz, and rubble deepens crumb by crumb.

Here they live. Hear them on their boulevards
beneath the attic flooring tread the shards
of panes from long ago, and Fiberglas
fallen to dust, and droppings, and dry clues
to crimes no longer news. The villains pass
with scrabbly traffic-noise; their avenues
run parallel to chambers of our own
where we pretend we're clean and all alone.

The Melancholy of Storm Windows

We touch them at the raw turns
of the year—November,
with its whipped trees and cellar sky,
and April, whose air
promises more than the earth
seems willing to yield.
They are unwieldy, of wood, and their panes
monotonously ask the same question—*Am I clean?*

No, the answer is.
They fit less well, we feel, each year.
But the weather lowers,
watery and wider than a tide,
and if a seam or leak of light shows, well,
nothing's perfect under Heaven.
Our mortal shell,
they used to call the body.

In need of paint, they heave
up from the cellar and back down again
like a species of cloud,
shedding a snow of flakes and grime.
They rotate heavy in our hands; the screwdriver
stiffly twirls; the Windex swipes evaporate
in air ominous of coming worse
or, at winter's end, of Easter entombment,
of cobwebbed storage among belittling ants
while the grasshopper world above basks.

Stacked, they savor of the crypt,
of the unvisitable nook
and the stinking pipe, irreparable.
In place, they merely mitigate

death's whisper at the margins,
the knifing chill that hisses how
the Great Outer cares not a pin for our skins
and the airtight hearts that tremble therein.

We, too, are warped each fall.
They resemble us, storm windows,
in being gaunt, in losing putty,
in height, transparency, fragility—
weak slabs, poor shields, dull clouds.
Ambiguous, we have no place
where we, once screwed, can say, *That's it.*

Calder's Hands

In the little movie
at the Whitney
you can see them
at the center of the spell
of wire and metal:

a clumsy man's hands,
square and mitten-thick,
that do everything
without pause:
unroll a tiny rug

with a flick,
tug a doll's arm up,
separate threads:
these hands now dead
never doubted, never rested.

The Grief of Cafeterias

Everyone sitting alone with a sorrow,
overcoats on. The ceiling was stamped
of tin and painted over and over.
The walls are newer, and never matched.
SALISBURY STEAK SPECIAL $1.65.
Afterwhiffs of Art Deco chrome,
and the space is as if the space
of the old grand railroad terminals
has been cut up, boxcarred out, and reused.
SOUP SALAD & SANDWICH $1.29.
Nobody much here. The happiness
of that at least—of vacancy, mopped.
Behind cased food, in Hopper light,
the servers attend to each other, forever.

Spanish Sonnets

I.

By the light of insomnia, truths
that by daylight don't look so bad—
one is over the hill, will die, and has
an appointment tomorrow that can't be broken—
become a set of slippery caves.
Bare facts that cast no shadow at noon
echo and shudder, swallow and loom.
To be alive is to be mad.

Can it be? Only Goya pictures it.
Those last brown paintings smeared in Madrid

fill a room with insomnia's visions,
a Spanish language rapid as a curse.
Prayer's a joke, love a secretion;
the tortured torture, and worse gets worse.

II.

He omits, Goya, not even the good news:
the pink-cheeked peasants in the ideal open,
the village health, the ring of children,
in days when everyone dressed like lords.
Carlos the Fourth wears a fool's mild smile,
and the royal family, a row of breeders,
are softly human, and in this style still
the white-shirted rebel throws up his arms.

The red scream darkens, the brushstrokes plunge
headlong into Rouault, where evil
faces are framed like saints' by lead.
The astonishing *Half-Hidden Dog*
for a sky has a Turner. Pain is paint
and people are meat, as for Francis Bacon.

III.

Yes, self-obsession fills our daily clothes,
bulges them outward like armor,
but at night self must be shed,
the room must be hollow, each lamp
and table crazily exact, and the door
snug in the frame of its silence. When we
can imagine the room when we are not there,
we are asleep. The world hasn't ended.

I worry for you a hemisphere away,
awaiting the edge of evening while I,

deep in midnight, plump the pillow,
turn on the light, and curse the clock.
The planet's giant motion overpowers us.
We cannot stop clinging where we are.

IV.

Each day's tour, I gather sandy castles,
cathedrals of marzipan gone bad,
baroque exploding sunbursts in Toledo,
filigreed silver crosses in Ávila,
like magnified mold proliferating.
The tragical stink of old religion—
greasy-eyed painters trying too hard,
crucifix-carvers gone black in the thumb.

And the Moor piled up brick and ochre,
and the Christian nailed iron in turn
to the gates of the city, and the land breathes green
under power lines hung upon windmills,
and I try to picture your body part by part
to supplant the day's crenellated loot.

V.

The land is dry enough to make the rivers
dramatic here. You say you love me;
as the answer to your thirst, I splash,
fall, and flow, a varied cool color.
Here fountains celebrate intersections,
and our little Fiats eddy and whirl
on the way to siesta and back.
They say don't drink tap water, but I do.

Unable to sleep, I make water at night
to lighten myself for a phantom trip.

My image in the mirror is undramatic,
merely old and nude—a wineskin.
Who could ever love me? Misread
road maps pour out of me in a stream.

VI.

Neumático punturado—we stopped
on the only empty spot in Spain,
a concrete stub road forgotten between
a steep grass slope up to an orange wall
and a froth of mustard veiling two poppies.
Blessedly, the native space held back,
the Fiat held mute while we puzzled through
its code of metal to the spare and the jack.

¡Milagro! It rose like a saint, the car,
on a stiff sunbeam; nuts fell from the wheel
with the ease of bread breaking. The change
achieved, we thankfully looked up. Three men
in sky-blue work clothes in a sky of green
in silence wielded sickles. They had seen.

VII.

All crises pass, though not the condition of crisis.
Today I saw Franco as a bookend, with Juan Carlos.
The king is much on television, and indeed
seems telegenic. Slept well last night,
with dreams in deeper colors than there are.
Imagine a cardinal's biscuit palace, friable,
from whose uncountable windows peep
hospital bedsteads painted lime-green:

I saw this in sunlight. The people
are clean, white, courteous, industrious.
To buy an inner tube, pay a traffic fine,

order Cinzano—this is civilization.
The streets, though dim, are safe at night. Lovers
touch, widows wear black, all is known.

VIII.

These islands of history amid traffic snarls—
Joanna the Mad in Tordesillas
played the harpsichord, leaned on the parapet,
saw a river, great fields, a single man
hooking a sheep who had gone the wrong way;
in Valladolid, Álvaro de Luna
knelt in the tiny, now dirty plaqued plaza
called Ochavo to be beheaded.

These souls thought the stars heaved with them.
My life has seamed shut; I sleep
as return to you dawns like a comet.
Rubber tires burn where martyrs bled,
the madness of sunshine melts the plain,
tulips outnumber truths in my Madrid.

To Ed Sissman

I.

I think a lot about you, Ed:
tell me why. Your sallow owlish face
with the gray wart where death had kissed it,
drifting sideways above your second gin
in Josèph's, at lunch, where with a what-the-hell
lurch you had commanded the waiter

to bring more poison, hangs in my mind
as a bloated star I wish to be brave on.

I loved your stuff, and the way
it came from nowhere, where poetry
must come from, having no credentials.
Your talk was bland, with a twist of whine,
of the obvious man affronted. You stooped
more and more, shouldering the dark for me.

II.

When you left, the ceiling caved in.
The impossible shrank to the plausible.
In that final room, where one last book
to be reviewed sat on your chest, you said,
like an incubus, transparent tubes
moved in and out of your veins
and nurses with volleyball breasts
mocked us with cheerleader health.

You were sicker than I, but I huddled in
my divorcing man's raincoat by your bed
like a drenched detective by the cozy fire
a genial suspect has laid in his manor,
unsuspecting he is scheduled Next Victim.
I mourned I could not solve the mystery.

III.

You told me, lunching at Josèph's,
foreseeing death, that it would be
a comfort to believe. My faith,
a kind of rabbit frozen in the headlights,
scrambled for cover in the roadside brush
of gossip; your burning beams passed by.
"Receiving communications from beyond": thus
you once described the fit of writing well.

The hint hangs undeveloped, like
my mental note to send you Kierkegaard.
Forgive me, Ed; no preacher, I—
a lover of the dust, like you,
who took ten years of life on trial
and lent pentameter another voice.

Ohio

I.

Rolling along through Ohio,
lapping up Mozart on the radio
(Piano
Concerto No. 21, worn but pure),
having awoken while dawn
was muddying a rainy sky,
I learned what human was:
human was the music,

natural was the static
blotting out an arpeggio
with clouds of idiot rage,
exploding, barking, blind.
The stars sit athwart our thoughts
just so.

II.

To be fair, though, about that day—
dull sky, scuds of goldenrod,
fields dried flat, the plain hinting
at a tornado,
the choleric sun
a pillowed sort of face upon

which an antic wisp of cirrus
had set a mustache—

at dawn, I remembered all day,
I had parked beneath an overpass
to check my lights, and breathed
the secret green, the rain.
Like hammered melody the empty road
soared east and west. No static. Air.

Iowa

White barns this morning match the trees
whitewashed by fog that tiptoed in
among the little hills and froze.
Was all land once so innocent?
Did all our country uncles come to rest
on such long porches fortified
by moats of lawn where fireflies and dew
compounded the smoke of their summer cigars?

Those fireflies! From gloomy aisles of corn,
from lakeside groves the lanterns come.
This winter holds them in it like a jar—
contours of ripeness cast in frost
like old lawn furniture of iron,
our fruited plain as virgin as the moon.

Waiting Rooms

Boston Lying-In

Here women, frightened, bring their sex
as black men bring their wounds to the nighttown ward,
red evidence of rampages they ask
abstracted doctors to forgive,
forgive and understand and heal.
That snubnose has a secret in her crotch;
she holds some kind of order slip, a clue
in triplicate, at a loss for the proper desk.

They will bleed her and splay her and bed her
in sheets too white, in a bed too narrow;
black women will tend her sardonically
while men with hands scrubbed too often will peer
into the heart of anfractuous love.
Our bottoms betray us and beg for the light.

Mass. Mental Health

The mad are mad for cigarettes;
slightly shouting in their brain-deaf way,
they bum from one another with angry eyes
that run on separate circuits from their mouths.
The men, a-twitch, in curious rags
of their own combining, seem to have shaved
at some half-lit hour when nothing counted.
Glowering, knotted, their brows are shamed.

The women are different—haughty tramps
exhaling. One wears a paper hat

and has good legs, though bitten nails.
She asks me, "You a doctor?" I say, "No,"
all agitated. When men crack, we expect
murder to out; when women crack, sex.

On the Way to Delphi

Oedipus slew his father near this muddy field
the bus glides by as it glides by many another,
and Helicon is real; the Muses hid and dwelled
on a hill, less than a mountain, that we could climb
if the bus would stop and give us the afternoon.

From these small sites, now overrun by roads and fame,
dim chieftains stalked into the world's fog and grew huge.
Where shepherds sang their mistaken kings, stray factories
mar with cement and smoke the lean geology
that wants to forget—*has* forgotten—the myths it bred.

We pass stone slopes where houses, low, of stone, blend in
like utterings on the verge of sleep—accretions scarce
distinguishable from scree, on the uphill way
to architecture and law. No men are visible.
All out: Parnassus. The oracle's voice is wild.

An Oddly Lovely Day Alone

The kids went off to school,
the wife to the hairdresser,
or so she said, in Boston—
"He takes forever. 'Bye."

I read a book, doing my job.
Around eleven, the rat man came—
our man from Pest Control,
though our rats have long since died.

He wears his hair rat-style—
cut short, brushed back—and told me
his minister had written a book
and "went on television with it."

The proceeds, however, unlike mine,
would be devoted, every cent,
to a missionary church
in Yucatán.

Time went by silently. For lunch,
I warmed up last night's pizza,
and added my plate to the dishwasher,
and soap, and punched FULL CYCLE.

A book, a box of raisins,
and bed. The phone rang once,
a woman whose grant had not come through,
no fault of mine.

"That's all right," I told her.
"Just yesterday,
I failed to win
the National Book Critics' Circle Prize."

The book was good. The bed was warm.
Each hour seemed a rubber band
the preoccupied fingers of God
were stretching at His desk.

A thump, not a dishwasher thump.
The afternoon paper: it said
an earthquake had struck Iran
mere minutes after the shah had left.

The moral seemed clear enough.
More time passed, darkening.
All suddenly unbeknownst,
the afternoon had begun to snow—

to darken, darken and snow:
a fantastic effect, widespread.
If people don't entertain you,
Nature will.

Taste

I have, alas, no taste—
taste, that Talleyrand, that ally of the minimal,
that foreign-accented intuiter
of what sly harmonies exist
betwixt the draped, the draper, and the drape:
that advocate of the *right* as it teeters
on its tightrope above the abyss of excess,
beneath the airy tent-top of not quite enough.

My first wife had taste.
White walls were her answer, and, Take that
to the attic. Nothing pleased her, quite,
save Cézanne and emptiness
and a shabby Oriental rug so full
of dust and virtue it made me sneeze,
descended as it was from her ancestors,

exemplary in piety and in the China trade.
Yet she was *right,* right in all things,
and draped herself in cocktail dresses
of utter black, her arms no less perfect than bones.

I know a man with taste.
He lives alone on a floor of a warehouse
and designs machines that make nothing
but vivid impressions of whirling,
of ellipticity, dazzle, and flow.
He cooks on a single burner
Suprèmes de Volaille aux Champignons,
has hung his brick walls with pencilled originals
by Impressionist masters,
and lives in smiling harmony with all that is there
and is not there,
minding only the traffic noise from the street.
He and my first wife would make a pair,
but they will never meet.

My second wife, that flatterer, says
I have taste.
All decisions as to pattern are deferred to me.
A chair, a car I chose is cheered
when it arrives, like a bugle note, on pitch
with all the still-humming chords
of our clamorous, congratulatory mingling.
It makes one blush, to be credited with taste.
Chipmunk fur, wave-patterns on sand, white asters—
but for these, and some few other exceptions,
Nature has no taste, just productivity.
I want to be, like Nature, tasteless,
abundant, reckless, cheerful. Go screw, taste—
itself a tasteless suggestion.

Penumbrae

The shadows have their seasons, too.
The feathery web the budding maples
cast down upon the sullen lawn

bears but a faint relation to
high summer's umbrageous weight
and tunnellike continuum—

black leached from green, deep pools
wherein a globe of gnats revolves
as airy as an astrolabe.

The thinning shade of autumn is
an inherited Oriental,
red worn to pink, nap worn to thread.

Shadows on snow look blue. The skier,
exultant at the summit, sees his poles
elongate toward the valley: thus

each blade of grass projects another
opposite the sun, and in marshes
the mesh is infinite,

as the winged eclipse an eagle in flight
drags across the desert floor
is infinitesimal.

And shadows on water!—
the beech bough bent to the speckled lake
where silt motes flicker gold,

or the steel dock underslung
with a submarine that trembles,
its ladder stiffened by air.

And loveliest, because least looked-for,
gray on gray, the stripes
the pearl-white winter sun

hung low beneath the leafless wood
draws out from trunk to trunk across the road
like a stairway that does not rise.

Revelation

Two days with one eye:
doctor said I had to wear a patch
to ward off infection
in the abraded cornea.

As hard to get used to as the dark:
no third dimension
and the swaddled eye
reporting a gauze blur to the brain.

You feel clumsy:
hearing and thinking affected also.
Only your sense of smell improves
in a world of foggy card-shapes.

When the patch came off on Monday,
the real world was alarming,
bulging every which way and bright:
a kind of a joke, a pop-up book.

The Shuttle

Sitting airborne on the
New York–to–Boston shuttle
for what seemed the thousandth time,
I recalled what seemed a poem:

In the time before jets,
when the last shuttle left
La Guardia at eleven,
I flew home to Logan

on a virtually empty DC-7
and one of the seven other passengers
I recognized as Al Capp.
Later, at a party,

one of those Cambridge parties
where his anti-Ho politics
were wrong, so wrong
the left eventually broke his heart,

I recalled the flight to him,
but did not recount how sleepy
he looked to me, how tired,
with his peg-legged limp

and rich man's blue suit
and Li'l Abner shock of hair.
He laughed and said to me,
"And if the plane had crashed,

can't you just see the headline?—
ONLY EIGHT KILLED.

ONLY EIGHT KILLED: everyone
would be so relieved!"

Now Al is dead, dead,
and the shuttle is always crowded.

Crab Crack

*In the
Pond*
The blue crabs come to the brown pond's edge
to browse for food where the shallows are warm
and small life thrives subaqueously,
while we approach from the airy side,
great creatures bred in trees and armed
with nets on poles of such a length
as to outreach that sideways tiptoe lurch
when, with a splash from up above, the crabs
discover themselves to be prey.
                                    We can feel
at the pole's other end their fearful
*In the
Bucket*
wide-legged kicking, like the fury of scissors
if scissors had muscle. We want
their sweet muscle. Blue and a multitude
of colors less easily named (scum-green,
old ivory, odd ovals of lipstick-red
where the blue-glazed limbs are hinged),
they rest in the buckets, gripping one another
feebly, like old men fumbling in their laps,
numb with puzzlement, their brains
a few threads, each face a mere notch
on the brittle bloated pancake of the carapace.

*In the
Pot*
But the passion with which they resist!
Even out of the boiling pot they come clattering
and try to dig holes in the slick kitchen floor

and flee as if hours parching in the sun
on the lawn beneath our loud cocktails
had not taught them a particle of despair.

On the
Table
Now they are done, red. Cracking
their preposterous backs, we cannot bear
to touch the tender fossils of their mouths
and marvel at the beauty of the gills,
the sweetness of the swimmerets. All is exposed,
an intricate toy. Life spins such miracles
by multiples of millions, yet our hearts
never quite harden, never quite cease
to look for the hand of mercy in
such workmanship. If when we die we're dead,
then the world is ours like gaudy grain
to be reaped while we're here, without guilt.
If not, then an ominous duty to feel
with the mite and the dragon is ours,
and a burden in being.

In the
Stomach
                          Late at night
the ghosts of the crabs patrol our intestines,
scampering sideways, hearkening *à pointe*
like radar dishes beneath the tide, seeking
the safe grave of sand in vain, turning,
against their burning wills, into us.

Nature

is such a touching child.
When his first wife and he
had their tennis court built,
they were going to plant cedars
transplanted from the field
all around the court, to make

a windscreen.
The digging proved hard,
the wheelbarrow awkward,
and they planted only one,
at the corner.
Now, years later, returning
to drop off a child,
he sees the forgotten cedar
has grown tall enough
to be part of a windscreen
if there were others with it,
if it had not grown alone.

The Moons of Jupiter

Callisto, Ganymede, Europa, Io:
these four, their twinkling spied by Galileo
in his new-invented telescope, debunked
the dogma of celestial spheres—great bubbles
of crystal turning one within another,
our pancake Earth the static, sea-rimmed center,
and, like a beehive, Purgatory hung below,
and angels scattered all throughout, chiming
and trumpeting across the curved interstices
their glad and constant news. Not so. *"E pur
si muove,"* Galileo muttered, *sotto
voce,* having recanted to the Pope.

Yet, it moves, the Earth, and unideal
also the Galilean moons: their motion
and fluctuant occlusions pierced Jove's sphere
and let out all the air that Dante breathed
as tier by singing tier he climbed to where
Beatrice awaited, frosting bride

atop the universal wedding cake.
Not Vergil now but Voyager, cloned gawker
sent spinning through asymptotic skies
and televising back celestial news,
guides us to the brink of the bearable.

Callisto is the outermost satellite
and the first our phantom footsteps tread.
Its surface underfoot is ancient ice,
thus frozen firm four billion years ago
and chipped and peppered since into a slurry
of saturated cratering. Pocked, knocked,
and rippled sullenly, this is the terrain
of unforgiven wrongs and hurts preserved—
the unjust parental slap, the sneering note
passed hand to hand in elementary school,
the sexual jibe confided between cool sheets,
the bad review, the lightly administered snub.
All, in this gloom, keep jagged edges fresh
as yesterday, and, muddied by some silicon,
the bitter spikes and uneroded rims
of ancient impact trip and lacerate
our progress. There is no horizon, just
widespread proof of ego's cruel bombardment.

Next, Ganymede, the largest of these moons,
as large as toasted Mercury. Its ice enchants
with ponds where we can skate and peek down through
pale recent crazings to giant swarthy flakes
of mineral mystery; raked blocks like glaciers
must be traversed, and vales of strange grooves cut
by a parallel sliding, implying
tectonic activity, a once-warmed interior.
This is the realm of counterthrust—the persistent
courtship, the job application, the punch

given back to the ribs of the opposing tackle.
A rigid shame attends these ejecta,
and a grim satisfaction we did not go under
meekly, but thrust our nakedness hard
against the skin of the still-fluid world,
leaving what is called here a ghost crater.

"Cue ball of the satellites"—so joked
the *National Geographic* of Europa.
But, landed on the fact, the mind's eye swims
in something somber and delicious both—
a merged Pacific and Siberia,
an opalescent prairie veined with beige
and all suffused by flickers of a rose
tint caught from great, rotating Jupiter.
Europa's surface stretches still and smooth,
so smooth its horizon's glossy limb betrays
an arc of curvature. The meteors here
fell on young flesh and left scars
no deeper than birthmarks; as we walk
our chins are lit from underneath, the index
of reflection, the albedo, is so high.
Around us glares the illusion of success:
a certain social polish, decent grades,
accreditations, memberships, applause,
and mutual overlookings melt together
to form one vast acceptance that makes us blind.

On Io, volcanoes plume, and sulphur tugged
by diverse gravitations bubbles forth
from a golden crust that caps a molten sea.
The atmosphere smells foul, and pastel snow
whips burningly upon us, amid the cold.
This is our heart, our bowels, ever renewed,
the poisonous churn of basic needs

suffering the pull of bodies proximate.
The bulblike limbic brain, the mother's breast,
the fear of death, the wish to kill, the itch
to plunge and flee, the love of excrement,
the running sore and appetitive mouth
all find form here. Kilometers away,
a melancholy puckered caldera
erupts, and magma, gas, and crystals hurl
toward outer space a smooth blue column that
umbrellas overhead—some particles
escaping Io's seething gravity.

Straining upward out of ourselves to follow
their flight, we confront the forgotten
witness, Jupiter's thunderous mass,
the red spot roaring like an anguished eye
amid a turbulence of boiling eyebrows—
an emperor demented but enthroned,
and hogging with his gases an empyrean
in which the Sun is just another star.
So, in a city, as we hurry along
or swiftly ascend to the sixtieth floor,
enormity suddenly dawns and we become
beamwalkers treading a hand's-breadth of steel,
the winds of space shining around our feet.
Striated by slow-motion tinted tumult
and lowering like a cloud, the planet turns,
vast ball, annihilating *other*,
epitome of ocean, mountain, cityscape
whose mass would crush us were we once
to stop the inward chant, *This is not real.*

Upon the Last Day
of His Forty-Ninth Year

Scritch, scratch, saith the frozen spring snow—
not near enough, this season or the last,
but still a skin for skiing on, with care.
At every shaky turn into the fall line
one hundred eighty pounds of tired blood
and innards weakly laced with muscle seek
to give themselves to gravity and ruin.
My knees, a-tremble with old reflex, resist
and try to find the lazy dancer's step
and pillowed curve my edges flirted with
when I had little children to amaze
and life seemed endlessly flexible. Now,
my heavy body swings to face the valley
and feels the gut pull of steep maturity.

Planting Trees

Our last connection with the mythic.
My mother remembers the day as a girl
she jumped across a little spruce
that now overtops the sandstone house
where still she lives; her face delights
at the thought of her years translated
into wood so tall, into so mighty
a peer of the birds and the wind.

Too, the old farmer still stout of step
treads through the orchard he has outlasted
but for some hollow-trunked much-lopped

apples and Bartlett pears. The dogwood
planted to mark my birth flowers each April,
a soundless explosion. We tell its story
time after time: the drizzling day,
the fragile sapling that had to be staked.

At the back of our acre here, my wife and I,
freshly moved in, freshly together,
transplanted two hemlocks that guarded our door
gloomily, green gnomes a meter high.
One died, gray as sagebrush next spring.
The other lives on and some day will dominate
this view no longer mine, its great
lazy feathery hemlock limbs down-drooping,
its tent-shaped caverns resinous and deep.
Then may I return, an old man, a trespasser,
and remember and marvel to see
our small deed, that hurried day,
so amplified, like a story through layers of air
told over and over, spreading.

The Fleckings

The way our American wildflowers hover
    and spatter and fleck the underlying ground
was understood the best by Winslow Homer;

with brush and palette knife he marred the somber
    foreground field of the mountainous *Two Guides*
and slashed the carpet green of *Boys in a Pasture*.

So all our art; these casual stabs of color—
    Abstract Expressionism ere it had a name—
proclaim the violence underfoot discovered.

East Hampton–Boston by Air

Oh dear,
the plane is so small the baggage
is stuffed into its nose

and under its wings,
like the sacs of a honeybee!
There are six of us, mostly women.

We crowd in, crouching
in our summer denims and shades;
we settle, buckle, inhale. Oh

no, we are aloft! like that,
with just a buzz, and Shelter Island
flattens beneath us, between

the forks of Long Island—the twisty
legs of a dancing man, foreshortened,
his head lost in a tan mist.

The plane is too little!
It rides the waves of air
like a rowboat, of aluminum,

sluing, dropping into the troughs;
it gives out a shuddering Frug motion
of its shoulders—one, two!

I sit facing
the women I am flying to Boston with,
only one of them my wife

but all of them grimacing,
shutting their eyes with a sigh, resting
forehead on fingertips as in sick prayer.

Eyeballs roll, breasts bounce,
nostril-wings turn pale, and hair
comes sweatily undone;

my wife signals
with mirthless terrified lips that only
I can read, "I hate this."

We tip! tip as a body,
skid above some transmitting antennae,
in Rhode Island it must be,

stuck in the Earth like knitting needles
into a ball of yarn: webbed
by wire stays, their eerie points rise.

We are high, but not so high
as not to feel high;
the Earth is too clear beneath us,

under glass that must not be touched,
each highway and house and the sites
of our graves but not yet,

not yet, no! Bright wind
toys with us,
tosses us,

our eyes all meet together
in one gel gaze of fear;
we are closer than in coitus;

the girl beside me,
young and Jewish, murmurs
she was only trying to get to Maine.

And now Boston
is its own blue street-map beneath us;
we can feel in the lurching the pilot

trying to pull in the city
like a great fish
by the throat of the runway.

What invisible castles
of turbulence rise
from the rooted, safe towers!

What ripples of ecstasy
leap
from the wind-whitened water!

The sea-wall, the side-streaming asphalt:
we are down, shouting out
defiance to our own momentum,

and trundle unbroken
back through the static gates
of life, and halt.

Had that been us, aloft?
Unbuckling, we trade
simpers and caresses of wry glance

in farewell, our terror
still moist on our clothes.
One by one

we crouch toward the open and drop,
dishevelled seatbelts left behind
us like an afterbirth.

Small-City People

They look shabby and crazy but not
in the campy big-city way of those
who really would kill you or really do
have a million dollars in the safe at home—
dudes of the absolute, swells of the dark.

Small-city people hardly expect to get
looked at, in their parkas
and their hunting caps and babushkas
and Dacron suits and outmoded
bouffants. No tourists come
to town to stare, no Japanese
or roving photographers.

The great empty mills, the wide main drag
with its boarded-up display windows,
the clouded skies that never quite rain
form a rock there is no out from under.

The girls look tough, the men look tired,
the old people dress up for a circus called off
because of soot, and snarl
with halfhearted fury, their hats
on backwards. The genetic pool
confluxes to cast up a rare beauty,
or a boy full of brains:
these can languish as in a desert

or eventually flourish, for not being
exploited too soon.

Small cities are kind, for
failure is everywhere, ungrudging;
not to mention free parking
and bowls of little pretzels in the ethnic bars.
Small-city people know what they know,
and what they know is what you learn
only living in a place
no one would choose but that chose you,
flatteringly.

L.A.

Lo, at its center one can find oneself
atop a paved and windy hill, with weeds
taller than men on one side and on the other
a freeway thundering a canyon's depth below.
New buildings in all mirror-styles of blankness
are being assembled by darkish people while
the old-time business blocks that Harold Lloyd
teetered upon crouch low, in shade, turned slum.

The lone pedestrian stares, scooped at by space.
The palms are isolate, like psychopaths.
Conquistadorial fevers reminisce
in the adobe band of smog across the sky,
its bell of blue a promise that lured too many
to this waste of angels, of ever-widening gaps.

Plow Cemetery

The Plow: one of the three-mile inns that nicked
the roads that led to Reading and eased the way.
From this, Plow Hill, Plowville—a little herd
of sandstone, barn and house like cow and calf,
brown-sided—and, atop the hill, Plow Church,
a lumpy Lutheran pride whose bellied stones
Grandfather Hoyer as a young buck wheeled
in a clumsy barrow up the bending planks
that scaffolded around the rising spire.
He never did forget how those planks bent
beneath his weight conjoined with that of rock,
on high; he would tell of it in the tone
with which he recounted, to childish me,
dental pain he had endured. The drill,
the dentist warned him, would approach the nerve.
"And indeed it did approach it, very close!"
he said, with satisfaction, savoring
the epic taste his past had in his mouth.

What a view he must have commanded then,
the hickory handles tugging in his palms!—
the blue-brown hills, Reading a red-brick smudge
eleven winding miles away. The northward view
is spacious even from the cemetery,
Plow Cemetery, downhill from the church.
Here rest my maternal forebears underneath
erect or slightly tipping slender stones,
the earliest inscribed *Hier ruhe*, then
with arcs of sentimental English set
afloat above the still-Germanic names
in round relief the regional soft rock
releases to the air slow grain by grain
until the dates that framed a brisk existence

spent stamping amid animals and weather
are weathered into timelessness. Still sharp,
however, V-cut in imported granite,
stand shadowed forth John Hoyer's name, his wife's,
his daughter's, and his son-in-law's. All four
mar one slab as in life they filled one house,
my mother's final year left blank. Alert
and busy aboveground, she's bought a plot
for me—for *me*—in Plow Cemetery.

Our earth here is red, like blood mixed with flour,
and slices easy; my cousin could dig
a grave in a morning with pick and shovel.
Now his son, also my cousin, mounts
a backhoe, and the shuddering machine
quick-piles what undertakers, for the service,
cloak in artificial turf as tinny
as Christmas. New mounds weep pink in the rain.
Live moles hump up the porous, grassy ground.
Traffic along Route 10 is quieter now
the Interstate exists in parallel,
forming a four-lane S in the middle view
that wasn't there before, this side the smudge
red Reading makes between its blue-brown hills.
Except for this and ever-fresher graves,
all changes are organic here. At first,
I did resent my mother's heavy gift,
her plot to bring me home; but slowly I
have come to think, Why not? Where else? I will
have been away for fifty years, perhaps,
but have forever to make my absence up.
My life in time will seal shut like a scar.

Spring Song

The fiddlehead ferns down by our pond
stand like the stems of violins
the worms are playing beneath the moss.

Last autumn's leaves are pierced by shoots
that turn from sickly-pale to green.
All growth's a slave, and rot is boss.

Accumulation

Busbound out of New York
through New Jersey,
one sees a mountain of trash,
a hill of inhuman dimension, with trucks
filing up its slopes like ants
and filing down empty, back to the city
for more.
Green plastic flutters from the mountain's sides,
and flattened tin glints through the fill
that bulldozer treads have tamped
in swatches like enormous cloth.
One wonders, does it have a name,
this hill,
and has any top been set
to its garbagy growing?

Miles pass.
A cut by the side of the eight-
lane concrete highway
(where spun rubber and dripped oil
accumulate)

has exposed a great gesture of shale—
sediment hardened, coarse page by page,
then broken and swirled like running water,
then tipped and infolded by time,
and now cut open like a pattern of wood
when grain is splayed to make a butterfly.
Gray aeons stand exposed in this gesture,
this half-unfurling
on the way to a fuller unfurling
wherein our lives will have been of less moment
than grains of sand tumbled back and forth
by the solidifying tides.

Our past
lies at the end of this journey.
The days bringing each their detritus,
the years minute by minute have lifted
us free of our home,
that muck whose every particle—
the sidewalk cracks, the gravel alleys—
we hugged to our minds as matrix,
a cozy ooze.
What mountains we are,
all impalpable, and
perishable as tissue
crumpled into a ball and tossed upon the flames!
Lives, piled upon lives.
The faces outside the stopped bus window
have the doughy, stoic look of those
who grew up where I did,
ages ago.

Styles of Bloom

One sudden week (the roads still salty,
and only garlic green) forsythia
shouts out in butter-yellow monotone
from hedge to hedge and yard to yard,
a shout the ochre that precedes
maple leaves echoes overhead.

The dogwood's blossoms float sideways
like stars in the dark that teatime brings
to the side of the tall brick house,
but almost vanish, melting flakes,
in morning's bald spring sun.

Lilac: an explosion of ego
odorous creamily, each raceme
dewy till noon, then overnight
turned papery and faded—a souvenir.

In arches weighed by fragile suds,
the bridal wreath looks drenched.
White as virtue is white, plain
as truth is plain, the bushes can't wait
to shed their fat bundles of sequins;
burdensome summer has come.

Natural Question

What rich joke does
the comically spherical peony bud—
like the big button on a gong striker—

hold, that black ants
crawl all over its tie-dyed tightness,
as if to tickle it forth?

Two Hoppers

Displayed in the Thyssen-Bornemisza Collection

The smaller, older *Girl at a Sewing Machine*
   shows her, pale profile obscured by her hair,
at work beneath an orange wall while sky

in pure blue pillars stands in a window bay.
   She is alone and silent. The heroine
of *Hotel Room,* down to her slip, gazes

at a letter unfolded upon her naked knees.
   Her eyes and face are in shadow. The day
rumbles with invisible traffic outside

this room where a wall is yellow, where
   a bureau blocks our way with brown and luggage
stands in wait of its unpacking near

a green armchair: sun-wearied, Thirties plush.
   We have been here before. The slanting light,
the woman alone and held amid the planes

of paint by some mysterious witness we're
   invited to breathe beside. The sewing girl,
the letter. Hopper is saying, *I am Vermeer.*

Two Sonnets Whose Titles
Came to Me Simultaneously

The Dying Phobiac Takes His Fears with Him

Visions of flame fanned out from cigarette
or insecure connection to engulf
all carpets, floors, and sleepers in their beds
torment no longer the shadow in his tent
of sterile plastic, his oblivious lungs
laboring to burn last oxygen,
his fear of heights dissolving as he hangs
high above hissing nothingness.
The dread of narrow places fails to visit
his claustral tent, and hydrophobia,
amid the confluence of apparatus,
runs swirling down a drain. His nerves and veins
release their fibrous demons; earth and air
annul their old contract and set him free.

No More Access to Her Underpants

Her red dress stretched across the remembered small
of her dear bare back, bare for me no more,
that once so nicely bent itself in bed
to take my thrusts and then my stunned caress,
disclosing to my sated gaze a film
of down, of sheen, upon the dulcet skin—
her red dress stretched, I say, as carapace
upon her tasty flesh, she shows a face
of stone and turns to others at the party.

Her ass, its solemn cleft; her breasts, their tips
as tender in color as the milk-white bit
above the pubic curls; her eyes like pits
of warmth in the tousled light: all forfeit,
and locked in antarctic ice by this bitch.

Long Shadow

Crossing from a chore as the day
was packing it in, I saw my long shadow
walking before me, bearing in the tilt
of its thin head autumnal news,
news broadcast red from the woods to the west,
the goldleaf woods of shedding branch and days
drawing in like a purse being cinched,
the wintry houses sealed and welcoming.

Why do we love them, these last days of something
like summer, of freedom to move in few clothes,
though frost has flattened the morning grass?
They tell us we shall live forever. Stretched
like a rainbow across day's end, my shadow
makes a path from my feet; I am my path.

Aerie

By following many a color-coded corridor
and taking an elevator up through the heart of the hospital
amid patients with the indignant stare of parrots
from within their cages of drugs,
one can arrive at the barbershop

which the great institution keeps as a sop to the less-than-
    mortal needs
of its captive populace, its serried ranks of pain.

Here, a marvel: a tiny room, high above Boston,
lined with Polaroid photographs of happy, shorn customers,
and the barber himself asleep in two chairs,
snoring with the tranquillity of a mustached machine.
Nor is that all: opposite me,
not ten feet away from where I stood wondering what
    happened next,
a seagull on the ledge outside the windows with so dazzling
    a view
worried at the same problem. With his beak
he rapped at the glass. Once. Twice. Hard.

We two framed the problem, two sentient bookends
with slumber's fat volume between us.
The gull was accustomed to being fed stale breadcrusts, and
    the back
of my neck tickled unendurably, and the tops of my ears.
One man with an oblivious mustache between us held the
    answer
to both of our problems, but until he awoke
our gazes interlocked like the strengths of sumo wrestlers too
    caught up
in the effort of contention even to grunt.

And the sky swooped at the blue harbor, and the great green
    steel bridge
trembled with its traffic, and the machines
keeping alive the terrified and comatose beneath us hummed,
and the icons of old haircuts grinned in fading color,
and all was as the earth is, poised in space between
    contending wishes,
until a sharper rap from the intelligent gull, or else

a more pointed clearing of my throat, awoke
the Demiurge, who, with not
a further wink, sized us both up
and nimbly reached for his bag of old bread and his scissors.

The Code

Were there no rain there would be little noise,
no rustle on the roof that we confuse
with our own bloodbeat on the inner ear,
no braided gurgle in the gutter, no breathing
within the tree whose shelved and supple bulk
sifts the rain to a mist of small descents.

A visitor come from a cloudless planet
would stand amazed by the tumults of our water
and feel bereaved. Without the rain
the taxi wheels would pass like wind on sand
and all the splashing that excites our lovers
fresh from drinks would be a chastening calm;

the sky would be devoid of those enormous
witnesses who hang invisible
until our wish to see brings forth in focus
their sliding incandescent shapes.
Without the rain the very links of life
would drift still uncemented, a dream of dust.

Were there no rain the windowpanes
would never tick as if a spy outside,
who once conspired with us to ferret out
the secret code, the terms of full concord
with all that is and will be, were signalling
with a fingernail, *I'm back, I've got the goods.*

Island Sun

When the albums of this century's intermingling
are assembled, I hope a page will show
two sunburned young honeymooners from Woonsocket,
Rhode Island, or an aged duo from Short Hills,
New Jersey (he in green pants, she in pink pleats),
gazing into the teeth of a black steel band
beating away and pealing in full flight
while the tropical moon leans lopsided overhead—

lopsided because its face is tilted differently
at these holiday latitudes, just as the air
yields different constellations, and summer
is not a season to be earned but always there:
outside the louvered door, the vertical sunlight
like a face of childhood, too good to be true.
The steel band wears mismatching tank tops
and speaks an English too liquid to understand.

Ghosts, we flit through a phantasmal summer
we have earned with dollar-shaped months of living
under clouds, in cold cities that are clouds.
We burn. Our noses have been painted red!
For the white translucent fish that flutter
away from our glass masks, the turquoise water
is paradise; but what of the mahogany man
entranced in his shack by the sea-grape tree?

His irises are like licked Lifesavers, so thin.
He smiles to see us rob him of the sun,
the golden pain he has anesthetized with rum.
Let's play that he's invisible. Six days
of sand like sugar, salt baths, and soft nights,

and you have learned to love your body again:
as brown as a stranger beheld in a mirror
whose back is gilded each time the planet turns.

Pain

Pain flattens the world—its bubbles
of bliss, its epiphanies, its upright
sticks of day-to-day business—
and shows us what seriousness is.

And shows us, too, how those around us
cannot get in; they cannot share
our being. Though men talk big
and challenge silence with laughter

and women bring their engendering smiles
and eyes of famous mercy,
these kind things slide away
like rain beating on a filthy window

when pain interposes.
What children's pageant in gauze
filled the skull's ballroom before
the caped dark stranger commanded, *Freeze*?

Life is worse than mere folly. We live
within a cage wherefrom escape
annihilates the captive; this, too,
pain leads us to consider anew.

Sleeping with You

One creature, not the mollusk
clamped around an orgasm, but
more loosely biune, we are linked
by tugs of the blanket and dreams whose disquiet
unsettles night's oily depths, creating
those eddies of semi-wakefulness wherein
we acknowledge the other is there
as an arm is there, or an ancestor,
or any fact admitted yet not known.

What body is warm beside mine,
what corpse has been slain
on this soft battlefield where we wounded
lift our heads to cry for water
and to ask what forces prevailed?
It is you, not dead, but entrusted
at my side to the flight the chemical mind
must take or be crazed, leaving the body
behind like matériel in a trench.

The moon throws back sunlight into the woods,
but whiter, cleansed by its bounce
amid the cold stars, and the owls
fly their unthinkable paths to pluck
the velvet mole from her tunnel of leaves.
Dreaming rotates us, but fear
leads us to cling each to each as a spar
is clung to by the shipwrecked
till dawn brings sky-fire and rescue.

Your breathing, relaxed to its center,
scrapes like a stone on rough fiber,
over and over. Your skin, steeped

in its forgetting, sweats,
and flurries of footwork bring you near
the surface; but then your rapt lungs slip
with a sigh back into the healing,
that unpoliced swirling of spirit
whose sharing is a synonym for love.

Richmond

The shadows in his eye sockets like shades
upon a bearded hippie, Stonewall Jackson
stares down Monument Avenue toward where Lee
sits on an even higher horse. The cause
was lost but lingers in the faintly defiant
dignity of the pale-gray, Doric dollhouse
from whence Jeff Davis, conscientious Satan,
directed our second rebellion: a damn good try.

Brick graciousness prevails; across the James
wood houses hold black pensioners, and Poe's
ghost haunts a set of scattered tombs, *musei*
exposing to Northern visitors his quills,
a model of his muddy city, and
an etching of, wry-necked in death, Virginia.

Gradations of Black

(Third Floor, Whitney Museum)

Ad Reinhardt's black, in *Abstract Painting 33*,
seems atmosphere, leading the eye into
that darkness where, self-awakened, we

grope for the bathroom switch; no light comes on,
    but slowly we perceive the corners of his square
black canvas to be squares just barely brown.

Frank Stella, in *Die Fahne Hoch,* aligns
    right-angled stripes, dark gray, upon black ground
granular and lustrous, like the magnified

skin of a tattooed noble from Niger.
    The black of Mark Rothko's *Four Darks in Red*
holds grief; small lakes of sheen ebb away,

and the eye, seeking to sink, is rebuffed
    by a much-worked dullness, the patina of a rag
that oily Vulcan uses, wiping up.

While Clyfford Still, in his tall *Untitled,*
    has laid on black in flakes of hardening tar,
a dragon's scales so slick the viewer's head

is mirrored, a murky helmet, as he stands
    waiting for the flame-shaped passion to clear.
With broad housepainter's brush and sweeping hands

Franz Kline, in *Mahoning,* barred radiance; now each
    black gobby girder has yielded cracks to time
and lets leak through the dead white underneath.

The Furniture

To things we are ghosts, soft shapes
in their blindness that push and pull,
a warm touch tugging on a stuck drawer,

a face glancing by in a mirror
like a pebble skipped across a passive pond.

They hear rumors of us, things, in their own rumble,
and notice they are not where they were in the last century,
and feel, perhaps, themselves lifted by tides
of desire, of coveting; a certain moisture
mildews their surfaces, and they guess that we have passed.

They decay, of course, but so slowly; a vase
or mug survives a thousand uses. Our successive
ownerships slip from them, our fury
flickers at their reverie's dimmest edge.
Their numb solidity sleeps through our screams.

Those photographs Victorian travellers
produced of tombs and temples still intact
contain, sometimes, a camel driver, or beggar; a brown
man in a gallabiya who moved his head, his life
a blur, a mere smear on the unflinching stone.

Seven Odes to Seven Natural Processes

Ode to Rot

Der gute Herr Gott
said, "Let there be rot,"
and hence bacteria and fungi sprang
into existence to dissolve the knot
of carbohydrates photosynthesis
achieves in plants, in living plants.
Forget the parasitic smuts,

the rusts, the scabs, the blights, the wilts, the spots,
the mildews and aspergillosis—
the fungi gone amok,
attacking living tissue,
another instance, did Nature need another,
of predatory heartlessness.
Pure rot
is not
but benign; without it, how
would the forest digest its fallen timber,
the woodchuck corpse
vanish to leave behind a poem?
Dead matter else would hold the elements in thrall—
nitrogen, phosphorus, gallium
forever locked into the slot
where once they chemically triggered
the lion's eye, the lily's relaxing leaf.

All sparks dispersed
to that bad memory wherein the dream of life
fails of recall, let rot
proclaim its revolution:
the microscopic hyphae sink
their fangs of enzyme into the rosy peach
and turn its blush a yielding brown,
a mud of melting glucose:
once-staunch committees of chemicals now vote
to join the invading union,
the former monarch and constitution routed
by the riot of rhizoids,
the thalloid consensus.

The world, reshuffled, rolls to renewed fullness;
the oranges forgot
in the refrigerator "produce" drawer
turn green and oblate

and altogether other than edible,
yet loom as planets of bliss to the ants at the dump.
The banana peel tossed from the Volvo
blackens and rises as roadside chicory.
Bodies loathsome with their maggotry of ghosts resolve
to earth and air,
their fire spent and water there
as a minister must be, to pronounce the words.
All process is reprocessing;
give thanks for gradual ceaseless rot
gnawing gross Creation fine,
the lightning-forged organic conspiracy's
merciful counterplot.

To Evaporation

What lifts the ocean into clouds
and dries our ink upon the page?
What gives the porous pavement, an hour after rain,
its sycamore-bark-splotchy steaminess
as molecules of H_2O leap from the fading film
to find lodging in air's loose lattices?
Evaporation,
that random breach of surface tension
by molecules "which happen to acquire exceptionally high
velocities." Brave "happening"!—they fly
the minute distance across
and join another state of matter,
sacrificing, as they depart, heat
to the attraction of the molecules still water,
like a wedlocked beauty leaving behind
her jewels as she flees to a better lover.

Fidelity of process!
The housewife trusts

the sheets left out upon the line to dry,
and on Anguilla, where I spent a winter once,
the natives trusted
the great salt pond behind our home to yield
its annual harvest of sublimated salt.
All around us, water is rising
on invisible wings
to fall as dew, as rain, as sleet, as snow,
while overhead the nested giant domes
of atmospheric layers roll
and in their revolutions lift
humidity north and south
from the equator toward the frigid, arid poles,
where latitudes become mere circles.
Molecular to global, the kinetic order rules
unseen and omnipresent,
merciful and laughingly subtle like the breathing of naiads.
The ladies of Anguilla, lilting in their kerchiefs,
with pale-nailed black hands would spread
their festive damp wash
on the bushes around their shacks to dry,
the scents of skin and soap and oleander confounded
in this process as elemental
as the rain showers that would fall so quickly that
sun, caught shining,
made of each hurtling drop a spear of fire.

As a child I—
I,
the tiniest of nominatives, the atom that "happens"—
watched the blood dry on my wounds
and observed how a cup of spilled water
would certainly vanish
with no more cause than time,
leaving behind as stain
only the dust its tumble of molecules had gathered

or, if the cup had been sweet, the sugar
left faintly behind as precipitate.
Trivial matters!
But I exulted
in the sensation of delivery,
of vapor carrying skyward, just as gravity
hurled water, twisting, down the sink and scummed gutter;
these processes
transpiring without my guilt or willing
were pure pleasure:
unseeable wheels interlocking beyond
all blame and duty and self-exertion,
evaporation
as delicate as mist,
more mighty than a waterfall.

Ode to Growth

Like an awl-tip breaking ice
the green shoot cleaves the gray spring air.
The young boy finds his school-pants cuffs
too high above his shoes when fall returns.
The pencilled marks on the bathroom doorframe climb.
The cells rereplicate,
somatotropin
comes bubbling down the bloodstream, a busybody
with instructions for the fingernails,
another set for the epiderm,
a third for the budding mammae,
all hot from the hypothalamus
and admitting of no editing,
lest dwarves result, or cretins, or neoplasms.
In spineless crustaceans

the machinery of molting is controlled
by phasing signals from nervous ganglia
located, often, in the eyestalks, where these exist.
In plants
a family of auxins,
shuttling up and down,
inhibit or encourage cell elongation
as eventual shapeliness demands,
and veto lateral budding while apical growth proceeds,
and even determine abscission—
the falling of leaves.
For death and surrender
are part of growth's package.

"It's just the eye's way of growing,"
my ophthalmologist euphemizes
of the lens's slow stiffening
and irreversible presbyopia.
Skin goes keratinous,
the epiphyses of the long bones unite with the shaft,
and "linear growth comes to an end."
Comes to an end!
Our aging's a mystery, as is our sleep:
the protein codes, transactions more elaborate
than the accounts of a thousand dummy trusts,
have their smuggling secrets still.

The meanwhile, let us die
rejoicing,
as around us uncountable husks
are split and shed by the jungle push of green
and the swell of fresh bone
echoes the engendering tumescence.
Time's line being a one-way street,
we must walk the tight rope or fly.
Growth is life's lockstep;

we shall never again sit next to Peggy Lutz
in third grade, her breasts
a mere glint on the curve of her tomboy vigor
and our whiskery doom
within us of less dimension than a freckle.

To Fragmentation

Motion, motion.
Within the body cells
each nucleus rotates widdershins
and mitochondria hustle round and round.
All things move, even the continents and Polaris,
those epitomes of stability.
Sun and gravity
push and pull.
Moisture seeps, and night-frost splits.
Glaciers rub a sandpaper of boulders
down U-shaped valleys,
and tectonic uplift
in slow motion shatters the friable shelves of shale.
Carbon dioxide is washed from the air
or the roots of plants:
the resultant carbonic acid
pries loose the glittering grip of flint upon flint.
Dampness evaporates
rapidly from the skin of stone but lingers within,
transforming granite into clay,
which swells,
spalling loose thin flakes like bark from a rotting tree.

At the cliff's base builds a slope of scree.
At the ocean's edge

the waves in a Shakespearean tumult pummel with pebbles
gripped in the fingers of their froth
the shore;
their millennial frenzy carves
the dizzying gills
and the stacks of stratified sediment
we marvelled at, visiting Caithness.
Remember, Martha?
The grass-bearing, cow-feeding turf
worn by those cliffs like a wind-lifted cape?

Breaking, breaking,
eaten, eaten,
the mother rock yields her sands and silts,
each grain of sand a monolith,
each Matterhorn a heap of potential till.
"The eternal mountains were scattered,
the everlasting hills sank low."
The pompous rivers conduct their symphonies of erosion,
and the mites in the subterrene dark
mince finer their mineral meal.
No, nothing is "too, too solid."
All things mundane must slide and weather.
Heat and cold saw back and forth,
and wet and dry;
wind and water and ice and life
have powdered our planet's obdurate skin.
But
had not Earth's aboriginal rock
submitted to fragmentation's lash,
no regolith would have seasoned into soil,
and the imaginary
would never have taken root.

Ode to Entropy

Some day—can it be believed?—
in the year 10^{70} or so,
single electrons and positrons will orbit
one another to form atoms bonded
across regions of space
greater than the present observable universe.
"Heat death" will prevail.
The stars long since will have burnt their hydrogen
and turned to iron.
Even the black holes will have decayed.
Entropy!
thou seal on extinction,
thou curse on Creation.
All change distributes energy,
spills what cannot be gathered again.
Each meal, each smile,
each foot-race to the well by Jack and Jill
scatters treasure, lets fall
gold straws once woven from the resurgent dust.
The night sky blazes with Byzantine waste.
The bird's throbbling is expenditure,
and the tide's soughing,
and the tungsten filament illumining my hand.

A ramp has been built into probability
the universe cannot reascend.
For our small span,
the sun has fuel, the moon lifts the lulling sea,
the highway shudders with stolen hydrocarbons.
How measure these inequalities
so massive and luminous
in which one's self is secreted

like a jewel mislaid in mountains of garbage?
Or like that bright infant Prince William,
with his whorled nostrils and blank blue eyes,
to whom empire and all its estates are already assigned.
Does its final diffusion
deny a miracle?
Those future voids are scrims of the mind,
as academic as blackboards.

Did you know
that four-fifths of the body's intake goes merely
to maintain our temperature of 98.6°?
Or that Karl Barth, addressing prisoners, said
the prayer for stronger faith is the one prayer
that has never been denied?
Death exists nowhere in nature, not
in the minds of birds or the consciousness of flowers,
not even in the numb brain of the wildebeest calf
gone under to the grinning crocodile, nowhere
in the mesh of woods or the tons of sea, only
in our forebodings, our formulae.
There is still enough energy in one overlooked star
to power all the heavens madmen have ever proposed.

To Crystallization

The atom is a crystal
of a sort; the lattices
its interlockings form
lend a planarity most pleasing
to the abysses and cliffs, much magnified,
of (for example) salt and tourmaline.
Arise, order,
out of necessity!

Mock, you crystals,
with all appearance of chiselled design,
our hope of a Grand Artificer.
The graceful layered frost-ferns the midnight elves
left on the Shillington windowpanes
for my morning astonishment were misinformation,
as is
the glittering explosion of tinted quartz
discovered in earth like a heart of thought,
buried evidence
crying out for release to the workman's pick,
tangled hexagonal hair of an angel interred
where it fell, our earth still molten, in the Fall.

When, on those anvils at the center of stars
and those even more furious anvils
of the exploding supernovae,
the heavy elements were beaten together
to the atomic number of 94
and the crystalline metals with their easily lost
valence electrons arose,
their malleability and conductivity
made Assyrian goldsmithing possible,
and most of New York City.

Stendhal thought that love
should be likened to a bare branch crystallized
by a winter in the depths of the salt mines of Hallein:
"the tiniest twigs, no bigger
than a tomtit's claws, are spangled with an infinite
number of shimmering, glistening crystals."
Our mathematics and hope of Heaven
alike look to crystals;
their arousal, the mounting
of molecules one upon the other, suggests
that inner freezing whereby inchoate

innocence compresses a phrase of art.
Music rises in its fixed lattices
and its cries of aspiration chill our veins
with snowflakes of blood;
the mind grapples up an inflexible relation
and the stiff spheres chime—
themselves, the ancients thought, all crystal.
In this seethe of hot muck there is *something else:*
the ribs of an old dory emerge from the sand,
the words set their bevelled bite on the page,
the loved one's pale iris flares in silent assent,
the electrons leap, leaving positive ions
as the fish-scales of moonlight show us water's perfect dance.
Steno's Law, crystallography's first:
the form of crystal admits no angle but its own.

Ode to Healing

A scab
is a beautiful thing—a coin
the body has minted, with an invisible motto:
In God We Trust.
Our body loves us,
and, even while the spirit drifts dreaming,
works at mending the damage that we do.
That heedless Ahab, the conscious mind,
drives our thin-skinned hull onto the shoals;
a million brilliant microscopic engineers below
shore up the wound with platelets,
lay down the hardening threads of fibrin,
send in the lymphocytes, and supervise
those cheery swabs, the macrophages, in their clean-up.
Break a bone, and fibroblasts
knit tight the blastema in days.

Catch a cold, and the fervid armies
swarm to blanket our discomfort in sleep.
For all these centuries of fairy tales poor men
butchered each other in the name of cure,
not knowing an iota of what the mute brute body knew.

Logically, benevolence surrounds us.
In fire or ice, we would not be born.
Soft tissue bespeaks a soft world.
Yet, can it have been malevolence
that taught the skinned knuckle to heal
or set the white scar on my daughter's glossy temple?
Besieged, we are supplied,
from caustic saliva down,
with armaments against the hordes,
"the slings and arrows," "the thousand natural shocks."

Not quite benevolence.
Not quite its opposite.
A perfectionism, it would almost seem,
stuck with matter's recalcitrance,
as, in the realm of our behavior, with
the paradox of freedom.
Well, can we add a cubit to our height
or heal ourselves by taking conscious thought?
The spirit sits as a bird singing
high in a grove of hollow trees whose red sap rises
saturated with advice.
To the child as he scuffles up an existence
out of pebbles and twigs
and finds that even paper cuts, and games can hurt,
the small assemblage of a scab
is like the slow days' blurring of a deep disgrace,
the sinking of a scolding into time.
Time heals: not so;
time is the context of forgetting and of remedy

as aseptic phlegms
lave the scorched membranes,
the capillaries and insulted nerves.
Close your eyes, knowing
that healing is a work of darkness,
that darkness is a gown of healing,
that the vessel of our tremulous venture is lifted
by tides we do not control.
Faith is health's requisite:
we have this fact in lieu
of better proof of *le bon Dieu.*

March–April 1984

Switzerland

The orderly hand of man, hollowing
tunnels and culverts, and threading rails
across the map, and edging lakes, and laying
interlocking tiles, has busied itself
beneath the baleful Alpine stare
of giant limestone layers hurled
kilometers high into a world of snow—
spiked clouds like a negated, broken sun.

The stationmaster weeds his window box
while over his shoulder the Eiger leans,
too out of scale to lend advice. Here time
is tamed by many tiny, ticking hands,
and into silence falls the avalanche
when the desk clerk forgets what language he's speaking.

Munich

Here Hitler had his first success, disguised
as failure. No plaque commemorates the *Putsch*
or marks the hall where Chamberlain begged peace.
Broad avenues and gazing monuments
devoted to the Wittelsbachs and feats
of old Bavarian arms command perspectives
askew with frolicsome façades that mask
riots of silvered rococo within.

The bombs fell lightly here; a burnt-out church
alone eludes the grasp of restoration.
The beer halls smile, the traffic purrs, the young
look innocent as sleeping animals.
The vegetables are stacked like giant jewels
in markets far removed from earth and blood.

A Pear like a Potato

Was it worms, having once bitten
and then wilted away, or some canker
known only to nurserymen? Whatever the reason, the pear
fresh-plucked from my tree where it leans and struggles
in the garden's dappled corner
is a heavy dwarf-head whose faceless face
puckers and frowns around a multitude of old problems,
its furrowed brow and evil squint and pursy mouth
and pinched-in reptilian ear rescrambling,
feature for feature, as I rotate
this weight in my hand, this

friendly knot of fruit-flesh, this
pear like a potato.

It wanted to grow, and did. It
had a shape in mind, and if that shape
in transit was waylaid by scars, by cells that turned
too obdurate to join in with the general swelling
and stalled instead, leaving dents between bulges
like quilt-buttons, well, it kept on going
and rests here in my hand ripe and ready,
sun-warmed, to be eaten.

Not bad. The teeth must pick their spots,
between the potato-eyes. Sun's warmth
mingles sweetly with mine. Our brains
are like this, no doubt, having swelled
in spite of traumas, of languages
we never learned, of grudges never set aside but grown
         around,
like parasites that died but forever snapped
the rhythm whereby cell links up to cell
to make up beauty's smoothness. Plato's
was a manner of speaking, perfection's
an idea there at the start, that
the body and soul make a run at

and, falling short, fill the world instead
with the lopsided jumble that is: the congregation
of the failed yet not uncheerful,
like this poor pear
that never would do at the supermarket,
bubble-wrapped with symmetrical brothers, but
has given me a snack,
a nibble here and there, on my own land,
here in the sun of a somewhat cloudy morning.

Airport

Palace of unreality, where the place
we have just been to fades from the mind—shrinking
to some scribbled accounts, postcards unmailed,
and faces held dear, let go, and now sinking
like coins in clouded, forgetful water—
and the place we are heading toward hangs forestalled
in the stretched and colorless corridors,
on the travelling belts, and with the false-

smiling announcements that melt in mid-air:
to think, this may be our last reality.
Dim alcoves hold bars well-patronized but where
there is not that seethe of mating, each he and she
focused instead on a single survival.
To pass through, without panic: that is all.

From Above

These pink-white acres of overcast
have rivers and cliffs, seen from above.
A heavenly sight, such vapor grazed
by sunset-red; interstices
show baby-blue, a shadow of
the hazed and hidden earth.
Dead-level with our eyes, a horizon
of buff, a salmon line, defines

a smooth electric firmament—
a second sky we fliers see.
Leonardo, Bellini, and others arisen

as Christendom evaporated
first caught that tint, that cold blue-green
just there, where illusion ends.

Oxford, Thirty Years After

The emperors' heads around the Sheldonian
have been replaced: grotesque great noggins
Roman in style, modern in mocking manner,
sculptured lips ajar, drill-holed eyes a-goggle.
Well, it kept some Council artist busy
for a year or two, and off the dole.
The Fifties heads were rotten, eyeless, blackened,
the limestone leprous yet imperial—

the mind supplied what had been lost to time.
Elsewhere, little change; the long-revered
resists where the new succumbs. Our cafeteria
is gone, but cast-iron gates and hallowed archways
still say *keep out, not yours, all mine* beneath
old England's sky of hurrying gray stones.

Somewhere

Travelling alone through Europe,
one can make beautiful moments—
the pale bowl of fruit, the herringbone parquet,
the bare feet up on a marquetry table
in a slant of sun interlaced with sparrow
twitter and a trolley's distant squeal
(always, this silence of travelling alone

like a broad tinted mat that surrounds
some precise old engraving, the absence
of another voice a chance, once more,
to face one's life and to live solemnly,
with an eloquence, like a bow being drawn
across a cello the color of God's cigar—
to make, of this scuttle and heartbeat, art).

Sonnet to Man-Made Grandeur

The Pyramids rooted in a rubble of beggars and bored
    camels
the Parthenon eroding in the chemical nibble of Athenian
    exhaust
the Pantheon with its far square star of a leaking skylight
Chartres and its tilted old floor and darkening sad glass
St. Peter's that monstrous consumer of indulgences
swallowing angels upward in its cavernous blue vaults
St. Paul's the fog-gray of mothering London
its domed gallery whispering while the void below screams

Versailles paved to the horizon with its gardens and mirrors
Napoleon's tomb that orgy of marble *tout à gloire*
Neuschwanstein mad Ludwig's bankrupting fairy tale
and the Washington obelisk like a mote in God's eye:
Majesty! we have lifted you up on the backs of slaves
whose lives you still hold as the curved Earth holds worms

Klimt and Schiele Confront the Cunt

That women in their marble glory still
had pubic hair so startled Ruskin he
turned impotent, and had to be divorced.
The nineteenth century, for all its love
of facts, preferred its female hair to stream,
like emanations of divinity,
a ghostly river, solely from the head.

Vienna, though, was looking lower. Freud
sat giving ear above that mystic couch
where golden heads, and brown, materialized
to spill their minds' secretions; meanwhile, Klimt
and Schiele pencilled pussies blackly on
their nudes and even limned the labia
that frame the blameless hole men seek and dread.

For stylish Gustav Klimt, whose early work
shows much of Edvard Munch's hysteria—
such staring, snake-haired, toxic femmes fatales!—
the pubic patch (once lightly called,
by young Adele Astaire, the "Ace of Spades")
plays hide-and-seek beyond a bent-down head
or tucked between the buttocks, just a curl.

For Egon Schiele, born much closer to
la fin de siècle (*fin* is feminine,
men will observe), the pencil gouges deeper,
and something close to famine dulls the eyes
while fingers seek the masturbator's groove.
The flesh is gaunt and splotchy but alive,
and appetite torments its toothless mouth.

Returning Native

What can you say about Pennsylvania
in regard to New England except that
it is slightly less cold, and less rocky,
or rather that the rocks are different?
Redder, and gritty, and piled up here and there,
whether as glacial moraine or collapsed springhouse
is not easy to tell, so quickly
are human efforts bundled back into nature.

In fall, the trees turn yellower—
hard maple, hickory, and oak
give way to tulip poplar, black walnut,
and locust. The woods are overgrown
with wild-grape vines, and with greenbrier
spreading its low net of anxious small claws.
In warm November, the mulching forest floor
smells like a rotting animal.

A genial pulpiness, in short: the sky
is soft with haze and paper-gray
even as the sun shines, and the rain
falls soft on the shoulders of farmers
while the children keep on playing,
their heads of hair beaded like spider webs.
A deep-dyed blur softens the bleak cities
whose people palaver in prolonged vowels.

There is a secret here, some death-defying joke
the eyes, the knuckles, the bellies imply—
a suet of consolation fetched straight
from the slaughterhouse and hung out
for chickadees to peck in the lee of the spruce,
where the husks of sunflower seeds

and the peace-signs of bird feet crowd
the snow that barely masks the still-green grass.

I knew that secret once, and have forgotten.
The death-defying secret—it rises
toward me like a dog's gaze, loving
but bewildered. When winter sits cold and black
on Boston's granite hills, in Philly,
slumped between its two polluted rivers,
warmth's shadow leans close to the wall
and gets the cement to deliver a kiss.

.

Snowdrops 1987

Isn't it nice (Diane Keaton
singing in *Radio Days:* "*Sssso* nice"),
the way that snowdrops survive,
with many a nocturnal freeze-frame,
the cold days that follow their first thrusting
up through the dead-seeming dirt,
our dusty and stiff winter earth,
as the frost, rebounding, seals the ice
of the stars in their crazed inflexible pattern
and the rabbit curls tighter
in his burrow and the thought
    of a flower
seems quite as fantastic
as that of a warm-blooded God?

Through spring's intermissions
the snowdrops with their ovoid
hung heads on the delicate stems
don't lose faith, but advance
as little or much into bloom as the mood

of that day permits, till the bright days
in the cards come to bake their cool splash
against the stone foundation wall
and make life seem obvious: its tentative
yet implacable announcement as white
as her gown, a snow queen's, as she sings
"*Sssso* nice" (paradise) and lets her face
      come home to
her shy and grateful, pearl-pale smile.

Goodbye, Göteborg

The countries we depart will manage without us.
  The Swedes will rise tomorrow, brush their teeth,
  and go about their businesses. Beneath
the hiss of the street-sweeper's rotary brush
the footstep-peppered cobbles will resume
  their ancient shine; the citizens will seethe
  at dinging crosswalks and ruthlessly will keep
appointments made before our small hiatus.

We meant nothing. We were less to Sweden
  than a scratch on crystal. Their lovely English
  was a pose, a veneer applied by television;
like the thin ice of their eyes, it will be broken.
Behind our backs, all over Europe, men
  are picking up and carrying their languages,
  barbaric fossils, in their mouths; it is
as if they relish our absence from this Eden.

Hot Water

Imagine an empty house—a mansion, vast
and moon-caressed, apparently abandoned.
We tiptoe to a spidery bathroom
and turn on the tap. Out comes, first, rust,
with a belch that shakes pipes behind plaster,
then cold, then tepid water, and, lastly, hot.
Hot water! The house is alive, lived in
at least by the unswitched-off tall heater,
secreting its blue flame in the cellar.
And we ourselves, if you'd prick us, would gush
not scaldingly, but with a detectable
caloric investment. We are enough in our flesh
to warm the hands of another by; we are
hot water, here among the icy stars.

Squirrels Mating

In fits and starts around
and around the hickory's
adhesive trunk, they
chase one another—or
so it seems, though the male
must be doing the chasing
and the female the fleeing,
without ever seeming
to flee very far, or to be
quite out of it. Back in it,
rather. Around and
around the trunk in a
furry flurry, they stop
and start, up and down,

a double helix halted when,
deadpan, he mounts her, and
she, expressionless
in kind but palpably
alert and sensitive and strong,
supports their two linked weights
by clinging with her two
front feet, as frail as burrs,
to bark. The male, his tail
erect and quivering with faith,
hangs on to only her,
their four bright beady eyes
turned outward to the world.
Sun shines. Leaves shake. The slow
world turns. The moment passes,
the primal freeze-frame. Then,
as skittery as ever, they—
our innocent, unsatisfied
Sciuridae—resume
their chase in fits and starts.

Sails on All Saints' Day

One does not expect to see them, out there,
so late, on a sea so blue, beneath this sky
whose faint clouds seem to be remembering
yesterday's skywriting. True, the sails are few,
and the wind they are tilting in is a mystery.
A freighter stands out in Massachusetts Bay
like a small gray tab on a giant folder marked
FILE IN MEMORY. This calm at winter's edge.

More toward the foreground, trees, their blushing done,
look burnt, and the frost-defying roses

incongruous. The summer's last flies find
my warm white corner, where a leaning mop,
set out to dry, plays the hypotenuse
to its own slim shadow, mast-straight and blue.

Tulsa

Not Oral Roberts' city of heavenly glitz
(as are most dreams come true, in dreadful taste)
nor the Gilcrease Museum's thirty thousand
arrowheads and countless canvases
of melting cowboys in pathetic-prairie pink,
but vacant lots impressed me most: downtown
a wilderness of parking space and brave
renewal schemes—the least false note, pawn shops.

Oil money like a flash flood came and went;
one skyscraper was snapped off like a stick
when the big ebb hit. Now the Arkansas
pokes muddily along, and a rusty train
fills all that hollow downtown with a blast
the Cherokee street people blink away.

Washington: Tourist View

The protesters in their houses built of placards
and brandishing signs lettered with a paranoid fullness—
as crabbed as religious texts, in rainbows of emphasis—
would be hard for a Martian statesman to distinguish
from the drab desperadoes who flourish on the sidewalks
around the White House fence with their life-size cutouts
saying POSE WITH RON $5 USE YOUR OWN CAMERA or

(a cutout wrapped in plastic, a fad whose day is over)
POSE WITH OLLIE NORTH.
                                        He who is not with me is
against me; but who, amid all these façades,
is "me"? The marble show of power shows no center,
and on the Mall a mob of happy unempowered
toss Frisbees, tote balloons, and hug their souvenirs.

Behold the gleaming monuments, the stone celebrities
of Capitol and obelisk and sunken V
and Lincoln's stately outhouse, where he sits. Pure fame
ennobles the gilded air and bestows a gladness on
the long reflecting pool where freedom tosses trash.

So much! And yet, not quite enough, these radiant streets,
these gray museums where our loot and feats accrue:
always, for the buses of high-schoolers, and for
the troops of retirees in childish matching hats,
a sense that freedom has no center, and pulls at the legs,
and fails, among the Homers and dinosaur bones,
to yield its sweetest essence, the final word.
                                        Bums stained
or deep-dyed black like shadows sleep beneath cardboard
whose only message names some goods consumed, and cops
bulked out by guns and radios go rolling by
with the careful geared gait of robots: perhaps they,
or the Popsicle men, know where America
has tucked the goody half the planet craves, beneath
the cotton candy, the postermongers, the museum shops.

A spectral Ferris wheel lifts our egos to the height
of the obelisk tip and back down to the grass
worn bare by Sunday patriots and games of catch.

Back Bay

My adult unemployed son and I
(he composes electronic music)
for his birthday traversed the Back Bay
region of Boston, looking for suitable clothes
as a present. A leather jacket, he thought,
might be nice, but we had no idea where,
at this outset of summer, such an item
might be found. The Banana Republic,
on Newbury Street near Gloucester, offered
stone-washed denims and safari outfits in
a crinkly fabric that might be called pre-rumpled.
On Boylston beyond Berkeley, Eddie Bauer
was little better—committed to skimpy summer
and backpacking's sturdy orange canvas.
In Brooks Brothers, where Berkeley and Newbury meet,
my shy son, mirrored, posed in seersucker
but concluded it wasn't leather. I
was desperate to buy him something, he seemed
so shabby, shy and tall and broad; his shirt
baggy, his hairy belly peeping through,
his khaki trousers torn and smudged, his shoes
especially pitiful, scuffed gray dress shoes
he had found in a bin behind the building where
he lives with his equipment and his tapes.
These shoes brought back to me my father, who
dramatized his fear of poverty
by dressing himself in castoffs: dead man's shoes.

Also, as we traversed the area—saved
from the sea by landfill a century ago,
granite scraped from the top of Beacon Hill
and hauled by railroad to the fragrant flats

and dumped into the marsh, which at high tide
glittered just like the sea—I was haunted
by a woman I had once known, who had lived
in Back Bay and who loved to shop. Her wide hips.
Her slight hunch. Her big smile, eager to acquire.
Cancer had come and all her precious clothes,
the closetsful, the silken underwear,
had failed to shield her body cells. The day
was dazzling with white June sun for which
New England's wintry spring had not prepared us.
We were pale, and our pupils still open.
His shirt, my son's, sagged and flapped like a kite,
and I scanned the glittering crowds as if she
might pop into sight, by accident, grinning
in that way she had, displaying her gums.

An eeriness of the land-filled region
shimmered above the artificial flatness,
the alphabetical order of the cross-streets—
Arlington, Berkeley, Clarendon . . . Hereford.
It had been years since I had lived here, but
I remembered. Finally, at Bally's,
one of the swell small shops in Copley Plaza,
which we reached with a long walk along Boylston,
through clouds of construction dust as the city
piles ever more stones on the vanished marsh,
we found a jacket of black leather, for
eight hundred ninety dollars! But my son,
posing before the mirror with many head-cocks,
decided it made him look like an Italian
movie director. He settled for some slacks
and a new shirt back at Eddie Bauer's.
I didn't dare suggest new shoes, his own
as dead as my father and scuffed like a child's.
The bright streets struck us again, and I looked

for her, unable to grasp how gone she was
from this panorama, how she had existed,
as the living still did, less as a thing
than as a pattern or shimmer in what was seen
for a season or two, a ripple in water
that catches light, then spills it like a pod.

In Memoriam Felis Felis

The Pussycat on Causeway Street is closed.
Vacant the poster cases that proclaimed
RED HOT, ADULT, and UNINHIBITED.
Dusty and chained the glass doors opening
into the small slant lobby where a black
bored woman took your fiver and a turn-
stile yielded as if a subway lay beyond.
Dark, dark at noon the theatre had been,
its inky seats as silent as the tomb.
Your fear was sitting on a sleeping bum.
The screen would be ablaze with private parts,
and hollow breathless voices spelled a plot
whose only point was reached recurrently,
at bright pink junctures flecked with pubic hair.
The actors' voices smacked of youth, L.A.,
and nervousness subdued. The girls' bare forms,
most pallid in their bulges, testified
to mornings sunning on the beach before
the dawn of these exploitive afternoons.
Tans are an enemy of sex; the boys
were brown and fair and could not get it up
beneath the camera's cool lascivious eye,
though lapped and coaxed enough to rouse the dead.
The bits of film where actors, clothed, advanced
the feeble plot were touching—fumbled, mouthed

like Christmas pageants, Mary just a girl.
You knew you soon would see her stripped; in this
she was, this L.A. starlet, like a wife.

Your eyes grew accustomed; the flickering
picked out still shapes—men's heads, some bowed, some
     raised
and awash in the carnal, jerky glow,
but all well-spaced, no two adjacent, dumb
ruminants grazing their turf in dreamland.
Young males, their cheeks exuberant with acne,
in Boston for a toot; old Chinamen;
commuters with an hour before the train
dragged them home to suburban spice in frocks;
and alcoholics angels copulating
could not distract from stupor and their thirst:
as in an ill-attended church, our heads
in scatteration showed a stubborn faith,
a sly propensity to praise. What a thing
a woman is! No end to her sufferance,
her spirit of coöperation, or
her elasticity and rosy grace!
The tints of every rose from black to white,
from purple proud in her cleft to surface cream,
became her beauty; mercy swallowed shame.
Succumb to the wrecker's ball, closed Pussycat,
like a hooker jeering at her arrest.
There's more indecency than meets the eye.
Bald light will break into you like a drug
that kills the good bacteria with the bad;
a thousand furtive lusts will throng the sun
and form a cloud as fertile as the id.

Enemies of a House

Dry rot intruding where the wood is wet;
   hot sun that shrinks roof shingles so they leak
and bakes pane-putty into crumbs; the pet
   retriever at the frail screen door; the meek
small mice who find their way between the walls
   and gnaw improvements to their nests; mildew
in the cellar; at the attic window, squalls;
   loosening mortar; desiccated glue;
ice backup over eaves; wood gutters full
   of leaves each fall and catkins every spring;
     salt air, whose soft persistent breath
turns iron red, brass brown, and copper dull;
   voracious ivy; frost heaves; splintering;
     carpenter ants; adultery; drink; death.

Orthodontia

You see them everywhere, the grinning martyrs,
mere children, most of them, though some
are full-grown women, with breasts in bras, their teeth
tight-bound in silver and pried by tinsel bands
whose tensile strength does something to the eyes—
adds a fanatic gleam. What will the ages
not of our faith make of this glad torture?
The Iroquois and Aztecs had their games
and obsidian knives, and the blue Tuareg
sport stony scarifications, but nothing
claims quite the scope of all these chastised mouths
shining on streets and in schoolyards like stars.
To what end? Lips whose curves can barely cling
to parallel perfections that look false.

Condo Moon

When plans were announced to tear down
the garages behind the main street and put up
twelve units of condos, there was a protest
the board of aldermen narrowly overrode.
Now, as I stroll from behind the "convenience store,"
the moon like a tasteful round billboard
hangs wheat-field yellow over the far fake turret
of the condos' massed neo-shingle-style bulk.

The moon makes no protest. It rolls what it sees
into the scene it illumines, and lends its old weight—
afloat and paper-thin and scarred with *maria*—
to what men have thrown up as once it beamed benign
on Crusader castles, fern swamps becoming coal,
and the black ocean when no microbe marred it.

Pillow

Plump mate to my head, you alone absorb,
through your cotton skin, the thoughts behind my bone
skin of skull. When I weep, you grow damp.
When I turn, you comply. In the dark,
you are my only friend, the only kiss
my cheek receives. You are my bowl of dreams.
Your underside is cool, like a second chance,
like a little leap into the air when I turn
you over. Though you would smother me,
properly applied, you are, like the world
with its rotating mass, all I have. You accept
the strange night with me, and are depressed
when the morning discloses your wrinkles.

Seattle Uplift

Rain, now as all night, is tapping
in the alleyway that serves this hotel.
In my view, the skyscraper—the tallest west,
they boasted, of the Mississippi—where
last night I dined with the local rich,
dizzy (I) at the thinness of the glass
that held us back from flying out and falling,
half hides in the clouds, its steel head in a sulk.

More churlishly still, some unknown sport
has left a litter of dirty magazines
on a wet tar roof two stories below.
In the post-dawn gloom, I can make out skin,
its pinkness, and a dark patch or two,
but nothing distinct enough; I am still up too high.

The Beautiful Bowel Movement

Though most of them aren't much to write about—
mere squibs and nubs, like half-smoked pale cigars,
the tint and stink recalling Tuesday's meal,
the texture loose and soon dissolved—this one,
struck off in solitude one afternoon
(that prairie stretch before the late light fails)
with no distinct sensation, sweet or pained,
of special inspiration or release,
was yet a masterpiece: a flawless coil,
unbroken, in the bowl, as if a potter
who worked in this most frail, least grateful clay
had set himself to shape a topaz vase.
O spiral perfection, not seashell nor
stardust, how can I keep you? With this poem.

Charleston

A kind of wooden Boston, crowding toward
the ship-laden Atlantic down peninsular streets.
A square flat common shows, in January,
green blades of spring; a steeple-topping pillar
holds glowering Calhoun while Copa Lounge
(COPA DOLL REVUE FEATURING NICOLE)
and Tavern on the Green between them squeeze
a doorway-wide, one-windowed clapboard shack.

More seaward, like a prow awash with trees,
a fragrant park holds pyramided balls,
some stubby cannons, big blue paving stones
worn smooth by slaves' bare feet, and a prospect of
that horizontal smudge, Fort Sumter, where
six hundred thousand men began to die.

Frost

That snowless, warmthless January sucked
our lawn to the color of nothing, dead turf so hard
just seeing it made tears, sandpapering sight.
But, slowly, rimy patches caught my eye—
small doormats, as it were, of fibrous white,
like summer cobwebs bleached by dew the sky
has breathed upon them from above. But whence
did this small frost descend; or did it rise?
It was the breath, it was the very breath,
I in a revelation realized,
of creatures sleeping in the earth. Their holes,
now that I looked, were what the whiteness rimmed,
an inch or two all round: warm humid breath

from deep within the burrow's dark betrayed
the presence of some life besides my own,
bent down with murderous thought and tracker's glee,
my own breath a continuous white flag
declaring not truce but vital rivalry.
These sleeping were the gardener's enemy,
consumers of summer's stems and meaty roots;
a poison bomb would work within their dreams.
I counted four such furtive homes, each tingeing
with helpless vapor this abandoned lawn,
and let them be. Warm blood calls out to blood;
together we contest the deadly cold,
and if our heat of being hoists a flag,
our mazy respiration tells a tale,
salute it, listen to it, and forgive
intrusive life as we forgive our own.

To a Box Turtle

Size of a small skull, and like a skull segmented,
of pentagons healed and varnished to form a dome,
you almost went unnoticed in the meadow,
among its tall grasses and serrated strawberry leaves
your mottle of amber and umber effective camouflage.

You were making your way through grave distances,
your forefeet just barely extended and as dainty as dried
coelacanth fins, as miniature sea-fans, your black nails
decadent like a Chinese empress's, and your head
a triangular snake-head, eyes ringed with dull gold.

I pick you up. Your imperious head withdraws.
Your bottom plate, hinged once, presents a *No*
with its courteous waxed surface, a marquetry

of inlaid squares, fine-grained and tinted
tobacco-brown and the yellow of a pipe smoker's teeth.

What are you thinking, thus sealed inside yourself?
My hand must have a smell, a killer's warmth.
It holds you upside down, aloft, undignified,
your leathery person amazed in the floating dark.
How much pure fear can your wrinkled brain contain?

I put you down. Your tentative, stalk-bending walk
resumes. The manifold jewel of you melts into grass.
Power mowers have been cruel to your race, and creatures
less ornate and unlikely have long gone extinct;
but nature's tumults pool to form a giant peace.

Each Summer's Swallows

How do they know
                    the swallows each May
how to find in a continent of rooftops
                                        our garage
with no door to shut
                        them in or shut them out
and exposed rough rafters
                            and above-lintel cubbyholes
where a dozen earlier nests
                            shaped of mud and straw
memorialize earlier summers
                            How do they know
how to assemble
                the segments of mud
to make them shape up and cling
                                to a rough rafter
swooping all day in and out

                    to shape a cup to hold
the enigmatic eggs
                    the baby birds that peep
blue and brown above the edge
                         and to push
the tidy white packets of guano
                         over the edge
How do we know these
                    are last summer's swallows
and not their offspring
                    whose first careening flights
in air's bug-filled 3-D
                    astounded last July
for even the flight of birds
                    must be learned
or at least perfected
                    How do we know
one immortal diving dipping pair
                         does not always return
to our open garage
                    and then in August
before morning lifts the dew
                    again is not there

Fargo

"The fertillest soil this side of the Tigris
and Euphrates"—so the schoolchildren
of the countryside are taught, of their land
flat as a checkerboard to the hem of the sky.
The giant sky, pale green at dusk, stays black
long after morning cow-milking time.
Wind is incessant in winter, so
that snow falls sideways, like arctic sunshine.

This land of Lutherans and sugar beets
thickens its marvellous thinness here at the edge
of a Red River whose windings alone
betray the rectilinear. Downtown,
parking space is no problem, and grain-fed health
rewards those God's grandeur does not drive mad.

Fall

October 1989

The undertaker, who was with the local minister
and the neighboring farmer when they broke in,
made a wry face and hinted at damage
too dreadful to be viewed—"a cut in the eye,
a lot of blood." I took his kindly offer not
to view the corpse but looked, back in the house,
in the kitchen corner where she fell, head crushing
the paper bag she used for trash. She was eighty-five.
Her heart had floated to a stop and she dropped
without lifting a hand or averting her face.

What corner or edge might have given the gash?
I saw none, then saw her glasses, a circle and half
of plastic frames, the one lens popped
and skipped a foot away amid the dust.
I picked it all up, and the little wool hat
(it was getting to be fall) she wore for warmth,
with a spot of dried blood on the blue threads.
She seemed so very small in these her remnants.
"Oh, Mama," I said aloud, though I never called
her "Mama," "I didn't take very good care of you."

The Millipede

Oi! oi! *noli me tangere,* no argument:
this hideous thing in the kitchen sink.
Moving across the countertop with that slinky
motion having a hundred legs imparts,

it hesitated by the breadboard, sensing
my spiritual presence, and I knocked it in,
with the roll of paper towels, thinking,
What do I do with the damned thing next?

Turning on the faucet was obvious,
but drowning is not a death I'd wish
for myself, wriggling against the splash
down a slimy vortex black with sludge.

Nature knows best, I thought, and abandoned
the problem to read the newspaper.
While I pursued the latest Boston rape
from page one to Section B, page eleven,

my wife, dear woman, entered the kitchen
and went to the sink. *Ooh,* she pronounced,
not loudly, and I heard a small skirmish whence
the sound of the trashmasher opening

proceeded, accepting a Scott towel used
to wipe away some stray organic matter.
Poor millipede—he must have been a he—
to catch the eye of the real housekeeper.

Generic College

The statue of the founder wears a green
cape of verdigris upon his epaulettes.
White pillars everywhere, and bricks, and streaks
of dawn seen through the hard-to-sleep-in campus
guest house's narrow-mullioned fenestration.
A professor toddles on the walk below,
emitting smoke puffs like a choo-choo train.
The lamps installed to discourage rape go out.

Within this guest house, the founder's portrait
portrays him aging. Velvet furniture
selected by committee shows no wear.
The latches, black and flat, remind me of
my boyhood home. This stately farce of learning—
well, time to brush the teeth and face the students.

Perfection Wasted

And another regrettable thing about death
is the ceasing of your own brand of magic,
which took a whole life to develop and market—
the quips, the witticisms, the slant
adjusted to a few, those loved ones nearest
the lip of the stage, their soft faces blanched
in the footlight glow, their laughter close to tears,
their tears confused with their diamond earrings,
their warm pooled breath in and out with your heartbeat,
their response and your performance twinned.
The jokes over the phone. The memories packed
in the rapid-access file. The whole act.
Who will do it again? That's it: no one;
imitators and descendants aren't the same.

Working Outdoors in Winter

It can be done. The seal of frost
imposed upon the windows can
be broken, and a depth of air revealed.
Trees follow one another, one by one—
birch, beech, white oak, a hickory or ash—
and make a space to move in, space
like that inside your clothes,
which can be warmed.
                  The poison ivy dormant,
mosquitoes dead, and leaves' green suffocation
lifted, you wield the clipper, swing the ax
in an atmosphere of freedom earned, of nature
as calligraphy, transparent to the will.
You overheat, at last, and seem to wound
the virgin quiet as a glowing poker
wounds the water it is plunged into.

To build a fire in winter's heart!
Now, *there* is self-assertion, gathering
the heap of brush, the castoff branches,
the kindling wood and match, and tools
to keep the orange pet in bounds, its roar
and snap and snarl and singing hiss all yours,
Der Feuermeister.
                  The blue smoke soils
blue sky, an ascent of sparks describes an S
baroque as the sound holes in a violin,
and a bed of frozen earth is fried,
with all its sleeping worms. The cold day sinks
to its ruddy ash of dusk while you recall
in bone and vein what tough machines
men are, their burning gristle built to push
against the zero waiting all around.

Indianapolis

A passion for Roman order seized the plains.
Desire to woo the American Legion raised
not one but two imperial monuments
to the oft-regretted dead. In World War One
Das Deutsche Haus became, to lick the Huns,
another Athenaeum. The spreading city hangs
between brick-striped solidity and dim
apology for being there at all.

Metropolis of writers—Tarkington,
James Whitcomb Riley, Vonnegut, and more
who fled and fed New York's ungrateful maw.
Why flee? Come, stay beside the Hoosier Dome,
its alabaster bubble, citizen,
and dream your fill of plain civility—
of logical maps, and unimpeded streets,
and porch-swing sex like a window box in bloom.

Zoo Bats

In the Central Park Zoo, just past the ants
being televised by tiny cameras,
the bats flutter and swoop in a glassed-in gloom.
You don't see bats this close up very often.

Yet they are hard to see, too quick, too faint,
and their shapes disagree with the eyes—
appall us, really, though we approach and peer
determined not to be appalled, to be liberal and just

toward this creature that is, after all,
remarkably successful, if quietly so.
One seventh of all mammalian species
are Chiroptera, and their mortality rate

is low, their predators no problem, and
their child-rearing habits more constant than ours.
Who begrudges them their diet of bugs?
Their digestions are rapid, to keep themselves light.

For all this Fourierism, this favorable press,
these bats in the flesh are worse than we dreamed;
if we dreamed of them often, we would swap
such sleep for death, its featureless white glare.

They are shapeless in flight and in repose—
small broken umbrellas that grab the air
like brown-gloved skeletal hands, and latch
their sticky feet to a roost with a vile

tenacity, and tremblingly hang; or else
they drop to a ledge like a sudden deposit
of excrement, shit out of nowhere, a
product of this intestinal gray gloom.

No doubt they have dear faces—with nose-flaps,
some of them, to aid echolocation,
and snouts, like the hog-nosed bat of Thailand,
small as a bumblebee. The common bat

that haunts our mauve suburban twilights with
its airborne evening meal—connect the dots—
weighs one third of an ounce, or less. How minor
a mass for so disquieting a shadow!

Perhaps to fly with webbed and lengthened fingers
sits worse, with nature, than to do it with
thoracic chitin-scales or feathered arms.
A bird is a new shape, a fish of the sky;

a bat, a squeaking face between a pair
of agitated hands, that's all. I once
was at a party when a bat broke in.
It dipped from room to room as people screamed.

The host at last opened a door, and out
it went. To make his teary daughter laugh,
I said, "It looked like this," and did a face—
a-squint, stretch-mouthed. She laughed and said, "It did!"

We see them better than we know, like the
subliminal bits on television.
They are subconscious, bats, and bubble up
like prejudices. Another time, one night,

I saw a bat sail like a flung black stone
behind my stepson's head. He and my wife
reacted violently, and, slamming doors,
delegated me to be the bat

eliminator. Trapped, I crept upstairs,
through hall and bedroom (nothing there) into
the bathroom where, all fearful of its flying
Dracula-fanged and rabid at my face,

I found it hanging, folded, to a towel.
Resigned and upside down, the bat had sensibly
amid our panic put itself to sleep.
Stealthy as a parent, I wrapped it gently up;

it chirruped, exerting a questioning pressure
back through the towel like the throb of a watch.
Up, window. Up, screen. I gave the bat back
to the night like a cup of water to the sea.

Landing in the Rain at La Guardia

The death-grip of the chalky clouds lets slip,
within our oval view, a glimpse of ground:
six city autos snug in their snail's pace
on rain-licked streets that we will never cruise.
The clouds return, a hurtling wisp or two
to measure our distressing speed; then space
opens again beneath our belly-drone
like a wound, damp and lucidly detailed—

flat factory roofs and empty parking lots,
a cemetery's ragged crowded rows.
What meaningless angel are we thus to loom
above the sleeping, crawling map of Queens?
The World's Fair globe, a toy. Shea Stadium.
Upreaching stony water. *Whumppf:* we're down.

Mouse Sex

In my cellar the poisoned mice, thirsty to death,
come out to die on the cement, in the center
of the floor. This particular corpse seemed fat,
so sideways-plump that pregnancy crossed my mind,
and, picking it up by the tail, I saw, sure enough,
at the base of the tail her tiny neat vagina,

a pumpkin-seed-shaped break in the dulcet fur.
I had murdered a matriarch, with d-Con.

Revelation of the vagina's simplicity
had come to me before. Tossing the tiny body
into the woods, I remembered another
woods-surrounded house, where I and another
lay together upstairs, and had heard
a sound downstairs, her husband or the wind.
The phantom sound, like an alchemist's pinch,
turned my erection inconvenient.

We listened, our love-flushed faces an inch apart.
The sound was not repeated. In the silence,
as the house resumed its enclosing, she said,
her voice thickened and soft and distinct,
"Put it in me." In my wild mind's eye I saw
the vagina as a simple wanting, framed in fur,
kept out of sight between the legs but always there,
a gentle nagging, a moist accommodacy.

A man and not a mouse, but with a bed-squeak,
I fell to my duty, our ungainly huddle
and its tense outcome less memorable
than the urgent, imperilled invitation.
How dear she was—her husband, that creep,
creeping about for all we knew—to sock it to
herself and give me in words the carte blanche
boys dream of but seldom receive spelled out.

I loved her for it, and for afterwards
with a touch of a blush confessing,
"I don't want to be coarse for you," as if women
could be as bluntly brutes as men.
Until that moment I did not suspect

that sex had an equitable basis.
The cat creeps below, but lady mice
still put their dulcet selves at risk, and die.

Suppose that moment, frozen, were Heaven or Hell:
our hearts would thump until the death of stars,
the trees outside would stir their golden edges,
the bed would squeak, the frightened inch
between our skins would hold the headboard's grain,
her brazen thighs would simply, frankly part,
our eyes and breath would forever entertain
our mutual inquisition. *Put it in.*

Suspended above the abyss of her desire,
I feel as far-flung as a constellation.
Colors: the golden-edged trees, the lilac sheets,
the mousy green of her self-startled eyes.
We are furtive, gigantic, our stolen hour
together a swollen eternity.
We enter into one another; the universe
rises about us like a hostile house.

Granite

New England doesn't kid around;
it wears its bones outside.
Quartz-freckled, time-rumpled granite—
your tombstone everywhere.

At night I wake and warily gaze
at outcroppings on my lawn.
These moonlit humpbacks, do they sleep
or do their blanched surfaces sense my eyes?

By day, you can see how earth
engenders itself over aeons—
pine needles silt in, and tender weeds
take hold in the cracks, then wild roses

and hairy-stemmed sumacs find enough
for a footing, and oak rootlets,
and out of the mesh comes a mulch, a soil—
trapped particles breed trapped life.

There is no way not to die,
can it be? What do these stones
coldly know? Or is moonlight warm,
and the granite a pledge

to which consciousness clings?
Better rock than the mud
of a meaningless mercy, such as men
would devise. This outcrop

is a wide gray glow the night has grown.
I think with awe of the man
who will gaze down upon it, awake,
when I'm blinder than stone.

Relatives

Just the thought of them makes your jawbone ache:
those turkey dinners, those holidays with
the air around the woodstove baked to a stupor,
and Aunt Lil's tablecloth stained by her girlhood's gravy.
A doggy wordless wisdom whimpers from
your uncles' collected eyes; their very jokes

creak with genetic sorrow, a strain
of common heritage that hurts the gut.

Sheer boredom and fascination! A spidering
of chromosomes webs even the infants in
and holds us fast around the spread
of rotting food, of too-sweet pie.
The cousins buzz, the nephews crawl;
to love one's self is to love them all.

Thin Air

By holding one's head stock-still and measuring
on a window edge the snail's pace at which
the plane in its airy trudge eats up
the luminous noodles of roadway—wet boughs
with speckled leaves and globular fruit
(sports stadia? new-opened malls?)
one gauges, abstractly, a speed outracing
headlights and in seconds eclipsing cities
spun underneath us like irregular webs
bespangled with life's bright dew—lives passing
from cradle to coffin in local ignorance.

But as we land, this speed turns non-abstract:
the flashing grope of water, the coded lights
that cry *Come home!*, the runway like a card
the magician slips from the bottom of the deck
murderously fast. We would die,
squashed snails, were the world one shade more solid.

November

The light the sun withdraws the leaves replace
in falling, sweeping clean the clouded sky.
This brightness shocks the window like a face.

Our eyes contract to hold the sudden space
of barrenness—bare branches, blue, up high.
The light the sun withdrew has been replaced.

The tiny muscles of the iris taste
past time—old falls, slant light—recalling why
this brightness shocks the window like a face.

To children, years are each a separate case,
enormous, full of presents and surprise:
the light the sun withdraws the leaves replace.

For grown-ups, reminiscence scores the days
with traces veteran nerve-ends recognize
when brightness shocks the window like a face.

November, we know you—the grudging grace
of clarity you grant the clouded eye.
The light the sun withdraws the leaves replace
with brightness at the window like a face.

Light Switches

Lord, but one wearies of flipping them,
or turning them, or punching or,
with certain rheostatted switches, sliding them.
Nipples on the walls' flat chests,

they yield the milk of light—the creamy
incandescence of resistant tungsten,
and lo-fat fluorescence that comes
in brimming, humming tubes. A modern
miracle, O.K.; but miracles wear
over a man's and/or a woman's lifetime
to mere routines—to recurrent details
that acquire no-meaning's muffled sense
of a gap between purpose and sign
like the gap inside a careful package
stuffed with newspapers wadded into nonsense,
the language they were printed in no matter.
Off. On. It goes without saying.
And the sockets get boring, too—their twin mouths
and little flat-sided eye for the grounding prong.
The walls are threaded with magic, so what?
It's magic merely our own, cooked up
so we can watch inane commercials—
never a lightning arising from a sky
beyond our brains, where electric-blue Zeus
hurls laughing bolts that weld amino acids
to a fantastic random hunger.
Instead, these mechanisms we understand,
these diagrams whose starkness shocks the soul.
Off, on—there must be something else,
some middle way, third eye, or *shakti* current.
These tilted blond clitorises
of plastic, their pure thrill palls
with the morning shave and the midnight douche.

Miami

As in some car chase on Sunday-night TV,
Art Deco collides with postmodern glass

above pink-plaster, low-slung *barrio;*
nothing crumples like passé luxury.
Miami Beach is now a hustling strip
where college kids rub naked shoulders with
the Caribbean's shadows, high on hopes
of cutting some sweet deal with Uncle Sam.

Street murder scents the gentle, saline air.
SUN SPOT EXPLODES, BECOMES METROPOLIS.
White millionaires' drab palaces still peep
behind the drooping bougainvillea, but
the crash, as in slow motion, widens out;
the moon keeps skidding through the gilded clouds.

Fly

What have we done this winter to deserve
this plague of giant flies? They breed in the house,
being born to batter and buzz at the glass
of windows where sunshine shows a world of snow.

Stupid out of season, they are easy to swat,
and some can't seem to fly, but run across
the kitchen linoleum in a comical hurry,
more like a frantic man than you would think.

Stupid myself one noon, I watched one primp
head-down on a sunstruck kitchen wall.
He rubbed his face on his rotating head
with forelegs finer than a pencil line;

a cleansing seemed in progress, bit by bit.
He held each wing out stiff, its rainbow shadow

projected down the wall diagonally,
and scrubbed the membranes with a fussy leg.

All creatures groom, but who would figure that
a fly, which thrives on dirt, could be so nice?
His head and legs were like a watchworks ticking,
but spaced by intervals of what seemed thought.

His interlocking parts' complexity
was photocopied by his lengthened shadow,
a sharp mechanical drawing sunshine drew:
each twitch, each quick caress of mouth-parts,

each hinge of animate anatomy.
Up from a maggot had arisen this tower
of microcosmic beams, their third dimension
craned outward to contain a fourth, called life.

So how can I crush construction so rare?
A bomber flattens cities but cannot see
the child in the map, the network of girders.
Swat not, not I at the moment, all eye.

Flurry

There is an excited nonserious species of snowstorm,
flurrying flakes thick as goosefeathers, actualized air,
that dies in an instant, succeeded by watery sunshine
and the ponderous dull of a gray winter day, like a flurry
of love some old gentleman once underwent, to think
    back on,
his duty to Eros fulfilled, and the world none the worse
    for it.

Bindweed

Intelligence does help, sometimes;
the bindweed doesn't know
when it begins to climb a wand of grass
that this is no tree and will shortly bend
its flourishing dependent back to earth.

But bindweed has a trick: self-
stiffening, entwining two- or three-ply,
to boost itself up, into the lilac.

Without much forethought it manages
to imitate the lilac leaves and lose
itself to all but the avidest clippers.

To spy it out, to clip near the root
and unwind the climbing tight spiral
with a motion the reverse of its own
feels like treachery—death to a plotter
whose intelligence mirrors ours, twist for twist.

July

Deep pools of shade beneath dense maples,
the dapples as delicious as lemon drops—
textures of childhood, and its many flavors!
The gratefulness of cool, the bottles of
sarsaparilla and iodine-red cream soda
schooled like fish, on their sides,
in the watery ice of the zinc-lined cooler
in the shade of the cherry trees
planted by the town baseball diamond,

where only grown-ups cared what the score was
and the mailman took his ups with a grunt
that made the crowd in its shirtsleeves laugh.
The sun kindled freckles like a match
touching straw, and beneath a tree
a quality reigned like the sound of a gong,
solemn and sticky and calm. Then the grass
bared the hurry of ants, and each blade
bent to some weight, some faint godly tread
we could not see. The dapples
were not holes in the shade but like pies,
bulging up, and air tasted of water,
and water of metal, and metal of what
would never come—real change, removal
from this island of stagnant summer,
the end of sarsaparilla and its hint
of licorice taste, of sassafras twig,
of things we chewed with the cunning of Indians,
to whom all trees had souls, the maples no more
like birches than clouds are like waterfalls.
The dying grass smelled especially sweet
where sneakers had packed it flat,
or out of the way, in the playground corner,
where the sun had forgot to stop shining.
This was the apogee, July, a month
like the piece of a dome where it flattens
and reflects in a smear high above us,
the ant-children busy and lazy below.

To a Dead Flame

Dear X, you wouldn't believe how curious
my eyebrows have become—jagged gray wands
have intermixed with the reddish-brown, and poke

up toward the sun and down into my eyes.
It hurts, a self-caress that brings tears
and blurred vision. Aches and pains! The other day
my neck was so stiff I couldn't turn my head
to parallel-park. Another man
would have trusted his mirrors, but not I;
I had the illusion something might interpose
between reality and its reflection, as happened with us.

The aging smell, X—a rank small breeze wafts upward
when I shed my underwear. My potency,
which you would smilingly complain about,
has become as furtive as an early mammal.
My hair shows white in photographs, although
the barber's clippings still hold some brown.
At times I catch myself making that loose mouth
old people make, as if one's teeth don't fit,
without being false. *You're well out of it—*
I tell you this mentally, while shaving
or putting myself to bed, but it's a lie.

The world is still wonderful. Wisps of mist
were floating off your old hill yesterday,
the hill where you lived, in sight of the course
where I played (badly) in a Senior Men's
Four-Ball in the rain, each green a mirage.
I thought of us, abed atop that hill,
and of how I would race down through your woods
to my car, and back to my life, my heart
enormous with what I newly knew—
the color of you naked, the milk of your sighs—
through leaves washed to the glisten of fresh wounds.

What desperate youthful fools we were, afraid
of not getting our share, our prize in the race,
like jostling marathoners starting out,

clumsy but pulsingly full of blood.
You dropped out, but we all drop out, it seems.
You never met my jealous present wife;
she hates this poem. The living have it hard,
not living only in the mind, but in
the receding flesh. Old men must be allowed
their private murmuring, a prayer wheel
set spinning to confuse and stay the sun.

Back from Vacation

"Back from vacation," the barber announces,
or the postman, or the girl at the drugstore, now tan.
They are amazed to find the workaday world
still in place, their absence having slipped no cogs,
their customers having hardly missed them, and
there being so sparse an audience to tell of the wonders,
the pyramids they have seen, the silken warm seas,
the nighttimes of marimbas, the purchases achieved
in foreign languages, the beggars, the flies,
the hotel luxury, the grandeur of marble cities.
But at Customs the humdrum pressed its claims.
Gray days clicked shut around them; the yoke still fit,
warm as if never shucked. The world is so small,
the evidence says, though their hearts cry, "Not so!"

Literary Dublin

Damn near where'er you look, a writer's ghost:
round plaques declaring Oscar Wilde slept here,
or Brendan Behan took a drink, or Patrick
O'Scrittore boarded for a year

as debt and desperate hopes revolved him through
the tattered brown-bricked streets, the blank-faced
Georgian rows, no pair of doors alike.
The scandal of them all, James Joyce, who sinned
against the Holy Spirit, said the Church,
is now a tourist souvenir, can you believe
it?—a bust in St. Stephen's Green, Bloom's route
all traced in a tidy pamphlet by some Yank,
and Daedalus's execration hung
above the city like a blind man's blessing.

Elderly Sex

Life's buried treasure's buried deeper still:
a cough, a draft, a wrinkle in the bed
distract the search, as precarious as
a safecracker's trembling touch on the dial.
We are walking a slack tight wire, we
are engaged in unlikely acrobatics,
we are less frightened of the tiger than
of the possibility the cage is empty.

Nature used to do more—paroxysms
of blood and muscle, the momentous machine
set instantly in place, the dark a-swim,
and lubrication's thousand jewels poured forth
by lapfuls where, with dry precision, now
attentive irritation yields one pearl.

Celery

So near to air and water merely
and yet a food, green,
fibrous like a ribbed sky at sunset,
diminishing inward
in nested arcs to a shaving-brush heart
paler than celadon:
the Chinese love you, and dieters,
for you take away
more calories in the chewing
than your mass bestows,
and children, who march around the table
to your drumbeat,
marking crisp time with their teeth,
your dancer's legs long as they leap.

São Paulo

Buildings to the horizon, an accretion
big beyond structure: no glass downtown shimmering
with peacock power, just the elephantine
color of poured concrete repeated in clusters,
into the haze that foots the horizon of hills,
a human muchness encountering no bounds.

From the hotel window, ridged roofs of ruddy tile,
the black of corrugated iron, the green
and yellow of shopfronts, a triangular hut
revealed survival's piecemeal, patchwork logic.
All afternoon, the view sulked beneath my room
in silence—a city without a city's outcry.

And then a pronouncement—thunder?—overruled
the air conditioner's steady whir, and a tapping
asked me to *look*. The empty, too-full view
held thousands of foreshortened arrows: rain,
seen from above, a raying angelic substance.
I felt lifted up, to God's altitude.

If the rain was angelic, why not men and their works?
Their colorless habitations, like a drenched
honeycomb: men come in from the country
to the town's crowded hope, the town grown
to a chaos but still open to the arrows
of Heaven, transparently, all life a veil.

Rio de Janeiro

Too good to be true—a city that empties
its populace, a hundred shades of brown,
upon its miles of beach in morning's low light
and takes the bodies back when darkness quells
the last long volleyball game; even then,
the sands are lit for the soccer of homeless children.

A city that exults in nakedness:
"The ass," hissed to us a man of the élite,
"the ass has become the symbol of Rio."
Set off by suits of "dental floss," girls' buttocks
possess a meaty staring solemnness
that has us see sex as it is: a brainless act

performed by lumpy monkeys, mostly hairless.
Still, the herd vibrates, a loom of joy
threaded by vendors—a tree of suntan lotion

or of hats, or fried snacks roofed in cardboard—
whose monotonous cries in Portuguese
make the same carnival mock of human need.

Elsewhere, chaste squares preserve Machado's world
of understated tragedy, and churches
honored in their abandonment suspend
the blackened bliss of gold. Life to the living,
while politicians dazzling in their polish,
far off in Brasília's cubes, feign impotence.

Brazil

To go to the edge is to discover
the edge to be the center. Cabral
was on his way around Africa
and passed an unexpected, endless coast.
The king bestowed the land, but few
the *donatários* who cared to come.
Of those that did, most yearned to find gold
and go home. Still, life grew its holds—
churches, whores, the whole caboodle.
The Indians knew how to die, the slaves
had rolling, fetching eye-whites. Sugar paid,
and the sense of banishment dimly shifted.
To arrive at self's end is to embark again
upon love's narcissistic enterprise.

Upon Looking into
Sylvia Plath's *Letters Home*

Yes, this is how it was to have been born
in 1932—the having parents
everyone said loved you and you had to love;
the believing having a wonderful life began
with being good at school; the certainty
that words would count; the diligence with postage,
sending things out; the seeing Dreyer's silent *Joan*
at the Museum of Modern Art, and being
greatly moved; the courtship of the slicks,
because one had to eat, one and one's spouse,
that soulmate in Bohem-/Utop-ia.
You, dead at thirty, leaving blood-soaked poems
for all the anthologies, and I still wheezing,
my works overweight; and yet we feel twins.

At the End of the Rainbow

Is this the bliss for which you've tried to live?
The motel room, 10:45, alone,
the last book signed, the thunderous applause
still tingling in your body. The polite
exchanges with the distant relatives
who drove a hundred miles or so (as if
they didn't trust a thing but downright seeing),
the nervous banter with your guardian,
the bearded chairman of the writing program
(between you in the dark car like a dagger
his own slim oeuvre), the silken-faced coeds,

their smiles as warm as humid underpants,
all gone, endured. The square made bed. Hi-tech
alarm clock, digital. The john. The check.

Academy

The shuffle up the stairs betrays our age:
sunk to polite senility our fire
and tense perfectionism, our curious rage
to excel, to exceed, to climb still higher.
Our battles were fought elsewhere; here, this peace
betrays and cheats us with a tame reward—
a klieg-lit stage and numbered chairs, an ease
of prize and praise that sets sheath to the sword.

The naked models, the Village gin, the wife
whose hot tears sped the novel to its end,
the radio that leaked distracting life
into the symphony's cerebral blend.
A struggle it was, and a dream; we wake
to bright bald honors. Tell us our mistake.

LIGHT VERSE

Mountain Impasse

"I despise mountains," Stravinsky declared contemptuously, "they
don't tell me anything."

—Life

Stravinsky looks upon the mountain,
   The mountain looks on him;
They look (the mountain and Stravinsky)
   And both their views are dim.

"You bore me, mountain," says Stravinsky,
   "I find you dull, and I
Despise you!" Says the mountain:
   "Stravinsky, tell me why."

Stravinsky bellows at the mountain
   And nearby valleys ring:
"You don't confide in me—Stravinsky!
   You never tell me anything!"

The hill is still before Stravinsky.
   The skies in silence glisten.
At last, a rumble, then the mountain:
   "Igor, you never listen."

Solitaire

Black queen on the red king,
the seven on the black
eight, eight goes on nine, bring
the nine on over, place

jack on queen. There is space
now for that black king who,
six or so cards back,
was buried in the pack.
Five on six, where's seven?
Under the ten. The ace
must be under the two.
Four, nine on ten, three, through.
It's after eleven.

Duet, with Muffled Brake Drums

50 Years Ago Rolls met Royce—a Meeting that made Engineering History
—advertisement in *The New Yorker*

Where gray walks slope through shadows shaped like lace
Down to dimpleproof ponds, a precious place
Where birds of porcelain sing as with one voice
Two gold and velvet notes—there Rolls met Royce.

"Hallo," said Rolls. His umber silhouette
Seemed mounted on a blotter brushed when wet
To indicate a park. Beyond, a brown
Line hinted at the profile of The Town.

And Royce, his teeth and creases straight, his eye
A perfect match for that well-lacquered sky
(Has zenith since, or iris, been so pure?),
Responded, "Pleased to meet you, I am sure."

A graceful pause, then Rolls, the taller, spake:
"Ah—is there anything you'd care to make?
A day of it? A fourth at bridge? Some tea?"
Royce murmured, "If your afternoon is free,
I'd rather—*much*—make engineering history."

Player Piano

My stick fingers click with a snicker
    As, chuckling, they knuckle the keys;
Light-footed, my steel feelers flicker
    And pluck from these keys melodies.

My paper can caper; abandon
    Is broadcast by dint of my din,
And no man or band has a hand in
    The tones I turn on from within.

At times I'm a jumble of rumbles,
    At others I'm light like the moon,
But never my numb plunker fumbles,
    Misstrums me, or tries a new tune.

Snapshots

How good of Mrs. Metz! The blur
Must be your cousin Christopher.

A scenic shot Jim took near Lyme.
Those rocks seemed lovely at the time.

And here's a product of the days
When Jim went through his gnarled-tree phase.

The man behind the man in shorts—
His name is Shorer, Shaw, or Schwartz.

The kids at play. This must be Keith.
Can that be Wilma underneath?

I'd give my life to know why Josh
Sat next to Mrs. McIntosh.

Jim looked so well in formal clothes.
I was much slimmer than this shows.

Yes, Jim and I were so in love.
That hat: what *was* I thinking of?

This disappointed Mrs. Weicker.
I don't know why, it's very like her.

The dog is Skip. He loved to play.
We had to have him put away.

I guess these people are the Wrens.
An insect landed on the lens.

This place is where I was inspired
To—stop me, if your eyes are tired.

An Imaginable Conference

*(Mr. Henry Green, Industrialist, and Mr. Wallace Stevens,
Vice-President of the Hartford Accident & Indemnity Co.,
Meet in the Course of Business)*

Exchanging gentle grips, the men retire,
prologued by courteous bumbling at the door,
retreat to where a rare room deep exists
on an odd floor, subtly carpeted. The walls

wear charts like checkered vests and blotters ape
the green of cricket fields. Glass multiplies

the pausing men to twice infinity.
An inkstand of blue marble has been carven:

no young girl's wrist is more discreetly veined.
An office boy misplaced and slack intrudes,
apologizes speaking without commas
"Oh sorry sirs I thought" which signifies

what wellmeant wimbly wambly stuff it is
we seem to be made of. Beyond the room,
a gander sun's pure rhetoric ferments
embarrassments of bloom. The stone is so.

The pair confers in murmurings, with words
select and Sunday-soft. No more is known,
but rumor goes that, as they hatched the deal,
vistas of lilac weighted their shrewd lids.

Dilemma in the Delta

An extra quarter-inch on Cleopatra's nose would have changed the entire
course of history.

—Pascal, misquoted in a newspaper

Osiris pales; the palace walls
Blush east; through slatted arches falls
The sun, who stripes the cushions where
Empires have been tucked away.
Light fills her jewels and rims her hair
And Cleopatra ripens into day.

Awake, she flings her parakeets
Some chips of cinnamon, and beats

Her scented slave, a charming thing
Who chokes back almond tears. The queen,
Her wrist fatigued, then bids them bring
Her mirror, a mammoth aquamarine.

She rests the gem upon her thighs
And checks her features. First, the eyes:
Weight them with ink. The lips need rose
Tint: crush a rose. And something's wrong
Between her mouth and brow—her nose,
Her nose seems odd, too long. It *is* too long!

These stupid jokes of Ra! She sees,
Through veils of fury, centuries
Shifting like stirred-up camels. Men
Who wrought great deeds remain unborn,
Unthought-of heroes fight like ten,
And her own name is lost to praise or scorn.

While she lies limp, seduced by grief,
There enters, grand beyond belief,
Marc Antony, bronze-braceleted,
Beloved of Venus as of Mars.
A wreath of laurel girds his head;
His destiny hangs balanced in the stars.

"Now dies," she cries, "your love, my fame!
My face shall never seem the same!"
But Marc responds, *"Deorum artis
Laudemus! Bonum hoc est omen.*
Egyptian though your wicked heart is,
I can't resist a nose so nobly Roman!"

Shipbored

That line is the horizon line.
The blue above it is divine.
The blue below it is marine.
Sometimes the blue below is green.

Sometimes the blue above is gray,
Betokening a cloudy day.
Sometimes the blue below is white,
Foreshadowing a windy night.

Sometimes a drifting coconut
Or albatross adds color, but
The blue above is mostly blue.
The blue below and I are, too.

Song of the Open Fireplace

When silly Sol in winter roisters
And roasts us in our closed-up cloisters
Like hosts of out-of-season oysters,
 The logs glow red.

When Sol grows cool and solely caters
To polar bears and figure skaters
And homes are turned refrigerators,
 The flames are dead.

And when idyllically transpires
The merger every man desires
Of air that nips and wood that fires,
 It's time for bed.

The Clan

Emlyn reads in Dickens' clothes.
Tennessee writes fleshy prose;
William Carlos, bony poems.
Esther swims in hippodromes.
Ted likes hits but hates his fans;
Gluyas draws Americans.
Vaughan pens music, score on score;
Soapy sits as governor.
I trust everybody is
Thankful for the Williamses.

Youth's Progress

Dick Schneider of Wisconsin . . . was elected "Greek God" for
an interfraternity ball.

—Life

When I was born, my mother taped my ears
So they lay flat. When I had aged ten years,
My teeth were firmly braced and much improved.
Two years went by; my tonsils were removed.

At fourteen, I began to comb my hair
A fancy way. Though nothing much was there,
I shaved my upper lip—next year, my chin.
At seventeen, the freckles left my skin.

Just turned nineteen, a nicely molded lad,
I said goodbye to Sis and Mother; Dad
Drove me to Wisconsin and set me loose.
At twenty-one, I was elected Zeus.

Humanities Course

Professor Varder handles Dante
  With wry respect; while one can see
It's all a lie, one must admit
  The "splendor" of the "imagery."

Professor Varder slyly smiles,
  Describing Hegel as a "sage";
But still, the man has value—he
  Reflects the "temper" of his "age."

Montaigne, Tom Paine, St. Augustine:
  Although their notions came to naught,
They still are "crucial figures" in
  The "pageantry" of "Western thought."

V. B. Nimble, V. B. Quick

Science, Pure and Applied, by V. B. Wigglesworth, F.R.S., Quick Professor
of Biology in the University of Cambridge.
                     —a talk listed in the B.B.C.'s *Radio Times*

    V. B. Wigglesworth wakes at noon,
    Washes, shaves, and very soon
    Is at the lab; he reads his mail,
    Tweaks a tadpole by the tail,
    Undoes his coat, removes his hat,
    Dips a spider in a vat
    Of alkaline, phones the press,
    Tells them he is F.R.S.,
    Subdivides six protocells,
    Kills a rat by ringing bells,

Writes a treatise, edits two
Symposia on "Will Man Do?,"
Gives a lecture, audits three,
Has the Sperm Club in for tea,
Pensions off an aging spore,
Cracks a test tube, takes some pure
Science and applies it, finds
His hat, adjusts it, pulls the blinds,
Instructs the jellyfish to spawn,
And, by one o'clock, is gone.

Lament, for Cocoa

The scum has come.
   My cocoa's cold.
The cup is numb,
   And I grow old.

It seems an age
   Since from the pot
It bubbled, beige
   And burning hot—

Too hot to be
   Too quickly quaffed.
Accordingly,
   I felt a draft

And in it placed
   The boiling brew
And took a taste
   Of toast or two.

Alas, time flies
   And minutes chill;
My cocoa lies
   Dull brown and still.

How wearisome!
   In likelihood,
The scum, once come,
   Is come for good.

Pop Smash, Out of Echo Chamber

O truly, Lily was a lulu,
   Doll, and dilly of a belle;
No one's smile was more enamelled,
No one's style was more untrammelled,
   Yet her records failed to sell
      Well.

Her agent, Daley, duly worried,
   Fretted, fidgeted, complained,
Daily grew so somber clever
Wits at parties said whenever
   Lily waxed, poor Daley waned.
      Strained

Beyond endurance, feeling either
   He or Lily must be drowned,
Daley, dulled to Lily's lustre,
Deeply down a well did thrust her.
   Lily yelled; he dug the sound,
      Found

A phone, contacted Victor,
   Cut four sides; they sold, and how!
Daley disclaims credit; still, he
Likes the lucre. As for Lily,
   She is dry and famous now.
      Wow.

Sunglasses

On an olive beach, beneath a turquoise sky
And a limeade sun, by a lurid sea,
While the beryl clouds went blithely by,
We ensconced ourselves, my love and me.

O her verdant hair! and her aqua smile!
O my soul, afloat in an emerald bliss
That retained its tint all the watery while—
And her copper skin, all verdigris!

Pooem

Writing here last autumn of my hopes of seeing a hoopoe . . .
          —Sir Stephen Tallents in the London *Times*

I, too, once hoped to have a hoopoe
Wing its way within my scoopoe,
Crested, quick, and heliotroopoe,
   Proud *Upupa epops.*
   For what seemed an eternity,
I sat upon a grassy sloopoe,

Gazing through a telescoopoe,
Weaving snares of finest roopoe,
   Fit for *Upupa epops.*
   At last, one day, there came to me,
Inside a crusty enveloopoe,
This note: "Abandon hope, you doopoe;
The hoopoe is a misanthroopoe.
   (Signed) Your far-off friend, *U. e.*"

To an Usherette

Ah, come with me,
Petite chérie,
And we shall rather happy be.
I know a modest luncheonette
Where, for a little, one can get
A choplet, baby lima beans,
And, segmented, two tangerines.

Le coup de grâce,
My petty lass,
Will be a demi-demitasse
Within a serviette conveyed
By weazened waiters, underpaid,
Who mincingly might grant us spoons
While a combo tinkles trivial tunes.

Ah, with me come,
Ma mini-*femme,*
And I shall say I love you some.

Time's Fool

Frederick Alexander Pott
Arrives at parties on the dot.
The drinks have not been mixed, the wife
Is still applying, with a knife,
Extract of shrimp and chicken spread
To parallelograms of bread
When Pott appears, remarking, "I'm
Afraid I'm barging in on time."

For Frederick Pott is never late
For any rendezvous or date.
Arrange to meet at some hotel;
You'll find he's been there since the bell
Tolled the appointed hour. Not
Intending to embarrass, Pott
Says shyly, "Punctuality
Is psychological with me."

Pott takes the most preposterous pains
To suit the scheduled times of trains.
He goes to concerts, races, plays,
Allowing nicely for delays,
And at the age three score and ten
Pott plans to perish; doubtless then
He'll ask, as he has often done,
"This *was* the time agreed upon?"

Superman

I drive my car to supermarket,
    The way I take is superhigh,

A superlot is where I park it,
    And Super Suds are what I buy.

Supersalesmen sell me tonic—
    Super-Tone-O, for Relief.
The planes I ride are supersonic.
    In trains, I like the Super Chief.

Supercilious men and women
    Call me superficial—*me*,
Who so superbly learned to swim in
    Supercolossality.

Superphosphate-fed foods feed me;
    Superservice keeps me new.
Who would dare to supersede me,
    Super-super-superwho?

An Ode

(Fired into Being by Life's *48-Star Editorial,
"Wanted: An American Novel")*

STROPHE
*Ours is the most powerful nation in the world. It has had a decade
of unparalleled prosperity. . . . Yet it is still producing a literature
which sounds sometimes as if it were written by an unemployed
homosexual. . . .*

ANTISTROPHE
    I'm going to write a novel, hey,
        I'll write it as per *Life:*
    I'm going to say, "What a splendid day!"
        And, "How I love my wife!"

Let heroines be once again
    Pink, languid, soft, and tall,
For from my pen shall flow forth men
    Heterosexual.

STROPHE

Atomic fear or not, the incredible accomplishments of our day are surely the raw stuff of saga.

ANTISTROPHE

    Raw stuff shall be the stuff of which
        My saga will be made:
    Brown soil, black pitch, the lovely rich,
        The noble poor, the raid
    On Harpers Ferry, Bunker Hill,
        Forefathers fairly met,
    The home, the mill, the hearth, the Bill
        Of Rights, et cet., et cet.

STROPHE

Nobody wants Pollyanna literature.

ANTISTROPHE

    I shan't play Pollyanna, no,
        I'll stare facts in the eye:
    Folks come and go, experience woe,
        And, when they're tired, die.
    Unflinchingly, I plan to write
        A book to comprehend
    Rape, fury, spite, and, burning bright,
        A sunset at The End.

STROPHE

In every healthy man there is a wisdom deeper than his conscious mind, reaching beyond memory to the primeval rivers, a yea-saying to the goodness and joy of life.

A wise and not unhealthy man,
   I'm telling everyone
That deeper than the old brainpan
   Primeval rivers run;
For *Life* is joy and *Time* is gay
   And *Fortune* smiles on those
Good books that say, at some length, "Yea,"
   And thereby spite the Noes.

The Newlyweds

After a one-day honeymoon, the Fishers rushed off to a soft drink bottlers'
convention, then on to a ball game, a TV rehearsal and a movie preview.

                                          —*Life*

"We're married," said Eddie.
Said Debbie, "Incredi-

ble! When is our honey-
moon?" "Over and done," he

replied. "Feeling logy?
Drink Coke." "Look at Yogi

go!" Debbie cried. "Groovy!"
"Rehearsal?" "The movie."

"Some weddie," said Debbie.
Said Eddie, "Yeah, mebbe."

The Story of My Life

Fernando Valenti, enthusiast, Yale graduate, and himself repre-
sented by numerous recordings of Scarlatti.

—The Saturday Review

Enthused I went to Yale, enthused
I graduated. Still infused
with this enthusiasm when
Scarlatti called, I answered en-
thusiastically, and thus
I made recordings numerous,
so numerous that I am classed,
quite simply, as "enthusiast."

A Bitter Life

Dr. Ycas [of the Quartermaster Research and Development Center, in a
report to the National Academy of Sciences] holds that the ocean itself was
alive. There were no living creatures in it.

—The New York Times

O you Dr. Ycas you!
    In one convulsive motion
Your brain has given birth unto
    A viable young ocean.
All monsters pale beside the new:
    The Hydra, Hap, Garuda, Ra,
Italapas, Seb, Hua-hu
    Tiao, Gulltopr, Grendel's ma,
Quetzalcoatl, Kukulkan,
    Onniont, Audhumbla, Ix,

274

Geryon, Leviathan,
   666,
The ox Ahura Mazda made,
   The Fomors, deevs, Graeae,
And others of this ilk all fade
   Alongside Ycas' sea.
The straits were sinews, channelways
   Were veins, and islands eyes;
Rivers were tails, reefs bones, and bays,
   Depending on their size,
Fists, shoulders, heads, ears, mouths, or feet.
   The fjords, as fingers, froze
Sometimes, as did the arctic pate
   And pale antarctic toes.
O horrid, horrid Ocean! The
   Foul grandmother of Tyr,
Who had nine hundred crania,
   Did not look half so queer.
It whistled with a mournful hiss
   In darkness; scared and bored,
It lapped the land, yet every kiss
   Was stonily ignored.
A spheric skin, or blue-green hide,
   Alone the ocean kept
Our planet's house, yet when it died
   One aeon, no one wept.

A Wooden Darning Egg

The carpentered hen
unhinges her wings,
abandons her nest
of splinters, and sings.

. . .

The egg she has laid
is maple and hard
as a tenpenny nail
and smooth as a board.

The grain of the wood
adorns the thick shell
as brown feathers do
a young cockerel.

The hen lifts her hackles;
her sandpapered throat
unwarps as she cackles
Cross-cut! ka-ross-cut!

Beginning to brood,
she tests with a level
the angle, sits down,
and coos *Bevel bevel.*

Publius Vergilius Maro,
the Madison Avenue Hick

This was in Italy. The year was the thirty-seventh before the birth of
Christ. The people were mighty hungry, for there was a famine in the land.
—the beginning of a Heritage Club advertisement,
in *The New Yorker*, for *The Georgics*

It takes a heap o' pluggin' t' make a classic sell,
Fer folks are mighty up-to-date, an' jittery as hell;
They got no yen to set aroun' with Vergil in their laps
When they kin read the latest news in twenty-four-point
    caps.

Ye've got t' hit 'em clean an' hard, with simple predicates,
An' keep the clauses short becuz these days nobody waits
T' foller out a sentence thet all-likely lacks a punch
When in the time o' readin' they could grab a bite o' lunch.

Ye've got t' hand 'em place an' time, an' then a pinch o'
    slang
T' make 'em feel right comfy in a Latinate shebang,
An' ef your taste buds curdle an' your tum turns queasy—
    well,
It takes a heap o' pluggin' t' make a classic sell.

Tsokadze O Altitudo

Tsokadze has invented a new style—apparently without knowing it. He does not bend from the waist at all. His body is straight and relaxed and leaning far out over his skis until his face is only two feet above them, his arms at his side, his head up. His bindings and shoes are so loose that only his toes touch his skies. He gets enormous distances and his flight is so beautiful.

    —Thorlief Schjelderup, quoted in *The New York Times*,
            of a young Russian ski-jumper

Tsokadze leans unknowingly
    Above his skis, relaxed and tall.
    He bends not from the waist at all.
This is the way a man should ski.

He sinks; he rises, up and up,
    His face two feet above the wood.
    This way of jumping, it is good,
Says expert Thorlief Schjelderup.

· · ·

Beneath his nose, the ski-tips shake;
    He plummets down the deepening wide
    Bright pit of air, arms at his side,
His heart aloft for Russia's sake.

Loose are the bindings, stiff the knees,
    Relaxed the man—see, still he flies
    And only his toes touch his skies!
Ah, c'est beau, when Tsokadze skis.

The One-Year-Old

(After Reading the Appropriate Chapter in
Infant and Child in the Culture of Today,
    by Arnold Gesell and Frances Ilg)

Wakes wet; is promptly toileted;
Jargons to himself; is fed;

Executively grips a cup;
Quadrupedal, will sit up

Unaided; laughs; applauds; enjoys
Baths and manipulative toys;

Socializes (parents: shun
Excess acculturation);

Demonstrates prehension; will
Masticate yet seldom spill;

Creeps (gross motor drives are strong);
And jargons, jargons all day long.

Room 28

National Portrait Gallery, London

Remembered as octagonal, dark-panelled,
  And seldom frequented, except by me—
    Indeed, a bower
Attained down avenues where, framed and annalled,
  Great England's great with truculence outlive
    Their hour
And staringly put up with immortality—
  The room gave rest as some libraries give.

The visitor, approaching, brushed a girlish
  Bust of Lord Byron. Sir James George Frazer's head,
    An unarmed sentry,
Austere, tormented, brazen-browed, and churlish,
  Guarded with sternness fit for Stygian gates
    The entry
To harmless walls where men of letters lately dead
  Were hung. The envied spot was held by Yeats.

His mask, alone a mask among the paintings,
  Attracted to itself what little sun
    The sky admitted.
Half-bronze, half-black, his Janus-face at matins
  Amazed that dim arena of the less
    Weird-witted
Survivors of a blurred time: presbyters upon
  Whose faces grieved the ghost of earnestness.

The whites of Rider Haggard's eyes were showing
  When last I saw them. Conrad's cheeks were green,
    And Rudyard Kipling's
Pink profile burned against his brown works, glowing

With royalties and loyalty to crown.
        Fine stipplings
Limned the long locks that Ellen Terry, seventeen,
    Pre-Raphaelite, and blonde, let shining down.

There Stevenson looked ill and ill-depicted;
    Frail Patmore, plucked yet gamey; Henry James,
            Our good grammarian,
More paunched and politic than I'd expected.
    Among the lone-faced portraits loomed a trin-
            Itarian
Composite: Baring, Chesterton, Belloc. The frame's
    Embellished foursquare dogma boxed them in.

Brave room! Where are they now? In college courses,
    Perused in inferior light, then laid
            On library tables.
White knights mismounted on empirical horses,
    Flagbearers for a tattered heraldry
            Of labels,
They lacked the universe their vows deserved, and fade
    Here on the cusp, in neither century.

Philological

The British puss demurely mews;
His transatlantic kin meow.
The kine in Minnesota moo;
Not so the gentle Devon cows:
        They low,
As every schoolchild ought to know.

Mr. High-Mind

Then went the Jury out, whose names were Mr. *Blind-man,* Mr. *No-good,*
Mr. *Malice,* Mr. *Love-lust,* Mr. *Live-loose,* Mr. *Heady,* Mr. *High-mind,* Mr.
Enmity, Mr. *Lyar,* Mr. *Cruelty,* Mr. *Hate-light,* and Mr. *Implacable.*
              —*The Pilgrim's Progress*

Eleven rogues and he to judge a fool—
He files out with the jury, but distaste
Constricts his fluting nostrils, and his cool
Mind turns tepid with contempt. There is brought
A basin for him, in which to wash his hands.
Laving his palms and fingertips, he finds
An image of his white, proportioned thought
Plunged in the squalid suds of other minds.
Unmoved by Lust's requests or Hate's commands
Or Superstition's half-embarrassed bribe,
His brain takes wing and flutters up the course
First plotted by the Greeks, up toward the sphere
Where issues and alternatives are placed
In that remorseless light that knows no source.

Here, in this saddle-shaped, expanding void,
The wise alone have cause for breathing; here
Lines parallel on Earth, extended, meet.
Here priests in tweeds gyrate around the feet
Of Fact, their bride, and hymn their gratitude
That each toe of her ten is understood.
From this great height, the notion of the Good
Is seen to be a vulgar one, and crude.
High-mind as Judge descends to Earth, annoyed,
Despairing Justice. Man, a massy tribe,
Cannot possess one wide and neutral eye.
He casts his well-weighed verdict with a sigh
And for a passing moment is distressed
To see it coinciding with the rest.

Tax-Free Encounter

We have $3,000 savings to invest and believe in the dignity of
man. Box Y-920.

—Personal notice in *The Saturday Review*

I met a fellow in whose hand
Was hotly held a cool three grand.
"Inform me of," he said, "the best
Technique of gaining interest."

"Lend money at usurious rates,"
I said. "It soon accumulates."
"Oh no!" he cried. "That is unsound
Artistically. Read Ezra Pound."

"Invest," I then suggested. "Deal
Yourself a hand in U.S. Steel."
He snapped, "Big businessmen are sharks.
Peruse *Das Kapital*, by Marx."

"Then buy some U.S. Savings Bonds,
For Our Defense, which corresponds
To Yours and Mine." He told me, "Cease!
Defense degrades. Read *War and Peace.*"

He added, "Dignity of men
Is what we most believe in." Then
He slyly smiled and slowly backed
Away, his principal intact.

Scenic

O when in San Francisco do
As natives do: they sit and stare
And smile and stare again. The view
Is visible from anywhere.

Here hills are white with houses whence,
Across a multitude of sills,
The owners, lucky residents,
See other houses, other hills.

The meanest San Franciscan knows,
No matter what his sins have been,
There are a thousand patios
Whose view he is included in.

The Golden Gate, the cable cars,
Twin Peaks, the Spreckels habitat,
The local ocean, sun, and stars—
When fog falls, one admires *that*.

Here homes are stacked in such a way
That every picture window has
An unmarred prospect of the Bay
And, in its center, Alcatraz.

Capacity

CAPACITY 26 PASSENGERS
—*sign in a bus*

Affable, bibulous,
corpulent, dull,
eager-to-find-a-seat,
formidable,
garrulous, humorous,
icy, jejune,
knockabout, laden-
with-luggage (maroon),
mild-mannered, narrow-necked,
oval-eyed, pert,
querulous, rakish,
seductive, tart, vert-
iginous, willowy,
xanthic (or yellow),
young, zebuesque are my
passengers fellow.

Little Poems

OVERCOME, Kim flees in bitter frustration to her TV studio dressing room
where she angrily flings a vase of flowers to the floor and sobs in abandon
to a rose she destroys: "I'm tearing this flower apart like I'm destroying my
life." As she often does, she later turned the episode into a little poem.
—*photograph caption in* Life

I woke up tousled, one strap falling
Off the shoulder, casually.

284

In came ten *Time-Life* lensmen, calling,
   "Novak, hold that deshabille!"

I went to breakfast, asked for java,
   Prunes, and toast. "Too dark," they said.
"The film we use is slow, so have a
   Spread of peaches, tea, and bread."

I wrote a memo, "To my agent—"
   "Write instead," they said, " 'Dear Mum.' "
In conference, when I made a cogent
   Point, they cried, "No, no! Act dumb."

I told a rose, "I tear you as I
   Tear my life," and heard them say,
"Afraid that 'as' of yours is quasi-
   Classy. We like 'like.' O.K.?"

I dined with friends. The *Time-Life* crewmen
   Interrupted: "Bare your knees,
Project your bosom, and, for human
   Interest, look ill-at-ease."

I, weary, fled to bed. They hounded
   Me with meters, tripods, eyes
That winked and winked—I was surrounded!
   The caption read, "ALONE, Kim cries."

Popular Revivals 1956

The thylacine, long thought to be extinct,
Is not. The ancient doglike creature, linked
To kangaroos and platypi, still pounces
On his Tasmanian prey, the *Times* announces.

The tarpan (stumpy, prehistoric horse)
Has been rebred—in Germany, of course.
Herr Heinz Heck, by striking genetic chords,
Has out of plowmares beat his tiny wards.

The California fur seal, a refined
And gullible amphibian consigned
By profit-seeking sealers to perdition,
Barked at the recent Gilmore expedition.

The bison, butchered on our Western prairie,
Took refuge in our coinage. Now, contrary
To what was feared, the herds are out of danger
And in the films, co-starred with Stewart Granger.

Tune, in American Type

Set and printed in Great Britain by Tonbridge Printers, Ltd., Peach Hall
Works, Tonbridge, in Times nine on ten point, on paper made by John
Dickenson at Croxley, and bound by James Burn at Esher.
—colophon in a book published by Michael Joseph (London)

Ah, to be set and printed in
Great Britain now that Tonbridge Prin-
ters, Limited, employ old John
Dickenson, at Croxley. On

his pages is Times nine-on-ten-
point type impressed, and, lastly, when
at Peach Hall Works the job is done,
James Burn at Esher's job's begun.

    Hey nonny nonny nonny,
    Hey nonny nonny nay!

Tonbridge! Croxley! Esher! Ah,
is there, in America,
a tome contrived in such sweet towns?
No. English, English are the downs
where Jim Burn, honest craftsman, winds
beneath his load of reams; he binds
the sheets that once John Dickenson
squeezed flat from British pulp. *Hey non-*

    ny nonny, etc.

Due Respect

They [members of teen-age gangs] are respectful of their parents and
particularly of their mothers—known as "moo" in their jargon.
                —*The New York Times Magazine*

    Come moo, dear moo, let's you and me
    Sit down awhile and talk togee;
    My broo's at school, and faa's away
    A-gaaing rosebuds while he may.

    Of whence we come and whii we go
    Most moos nee know nor care to know,
    But you are not like any oo:
    You're always getting in a poo

Or working up a dreadful laa
Over nothing—nothing. Bah!
Relax. You love me, I love you,
And that's the way it shapes up, moo.

A Rack of Paperbacks

Gateway, Grove,
  and Dover say,
"Unamuno
  any day."

Beacon Press
  and Torchlight chorus,
"Kierkegaard
  does nicely for us."

"Willey, Waley,"
  Anchor bleats,
"Auden, Barzun,
  Kazin, Keats."

"Tovey, Glover,
  Cohen, Fry"
is Meridi-
  an's reply.

"Bentley's best,"
  brags Dramabooks.
Harvest brings in
  Cleanth Brooks.

All, including
  Sentinel,
Jaico, Maco,
  Arco, Dell,

Noonday, Vintage,
   Living Age,
Mentor, Wisdom—
   page on page

of classics much
   too little known
when books were big
   and bindings sewn—

agree: "Lord Raglan,
   Margaret Mead,
Moses Hadas,
   Herbert Read,

the Panchatantra,
   Hamsun's *Pan*,
Tillich, Ilg,
   Kahlil Gibran,

and Henry James
   sell better if
their spines are not
   austerely stiff."

Even Egrets Err

Egregious was the egret's error, very.
   Egressing from a swamp, the bird eschewed
No egriot (a sour kind of cherry)*
   It saw, and reaped extremest egritude.†

*Obs.
†Rare form of obs. Aegritude, meaning sickness.

Glasses

I wear them. They help me. But I
Don't care for them. Two birds, steel hinges
Haunt each an edge of the small sky
My green eyes make. Rim-horn impinges
Upon my vision's furry fringes;
Faint dust collects upon the dry,
Unblinking shield behind which cringes
My naked, deprecated eye.

My gaze feels aimed. It is as if
Two manufactured beams have been
Lodged in my sockets—hollow, stiff,
And gray, like mailing tubes—and when
I pivot, vases topple down
From tabletops, and women frown.

The Sensualist

Each Disc contains not more than ½ minim of Chloroform together with
Capsicum, Peppermint, Anise, Cubeb, Licorice, and Linseed.
                          —from a box of Parke-Davis throat discs

Come, Capsicum, cast off thy membranous pods;
Thy Guinea girlhood's blossoms have been dried.
Come, Peppermint, belovèd of the gods
(That is, of Hades; Ceres,,in her pride,
So Strabo says, transmogrified
Delicious Mintha, making her a plant).

Come, Anise, sweet stomachic stimulant,
Most umbelliferous of condiments,

Depart thy native haunt, the hot Levant.
Swart Licorice, or Liquorice, come hence,
And Linseed, too, of these ingredients
Most colorless, most odorless, most nil.

And Javan Cubeb, come—thy smokable
Gray pericarps and pungent seeds shall be
Our feast's incense. Come, Chloroform, née Phyll,
In demiminims dance unto the spree.
Compounded spices, come: dissolve in me.

In Memoriam

In the novel he marries Victoria but in the movie he dies.
—caption in Life

Fate lifts us up so she can hurl
    Us down from heights of pride,
Viz.: in the book he got the girl
    But in the movie, died.

The author, seeing he was brave
    And good, rewarded him,
Then, greedy, sold him as a slave
    To mean old M-G-M.

He perished on the screen, but thrives
    In print, where serifs keep
Watch o'er the happier of his lives:
    Say, Does he wake, or sleep?

Planting a Mailbox

Prepare the ground when maple buds have burst
   And when the daytime moon is sliced so thin
His fibers drink blue sky with litmus thirst.
   This moment come, begin.

The site should be within an easy walk,
   Beside a road, in stony earth. Your strength
Dictates how deep you delve. The seedling's stalk
   Should show three feet of length.

Don't harrow, weed, or water; just apply
   A little gravel. Sun and motor fumes
Perform the miracle: in late July,
   A branch post office blooms.

ZULUS LIVE IN LAND
WITHOUT A SQUARE

A Zulu lives in a round world. If he does not leave his reserve, he can live
his whole life through and never see a straight line.
              —headline and text from *The New York Times*

    In Zululand the huts are round,
    The windows oval, and the rooves
    Thatched parabolically. The ground
    Is tilled in curvilinear grooves.

    When Zulus cannot smile, they frown,
    To keep an arc before the eye.

Describing distances to town,
They say, "As flies the butterfly."

Anfractuosity is king.
Melodic line itself is banned,
Though all are hip enough to sing—
There are no squares in Zululand.

Caligula's Dream

Insomnia was his worst torment. Three hours a night of fitful sleep
was all that he ever got, and even then terrifying visions would haunt
him—once, for instance, he dreamed that he had a conversation with
the Mediterranean Sea.

—Suetonius

Of gold the bread on which he banqueted,
Where pimps in silk and pearls dissolved in wine
Were standard fare. The monster's marble head
Had many antic veins, being divine.
At war, he massed his men upon the beach
And bawled the coward's order, "Gather shells!"
And stooped, in need of prisoners, to teach
The German tongue to prostituted Gauls.
Bald young, broad-browed, and, for his era, tall,
In peace he proved incestuous and queer,
And spent long hours in the Capitol
Exchanging compliments with Jupiter;
He stalled his horse in ivory, and displayed
His wife undressed to friends, and liked to view
Eviscerations and the dance, and made
Poor whores supply imperial revenue.

. . .

Perhaps—to plead—the boy had heard how, when
They took his noble father from the pyre
And found a section unconsumed, the men
Suspicioned: "Poisoned hearts resist the fire."
It was as water that his vision came,
At any rate—more murderous than he,
More wanton, uglier, of wider fame,
Unsleeping also, multi-sexed, the Sea.

It told him, "Little Boots, you cannot sin
Enough; you speak a language, though you rave.
The actual things at home beneath my skin
Out-horrify the vilest hopes you have.
Ten-tentacled invertebrates embrace
And swap through thirsty ani livid seed
While craggy worms without a brain or face
Upon their own soft children blindly feed.
As huge as Persian palaces, blue whales
Grin fathoms down, and through their teeth are strained
A million lives a minute; each entails,
In death, a microscopic bit of pain.
Atrocity is truly emperor;
All things that thrive are slaves of cruel Creation."

Caligula, his mouth a mass of fur,
Awoke, and toppled toward assassination.

Bendix

This porthole overlooks a sea
    Forever falling from the sky,
The water inextricably
    Involved with buttons, suds, and dye.

Like bits of shrapnel, shards of foam
   Fly heavenward; a bedsheet heaves,
A stocking wrestles with a comb,
   And cotton angels wave their sleeves.

The boiling purgatorial tide
   Revolves our dreary shorts and slips,
While Mother coolly bakes beside
   Her little jugged apocalypse.

The Menagerie at Versailles in 1775

(Taken Verbatim from a Notebook Kept by
Dr. Samuel Johnson)

Cygnets dark; their black feet;
on the ground; tame.
Halcyons, or gulls.
Stag and hind, small.
Aviary, very large: the net, wire.
Black stag of China, small.

Rhinoceros, the horn broken
and pared away, which, I suppose,
will grow; the basis, I think,
four inches 'cross; the skin
folds like loose cloth doubled over his body
and 'cross his hips: a vast animal,
though young; as big, perhaps,
as four oxen.

            The young elephant,
with his tusks just appearing.

The brown bear put out his paws.
All very tame. The lion.
The tigers I did not well view.
The camel, or dromedary with two bunches
called the Huguin, taller than any horse.
Two camels with one bunch.

Among the birds was a pelican,
who being let out, went
to a fountain, and swam
about to catch fish. His feet
well webbed: he dipped his head,
and turned his long bill sidewise.

Reel

whorl (hwûrl; hwôrl), *n.* . . . . 2. Something that whirls or seems
to whirl as a whorl, or wharve . . .
—Webster's Collegiate Dictionary

Whirl, whorl or wharve! The world
   Whirls within solar rings
Which once were hotly hurled
   Away by whirling things!

We whirl, or seem to whirl,
   Or seem to seem to; whorls
Within more whorls unfurl
   In manners, habits, morals.

Wind whirls; hair curls; the worm
   Can turn, and wheels can wheel,
And even stars affirm:
   Whatever whirls is real.

Kenneths

Rexroth and Patchen and Fearing—their mothers
Perhaps could distinguish their sons from the others,
But I am unable. My inner eye pictures
A three-bodied sun-lover issuing strictures,
Berating "Tom" Eliot, translating tanka,
Imbibing espresso and sneering at Sanka—
Six arms, thirty fingers, all writing abundantly
What pops into heads each named Kenneth, redundantly.

Upon Learning That a Bird Exists Called the Turnstone

A turnstone turned rover
   And went through ten turnstiles,
Admiring the clover
   And turnsole and fern styles.

She took to the turnpike
   And travelled to Dover,
Where turnips enjoy
   A rapid turnover.

The Turneresque landscape
   She scanned for a lover;
She'd heard one good turnstone
   Deserves another.

In vain did she hover
   And earnestly burn
With yearning; above her
   The terns cried, "Return!"

In Extremis

I saw my toes the other day.
I hadn't looked at them for months.
Indeed, they might have passed away.
And yet they were my best friends once.
When I was small, I knew them well.
I counted on them up to ten
And put them in my mouth to tell
The larger from the lesser. Then
I loved them better than my ears,
My elbows, adenoids, and heart.
But with the swelling of the years
We drifted, toes and I, apart.
Now, gnarled and pale, each said, *j'accuse!*—
I hid them quickly in my shoes.

Blked

Labor—gas tove	$28.00
4¾ female ells	2.60
1¾ blk union	.80
4¾ × 2″ cplings	1.14
2¾ male tees	.72

—from a plumbing bill

At first, the euphemistic "blk"
Appeared to me to rhyme with "milk."
The labor done upon my tove
Had not, it seemed, been one of love.

And yet love's language ripples through

The reckoning; cplings, two by two,
Perhaps aroused some Puritan
To *balk* a union. Nasty man!

Or does the "union" mean The States,
Which Cold-War cost debilitates?
To boost the Free World's *bulk,* give $.80,
And be a *bulwark* of defense.

Toothache Man

The earth has been unkind to him.
   He lies in middle strata.
The time capsules about him brim
   With advertising matter.

His addled fossils tell a tale
   That lacks barbaric splendor;
His vertebrae are small and pale,
   His femora are slender.

It is his teeth—strange, cratered things—
   That name him. Some are hollow,
Like bowls, and hold gold offerings.
   The god may be Apollo.

Silver and gold. We think he thought
   His god, who was immortal,
Dwelt in his skull; hence, the devout
   Adorned the temple's portal.

Heraldic fists and spears and bells
   In all metallic colors

Invade the bone; their volume swells
  On backward through the molars.

This culture's meagre sediments
  Have come to light just lately.
We handle them with reverence.
  He must have suffered greatly.

Party Knee

To drink in moderation, and to smoke
  A minimal amount, and joke
  Reservedly does not insure
Awaking from a party whole and pure.

Be we as temperate as the turtledove,
  A soirée is an orgy of
  This strange excess, unknown in France,
And Rome, and Nineveh: the upright stance.

When more than four forgather in our land,
  We stand and stand, and stand and stand.
  Thighs ache; a drowsy numbness locks
The bones between our pockets and our socks.

We rue the night next morning; up from bed
  With addled knees and lucid head
  We crawl at dawn, and sob, and beg
A buffered aspirin for a splitting leg.

The Moderate

Frost's space is deeper than Poliakoff's and not as deep as that of Soulages.
—Patrick Heron in *Arts*

"Soulages's space is deep and wide—
Beware!" they said. "Beware," they cried,
"The yawning gap, the black abyss
That closes with a dreadful hiss!

"That shallow space by Poliakoff,"
They added, "is a wretched trough.
It wrinkles, splinters, shreds, and fades;
It wouldn't hold the Jack of Spades."

"But where?" I asked, bewildered, lost.
"Go seek," they said, "the space of Frost;
It's not too bonny, not too braw—
The nicest space you ever saw."

I harked, and heard, and here I live,
Delighted to be relative.

Deities and Beasts

Tall Atlas, Jupiter, Hercules, Thor,
Just like the antic pagan gods of yore,
Make up a too-erratic pantheon
For mortal men to be dependent on.

I much prefer, myself, the humble RAT,
The tiny Terrier, the short Hawk that
Makes secret flight, and the Sparrow, whose fall
Is never mentioned in the press at all.

Within a Quad

Within a quad of aging brick,
Behind the warty warden oak,
The Radcliffe sophomores exchange,
In fencing costume, stroke for stroke;
Their bare knees bent, the darlings duel
Like daughters of Dumas and Scott.
Their sneakered feet torment the lawn,
Their skirted derrières stick out.

Beneath the branches, needles glint
Unevenly in dappled sun
As shadowplay and swordplay are
In no time knitted into one;
The metal twitters, girl hacks girl,
Their educated faces caged.
The fake felt hearts and pointless foils
Contain an oddly actual rage.

In Praise of $(C_{10}H_9O_5)_x$

I have now worn the same terylene tie every day for eighteen months.
—From *Chemistry*, a Penguin book by Kenneth Hutton

My tie is made of terylene;
    Eternally I wear it,
For time can never wither, stale,
    Shred, shrink, fray, fade, or tear it.
The storms of January fail
    To loosen it with bluster;
The rains of April fail to stain
    Its polyester lustre;

July's hot sun beats down in vain;
  October's frosts fall futilely;
December's snow can blow and blow—
  My tie remains acutely
Immutable! When I'm below,
  Dissolving in that halcyon
Retort, my carbohydrates shed
  From off my frame of calcium—
When I am, in lay language, dead,
  Across my crumbling sternum
Shall lie a spanking fresh cravat
  Unsullied *ad æternum,*
A grave and solemn prospect that
  Makes light of our allotted
Three score and ten, for terylene
  Shall never be unknotted.

Milady Reflects

RADIO SIGNALS BOUNCED OFF VENUS
    —headline in *The New York Times*

When I was known as Aphrodite, men
  Were wont to bounce their prayers off my side.
  I shrugged, and granted some, and some denied,
And even slept with mortals now and then.

But then Jehovah stormed in on a star
  And put a rapid end to such requests.
  Well, cultures change; the gods are transient guests
On Earth. I made the sky my sole boudoir.

Just yesterday, I felt an odd caress,
  A tickle or a whisper or a hum

That smacked of Man—his opposable thumb,
His monkey face, his myths, his *humanness*.

Oh, dear. I'm not the girl he left alone.
　　I have my books, my chocolates, and my maid—
　　I know Mars thinks I've gotten rather staid.
I think I'll have them disconnect the phone.

The Fritillary

The fritillary,
Fickle, wary,
Flits from plant to plant with nary
A forethought as to where he
Alights, a butterfly.

And, what's extraordinary,
Is also an herb—
The same word serves.
Nothing disturbs
Its thick green nerves.

When one lights on the other it is very
Nice:
The spotted wings and the spotted petals, both spelled from
　　　the Latin *fritillus* [dice],
Nod together
Toward a center
Where a mirror
Might be imagined.
They are tangent,
Self to self, the same
Within a single name.
A miracle has occurred.

　　　　　　　　　　. · .

Alas! The wingèd word
With a blind flap leaves the leaved,
Unbereaved,
And bobbles down the breeze,
Careless of etymologies.

Thoughts While Driving Home

Was I clever enough? Was I charming?
　　Did I make at least one good pun?
Was I disconcerting? Disarming?
　　Was I wise? Was I wan? Was I fun?

Did I answer that girl with white shoulders
　　Correctly, or should I have said
(Engagingly), "Kierkegaard smolders,
　　But Eliot's ashes are dead"?

And did I, while being a smarty,
　　Yet some wry reserve slyly keep,
So they murmured, when I'd left the party,
　　"He's deep. He's deep. He's deep"?

Sonic Boom

I'm sitting in the living room,
When, up above, the Thump of Doom
Resounds. Relax. It's sonic boom.

The ceiling shudders at the clap,
The mirrors tilt, the rafters snap,
And Baby wakens from his nap.

. . .

"Hush, babe. Some pilot we equip,
Giving the speed of sound the slip,
Has cracked the air like a penny whip."

Our world is far from frightening; I
No longer strain to read the sky
Where moving fingers (jet planes) fly.
Our world seems much too tame to die.

And if it does, with one more *pop*,
I shan't look up to see it drop.

Tome-Thoughts, from the *Times*

The special merit of the two first novels up for discussion today is that they
are neither overly ambitious nor overly long. Both are deftly written,
amusing and intensely feminine. Both are the work of brightly talented
young women.

—Orville Prescott, in *The New York Times*

Oh, to be Orville Prescott
Now that summer's here,
And the books on tinted paper
Blow lightly down the air,
And the merciful brevity of every page
Becalms the winter's voluminous rage,
And unambition like lilac lies
On Prescott's eyes.

When heroines with small frustrations,
Dressed in transparent motivations,
Glimmer and gambol, trip and trot;
Then may the sensitive critic spy,

Beneath the weave of a gossamer plot,
The subtle pink of an author's thigh.
Oh bliss! oh brightly talented! oh neither
Overly this nor that—a breather!
Along the sands of the summer lists
The feminine first novelists
Go dancing, deft, and blessed twice over
By Prescott, deep in short-stemmed clover.

A Song of Paternal Care

A Lithuanian lithographer
   Who lived on lithia water
Was blessed, by lithogenesis,
   With a lithe and lithic daughter.

Said he beneath a lithy tree
   When she'd reached litholysis,
"It's time you thought of lithomarge,
   And even . . . lithophthisis."

She blushed, the lovely lithoglyph,
   And said, "I love a lithsman.*
I feel so litholyte when I'm,"
   She smiled, eliding, "wi' th's man."

"Go fetch the lithofellic fellow!"
   Her father boomed, with laughter.
She did. They lived in Lithgow, Austl.,
   Litherly† ever after.

*An unfortunately obsolete word meaning a sailor in the navy under the Danish kings of England.
†Another, meaning mischievous, wicked, or lazy.

Tropical Beetles

Composed of horny, jagged blacks
  Yet quite unformidable,
They flip themselves upon their backs
  And die beneath the table.

The Temperate wasp, with pointed moan,
  Flies straightway to the apple;
But bugs inside the Tropic Zone
  With idle fancies grapple.

They hurl themselves past window sills
  And labor through a hundred
Ecstatic, crackling, whirring spills—
  For what, I've often wondered.

They seek the light—it stirs their stark,
  Ill-lit imaginations—
And win, when stepped on in the dark,
  Disgusted exclamations.

Agatha Christie and Beatrix Potter

Many-volumed authoresses
In capacious country dresses,
Full of cheerful art and nearly
Perfect craft, we love you dearly.

You know the hedgerow, stile, and barrow,
Have sniffed the cabbage, leek, and marrow,
Have heard the prim postmistress snicker,
And spied out murder in the vicar.

You've drawn the berry-beaded brambles
Where Mrs. Tiggy-winkle rambles,
And mapped the attics in the village
Where mice plot alibis and pillage.

We love you both, for in these places
You give us cozy scares and chases
That end with innocence acquitted—
Except for Cotton-tail, who did it.

Young Matrons Dancing

Corinna foots it in bare feet;
Her toes are dusty but discreet
In sliding backwards from the shoes
Of Arthur Johnson Betelgeuse.

Anthea, married twice with three
Small children, softly smiles to see
Her jealous present husband frown
While talking stocks with Elmore Brown.

These pelves childbirth spread still twitch
In time to that too-narrow itch
That led their innocence down ways
Composed of endless working days;

Corinna and Anthea still
Can bend to Lester Lanin's will,
And mime with scarce-diminished grace
Perpetuation of the race.

Comp. Religion

It all begins with fear of *mana*.
    Next there comes the love of tribe.
Native dances, totems, ani-
    Mism and magicians thrive.

Culture grows more complicated.
    Spirits, chiefs in funny hats,
And suchlike spooks are sublimated
    Into gods and ziggurats.

Polyarmed and polyheaded,
    Gods proliferate until
Puristic-minded sages edit
    Their welter into one sweet Will.

This worshipped One grows so enlightened,
    Vast, and high He, in a blur,
Explodes; and men are left as frightened
    Of *mana* as they ever were.

Meditation on a News Item

Fidel Castro, who considers himself first in war and first in peace, was first
in the Hemingway fishing tourney at Havana, Cuba. "I am a novice at
fishing," said Fidel. "You are a lucky novice," replied Ernest.
                    —*Life*, in June 1960

Yes, yes, and there is even a photograph,
of the two in profile, both bearded, both sharp-nosed,
both (though the one is not wearing a cap
and the other is not carrying a cat)

magnificently recognizable (do
you think that much-photographed faces grow
larger, more deeply themselves, like flowers
in sunlight?). A great cup sits between their chests.

Life does not seem to think it very strange.
It runs the shot cropped to four inches,
and the explanation is given in full above.
But to me it seems immeasurably strange: as strange
to me as if there were found,
in a Jacobean archive, an unquestionably authentic
woodcut showing Shakespeare
presenting the blue ribbon for Best Cake Baked
to Queen Elizabeth.

And even the dialogue: so perfect—
"You are a lucky novice." Succinct,
wry, ominous, innocent: Nick Adams talking.
How did it happen? Did he,
convulsively departing from the exhausting regimen—
the rising at 6 a.m. to sharpen twelve pencils
with which to cut, as he stands at his bookcase,
269 or 312 or 451 more words into the paper
that will compose one of those many rumored books
that somehow never appear—did he abruptly exclaim,
"I must have a fishing tourney!"
and have posters painted and posted
in cabañas, cigar stores, and bordellos,
ERNEST HEMINGWAY FISHING COMPETITION,
just like that?

And did he receive, on one of those soft Havana mornings,
while the smoky-green Caribbean laps the wharf legs,
and the *señoritas* yawn behind grillwork,
and the black mailmen walk in khaki shorts,

an application blank stating CASTRO, Fidel?
Occupation: Dictator. *Address:*
Top Floor, Habana-Hilton Hotel (commandeered).
Hobbies: Ranting, U.S.-Baiting, Fishing (novice).

And was it honest? I mean, did Castro
wade down off the beach in hip boots
in a long cursing line of other contestants, Cubans,
cabdrivers, pimps, restaurant waiters, small landowners,
and make his cast, the bobbin singing,
and the great fish leap, with a splash
leap from the smoky-green waves,
and he, tugging, writhing, bring it in
and stand there, mopping the brow
of his somehow fragile, Apollonian profile
while the great man panted back and forth
plying his tape measure?

And at the award ceremony,
did their two so-different sorts of fame—
yet tangent on the point of beards and love of exploit—
create in the air one of those eccentric electronic disturbances
to which our younger physicists devote so much thought?
In the photograph, there is some sign of it:
they seem beatified, and resemble
two apostles by Dürer, possibly Peter and Paul.

My mind sinks down through the layers of strangeness:
I am as happy as if I had opened
a copy of "Alice in Wonderland"
in which the heroine *does* win the croquet contest
administered by the Queen of Hearts.

Cosmic Gall

Every second, hundreds of billions of these neutrinos pass through each square inch of our bodies, coming from above during the day and from below at night, when the sun is shining on the other side of the earth!
—from "An Explanatory Statement on Elementary Particle Physics," by M. A. Ruderman and A. H. Rosenfeld, in *American Scientist*

Neutrinos, they are very small.
　　They have no charge and have no mass
And do not interact at all.
The earth is just a silly ball
　　To them, through which they simply pass,
Like dustmaids down a drafty hall
　　Or photons through a sheet of glass.
　　They snub the most exquisite gas,
Ignore the most substantial wall,
　　Cold-shoulder steel and sounding brass,
Insult the stallion in his stall,
　　And, scorning barriers of class,
Infiltrate you and me! Like tall
And painless guillotines, they fall
　　Down through our heads into the grass.
At night, they enter at Nepal
　　And pierce the lover and his lass
From underneath the bed—you call
　　It wonderful; I call it crass.

A Vision

*(After Being Heavily Drugged with Inhalations
of Literary Criticism, circa 1960)*

Said Harvey Swados to Herbert Gold,
"American Fiction has to be bold."
Said Leslie Fiedler to Seymour Krim,
"American Fiction ought to have vim."
Said Alfred Kazin to Lionel Trilling,
"American Fiction must become willing
To take the reader upon its knee
And criticize Society."
So saying, all took pen in hand
And scratched away to beat the band
And wrote these splendid works themselves
And then arranged them on the shelves,
Proud row on row, immutable ranks.
American Fiction wept, and gave thanks.

Les Saints Nouveaux

Proust, doing penance
in a cork-lined room,
numbered the petals
in the orchards of doom
and sighed through the vortex
of his own strained breath
the wonderfully abundant
perfume called Death.

Brancusi, an anchorite
among rough shapes,

blessed each with his eyes
until like grapes
they popped, releasing
kernels of motion
as patiently worked
as if by the ocean.

Cézanne, grave man,
pondered the scene
and saw it with passion
as orange and green,
and weighted his strokes
with days of decision,
and founded on apples
theologies of vision.

The Descent of Mr. Aldez

Mr. Aldez, a cloud physicist, came down last year to study
airborne ice crystals.
                    —dispatch from Antarctica in the *Times*

That cloud—ambiguous, not
a horse, or a whale, but what?—
comes down through the crystalline mist.
It is a physicist!

Like fog, on cat's feet, tiptoeing
to where the bits of ice are blowing,
it drifts, and eddies, and spies
its prey through vaporous eyes

and pounces! With billowing paws
the vague thing smokily claws

the fluttering air, notes its traits,
smiles knowingly, and dissipates.

Upon Learning That a Town Exists in Virginia Called Upperville

In Upperville, the upper crust
Say "Bottoms up!" from dawn to dusk
And "Ups-a-daisy, dear!" at will—
I want to live in Upperville.

One-upmanship is there the rule,
And children learn about, at school,
The Rise of Silas Lapham and
Why gravitation has been banned.

High hamlet, ho!—my mind's eye sees
Thy ruddy uplands, lofty trees,
Upsurging streams, and towering dogs;
There are no valleys, dumps, or bogs.

Depression never dares intrude
Upon thy sweet upswinging mood;
Downcast, long-fallen, let me go
To where the cattle never low.

I've always known there was a town
Just right for me; I'll settle down
And be uplifted all day long—
Fair Upperville, accept my song.

Recital

ROGER BOBO GIVES
RECITAL ON TUBA
—headline in *The New York Times*

Eskimos in Manitoba,
    Barracuda off Aruba,
Cock an ear when Roger Bobo
    Starts to solo on the tuba.

Men of every station—Pooh-Bah,
    Nabob, bozo, toff, and hobo—
Cry in unison, "Indubi-
    Tably, there is simply nobo-

Dy who oompahs on the tubo,
Solo, quite like Roger Bubo!"

I Missed His Book, but I Read His Name

"The Silver Pilgrimage," by M. Anantanarayanan . . . 160 pages.
Criterion. $3.95.
    —*The New York Times*

Though authors are a dreadful clan
To be avoided if you can,
I'd like to meet the Indian,
M. Anantanarayanan.

I picture him as short and tan.
We'd meet, perhaps, in Hindustan.

I'd say, with admirable *élan*,
"Ah, Anantanarayanan—

I've heard of you. The *Times* once ran
A notice on your novel, an
Unusual tale of God and Man."
And Anantanarayanan

Would seat me on a lush divan
And read his name—that sumptuous span
Of "a"s and "n"s more lovely than
"In Xanadu did Kubla Khan"—

Aloud to me all day. I plan
Henceforth to be an ardent fan
Of Anantanarayanan—
M. Anantanarayanan.

On the Inclusion of Miniature Dinosaurs
in Breakfast Cereal Boxes

A post-historic herbivore,
I come to breakfast looking for
A bite. Behind the box of Brex
I find *Tyrannosaurus rex*.

And lo! beyond the Sugar Pops,
An acetate *Triceratops*.
And here! across the Shredded Wheat,
The spoor of *Brontosaurus* feet.

Too unawake to dwell upon
A model of *Iguanodon*,
I hide within the Raisin Bran;
And thus begins the dawn of *Man*.

The High-Hearts

Assumption of erect posture in man lifts the heart higher above the ground
than in any other animal now living except the giraffe and the elephant.
—from an article titled "Anatomy" in the *Encyclopaedia Britannica*

Proud elephant, by accident of bulk,
Upreared the mammoth cardiacal hulk
That plunged his storm of blood through canvas veins.
Enthroned beneath his tusks, unseen, it reigns
In dark state, stoutly ribbed, suffused with doubt,
Where lions have to leap to seek it out.

Herbivorous giraffe, in dappled love
With green and sunstruck edibles above,
Yearned with his bones; in an aeon or so,
His glad heart left his ankles far below,
And there, where forelegs turn to throat, it trem-
Bles like a blossom halfway up a stem.

Poor man, an ape anxious to use his paws,
Became erect and held the pose because
His brain, developing beyond his ken,
Kept whispering, "The universe wants men."
So still he strains to keep his heart aloft,
Too high and low at once, too hard and soft.

Marriage Counsel

WHY MARRY OGRE
JUST TO GET HUBBY?
—headline in the Boston *Herald*

Why marry ogre
   Just to get hubby?
Has he a brogue, or
   Are his legs stubby?

Smokes he a stogie?
   Is he not sober?
Is he too logy
   And dull as a crowbar?

Tom, Dick, and Harry:
   Garrulous, greedy,
And grouchy. They vary
   From savage to seedy,

And, once wed, will parry
   To be set asunder.
O harpy, why marry
   Ogre? I wonder.

The Handkerchiefs of Khaibar Khan

Arriving for a Paris vacation with a wardrobe which included . . . 818 handkerchiefs . . . Iran's Khaibar Khan explained with disarming candor: "I was fortunate to be born in the middle of an area where oil comes from."

—Life

In Nishapur did Khaibar Khan
With stately ease exclaim *"Kerchoo!"*
And Standard Oil dispatched its man
With bales of linen to Iran
To minister unto his flu.
The prince allowed, "O lucky me,
To have been born above a sea
Where microörganisms died
By barrelfuls and so supplied
The engines of the fabled West
With fuel for which I take the fee
In handkerchiefs my valet crams
In chests and filing cabinets
In order of their monograms,
Which range from 'K' to 'K,' " said he,
With candor, quite disarmingly.

Dea ex Machina

In brief, shapeliness and smoothness of the flesh are desirable because they are signs of biological efficiency.

—David Angus, The New York Times Book Review

My love is like Mies van der Rohe's
    "Machine for living"; she,

Divested of her underclothes,
    Suggests efficiency.

Her supple shoulders call to mind
    A set of bevelled gears;
Her lower jaw has been aligned
    To hinge behind her ears.

Her hips, sweet ball-and-socket joints,
    Are padded to perfection;
Each knee, with its patella, points
    In just the right direction.

Her fingertips remind me of
    A digital computer;
She couldn't be, my well-tooled love,
    A millimeter cuter.

Die Neuen Heiligen

Kierkegaard, a
cripple and a Dane,
disdained to marry;
the consequent strain
unsprang the whirling
gay knives of his wits,
which slashed the Ideal
and himself to bits.

Kafka, a lawyer
and citizen of Prague,
became consumptive
in the metaphysic fog

and, coughing with laughter,
lampooned the sad state
that judged its defendants
all guilty of Fate.

Karl Barth, more healthy,
and married, and Swiss,
lived longer, yet took
small comfort from this;
Nein! he cried, rooting
in utter despair
the Credo that Culture
left up in the air.

Miss Moore at Assembly

(Based Finically upon an Item in The New York Times
*Describing Marianne Moore's Lecture Appearance before
the Students of a Brooklyn High School)*

A "chattering, gum-snapping audience"
   held rapt by poetess, hat
      tricorn, "gigantic white orchid
fluttering at her shoulder"—that
      suffices, in mid-
century, to tax one's fittingness's sense.

But why? . . . Birds heard Francis. Who else could come
   to Eastern District High School
      ("slum," "bubble-gum-snapping") and stand—
tobacco-eschewer but Bol-
      lingen Prize–winner—and
say, "I've always wanted to play a snare drum"?

White Dwarf

Discovery of the smallest known star in the universe was announced today. . . . The star is about one half the diameter of the moon.

—*The New York Times*

Welcome, welcome, little star!
I'm delighted that you are
Up in Heaven's vast extent,
No bigger than a continent.

Relatively minuscule,
Spinning like a penny spool,
Glinting like a polished spoon,
A kind of kindled demi-moon,

You offer cheer to tiny Man
'Mid galaxies Gargantuan—
A little pill in endless night,
An antidote to cosmic fright.

Exposure

Please do not tell me there is no voodoo,
For, if so, how then do you
Explain that a photograph of a head
Always tells if the person is living or dead?

Always. I have never known it to fail.
There is something misted in the eyes, something pale,
If not in the lips, then in the hair—
It is hard to put your finger on, but there.

A kind of third dimension settles in:
A blur, a kiss of otherness, a milky film.
If, while you hold a snapshot of Aunt Flo,
Her real heart stops, you will know.

Exposé

LE CHAMP MAGNÉTIQUE DE VÉNUS
EST EXTRÊMEMENT FAIBLE
—headline in *Le Monde*

Le Monde regrets it must report—
  In simple duty to the nation,
    And favoring no clique or faction—
    That Venus' powers of attraction,
When measured coolly, fall far short
  Of their much-vaunted reputation.

"Extrêmement"—harsh word, but, then,
  Le monde, it is a brutal planet,
    Unsentimental, unromantic.
    Though *faible* Venus may be frantic
At this dismissal, mundane men
  Have hearts of unmagnetic granite.

Released from her depleted spell,
  Where shall we iron filings gather?
    Stern Mars is cold, Uranus gassy,
    And Saturn hopelessly *déclassé;*
Perhaps our lodestone lies in Hell.
  I still am drawn to Venus, rather.

Farewell to the Shopping District of Antibes

Next week, alas, BOULANGERIE
Will bake *baguettes*, but not for me;
The windows will be filled, although
I'm gone, with brandy-laced *gâteaux*.

TABAC, impervious, will vend
Reynos to others who can spend
Trois francs (moins dix centimes) per pack—
Forget me not, *très cher* TABAC!

Grim BOIS & CHARBONS & MAZOUT
Will blacken someone else's suit,
And FLEURS will romance with the air
As if I never had been there.

ALIMENTATION won't grieve
As it continues, *sans* my leave,
To garland *oignons*, peddle *pommes*,
And stack *endives* till kingdom come.

La mer will wash up on the sand
Les poissons morts regardless, and
JOURNAUX will ask, though I'm away,
"UN AUTRE MARI POUR B.B.?"

Some Frenchmen

Monsieur Étienne de Silhouette*
  Was slim and uniformly black;
His profile was superb, and yet
  He vanished when he turned his back.

Humane and gaunt, precise and tall
  Loomed Docteur J. I. Guillotin;†
He had one tooth, diagonal
  And loose, which, when it fell, spelled *fin*.

André-Marie Ampère,‡ a spark,
  Would visit other people's homes
And gobble volts until the dark
  Was lit by his resisting ohms.

Another type, Daguerre (Louis),§
  In silver salts would soak his head,
Expose himself to light, and be
  Developed just in time for bed.

Too brassy, *tout* Paris agreed
  Of Adolph Sax,‖ who, Belgian-born,
With cone-shaped bore and single reed,
  Was always tooting his own horn.

*1709–1767.
†1738–1814.
‡1775–1836.
§1789–1851.
‖1814–1894

Sea Knell

Pulsating Tones in Ocean
Laid to Whale Heartbeats
—*The New York Times*

There is a rapture on the lonely shore,
There is society, where none intrudes,
By the deep sea, and music in its roar. . . .
—Byron

I wandered to the surfy marge
    To eavesdrop on the surge;
The ocean's pulse was slow and large
    And solemn as a dirge.

"Aha," mused I, "the beat of Time,
    Eternally sonorous,
Entombed forever in the brine,
    A fatal warning for us."

"Not so!" bespoke a jolly whale
    Who spouted into view.
"That pulsing merely proves I'm hale
    And hearty, matey, too!

"Rejoice, my lad—my health is sound,
    The very deeps attest!
It permeates the blue profound
    And makes the wavelets crest!"

With that, he plunged, in sheer excess
    Of spirits. On the shore,
I hearkened with an ear much less
    Byronic than before.

Vow

*(On Discovering Oneself Listed on the Back of a Concert
Program as a "Museum Friend of Early Music")*

May I forever a Muse-
Um Friend of Early Music be;
May I be never loath to thrill
When three-stringed rebecs thinly trill,
Or fail to have a lumpish throat
When crumhorns bleat their fuzzy note.
I'll often audit, with *ma femme*,
Duets of psaltery and shawm;
Cross-flutes of pre-Baroque design
Shall twit our eardrums as we dine,
And Slavic guslas will, forsooth,
In harsh conjunction with the crwth
(Which is a kind of Welsh vielle,
As all us Friends know very well),
Lull both of us to sleep. My love,
The keirnines (Irish harps) above
Tune diatonically, and lyres
Augment august celestial choirs
That plan to render, when we die,
"Lamento di Tristano" by
Anonymous. With holy din
Recorder angels will tune us in
When we have run our mortal race
From sopranino to contrabass.

The Amish

The Amish are a surly sect.
They paint their bulging barns with hex
Designs, pronounce a dialect
Of Deutsch, inbreed, and wink at sex.

They have no use for buttons, tea,
Life insurance, cigarettes,
Churches, liquor, Sea & Ski,
Public power, or regrets.

Believing motors undivine,
They bob behind a buggied horse
From Paradise to Brandywine,
From Bird-in-Hand to Intercourse.

They think the Devil drives a car
And wish Jehovah would revoke
The licensed fools who travel far
To gaze upon these simple folk.

The Naked Ape

(Following, Perhaps All Too Closely,
Desmond Morris's Anthropological Revelations)

The dinosaur died, and small
    Insectivores (how gruesome!) crawled
From bush to tree, from bug to bud,
    From spider-diet to forest fruit and nut,

Forming bioptic vision and
    The grasping hand.

These perfect monkeys then were faced
    With shrinking groves; the challenged race,
De-Edenized by glacial whim,
    Sent forth from its arboreal cradle him
Who engineered himself to run
    With deer and lion—

The "naked ape." Why naked? Well,
    Upon those meaty plains, that *veldt*
Of prey, as pell-mell they competed
    With cheetahs, hairy primates overheated;
Selection pressure, just though cruel,
    Favored the cool.

Unlikeliest of hunters, nude
    And weak and tardy to mature,
This ill-cast carnivore attacked,
    With weapons he invented, *in a pack*.
The tribe was born. To set men free,
    The family

Evolved; monogamy occurred.
    The female—sexually alert
Throughout the month, equipped to have
    Pronounced orgasms—perpetrated love.
The married state decreed its *lex*
    Privata: sex.

And Nature, pandering, bestowed
    On virgin ears erotic lobes
And hung on women hemispheres
    That imitate their once-attractive rears:

A social animal disarms
    With frontal charms.

All too erogenous, the ape
    To give his lusts a decent shape
Conceived the cocktail party, where
    Unmates refuse to touch each other's hair
And make small "grooming" talk instead
    Of going to bed.

He drowns his body scents in baths
    And if, in some conflux of paths,
He bumps another, says, "Excuse
    Me, *please.*" He suffers rashes and subdues
Aggressiveness by making fists
    And laundry lists,

Suspension bridges, aeroplanes,
    And charts that show biweekly gains
And losses. Noble animal!
    To try to lead on this terrestrial ball,
With grasping hand and saucy wife,
    The upright life.

The Origin of Laughter

(Again, after Desmond Morris)

Hunched in the dark beneath his mother's heart,
The fetus sleeps and listens; dropped into light,
He seeks to lean his ear against the breast
Where the known rhythm holds its secret pace.
Slowly, slowly, through blizzards of dozing,
A face is gathered, starting with the eyes—

At first, quite any face; two painted dots
On cardboard stir a responsive smile. Soon
No face but one will serve: the mother's,
A mist, a cloud that clearly understands.
She teases him, pretends to let him drop.
He wants to cry but knows that she is good.
Out of this sudden mix, this terror rimmed
With half-protective flesh, a laugh is born.

The Average Egyptian Faces Death

(Based upon an Article in Life*)*

Anubis, jackal-headed god
of mummification, will tenderly
eviscerate my corpse, oil it, salt it,
soothe it with unguent gods' tears and honey.

My soul will be a ba-bird,
a shadow, free to move in and out
of my muralled house,
though it's no pyramid.

In the court of Osiris the gods
will weigh my heart
for virtue; in the Field of Reeds
baboons worship Re,
and barley grows, and
beetle-headed Khepri, god of early morning,
infuses with gold the misted canals.

Atum the creator has set
a smoky partition in the midst of things,
but the Nile flows through;
death has no other name than *ankh*, life.

Painted Wives

Soot, house-dust, and tar didn't go far
With implacably bathing Madame Bonnard;
Her yellowish skin has immortally been
Turned mauve by the tints she was seen floating in.

Prim, pensive, and wan, Madame Cézanne
Posed with her purple-ish clothes oddly on;
Tipped slightly askew, and outlined in blue,
She seems to be hearing, "Stop moving, damn you!"

All lilac and cream and pink self-esteem,
Young Madame Renoir made the sheer daylight dream;
In boas of air, without underwear,
She smiles through the brushstrokes at someone still there.

Skyey Developments

The clouds within the Milky Way
May well be diamonds, proudly say
Astronomers at U. of C.
The atmospheres of two or three
"Cool stars" could concentrate and freeze
More ice than winks at Tiffany's.

The pulsars, lately found to beep
Six times or so a sec., still keep
Themselves invisible, but are,
Perhaps, a kind of neutron star
So dense a cubic inch would tip
The scales against a battleship.

The moon, the men who jumped it swear,
Is like a spheric sandbox where
A child has dabbled; gray and black
Were all the colors they brought back.
The mad things dreamt up in the sky
Discomfort our philosophy.

Courtesy Call

We again thank you for your esteemed order and now wish to advise you
that the clothes are awaiting the pleasure of your visit.
                                        —card from a London tailor

My clothes leaped up when I came in;
    My trousers cried, "Oh is it
Our own, our prince?" and split their pleats
    At the pleasure of my visit.

My jacket tried to dance with joy
    But lacked the legs; it screamed,
"Though our confusion is deplored,
    Your order is esteemed!"

"Dear clothes," I cooed, "at ease. Down, please.
    Adjust your warp and weft."
Said they, "We love you." I: "I know,
    I was advised," and left.

Business Acquaintances

They intimately know just how our fortune lies
And share the murmured code of mutual enterprise,
So when we meet at parties, like lovers out of bed,
We blush to know that nothing real is being said.

Seven New Ways
of Looking at the Moon

July 21, 1969

I

Man, am I sick
       of the moon.
We've turned it into one big
       television screen,
one more littered campsite,
one more high-school yearbook
       signed, "Lots of luck,
              Richard Nixon."

II

Still, seeing Armstrong's strong leg
float down in creepy silhouette
       that first stark second
       was worth sitting up for.
Then it got too real, and seemed
       a George Pal Puppettoon
       called "Men on the Moon,"
mocked up on a Ping-Pong table.

III

Never again will I think of Houston
as full of rich men in cowboy hats:
          it is full
of numbers that like to talk
          and cajole.
They say, "Neil, start gathering rocks now,"
and, "Buzz, about time to get back into
          your module."

IV

And how about little Luna
          snooping around
like a rusty private eye
          casing the motel
where we'd set up the tryst?

V

There was a backyard something
          that happened after
they put up the flag and laid out
the solar tinfoil and dug some holes.
          I had been there before,
playing marbles under a line of wash,
skinning my knees on the lack of grass.

VI

Since St. Paul filed his bulletins
standing headlines have been claiming
          SECOND COMING.
Now the type was broken up and used:
          MOON SEDUCING,

one "c" turned sideways as a "u."
Since no one came, we went.

VII

Well, I don't know. The media
have swamped the message, but anyway
  God bless the men.
  I loved the way they ran,
like bear-foot ghosts let out of school to say
that Death is probably O.K.
if all it means is being in the sky.
  Which answers why.

Upon Shaving Off One's Beard

The scissors cut the long-grown hair;
 The razor scrapes the remnant fuzz.
Small-jawed, weak-chinned, big-eyed, I stare
 At the forgotten boy I was.

The Cars in Caracas

The cars in Caracas
create a ruckukus,
a four-wheeled fracacas,
taxaxis and truckes.

Cacaphono-comic,
the tracaffic is farcic;
its weave leads the stomach
to turn Caracarsick.

Insomnia the Gem of the Ocean

Now when I lay me down to sleep
My waterbed says, "Gurgle gleep,"
And when I readjustment crave
It answers with a tidal wave
That lifts me like a bark canoe
Adrift in breakers off Peru.

Neap to my spring, ebb to my flow,
It turns my pulse to undertow,
It turns my thoughts to bubbles, it
Still undulates when I would quit;
Two bags of water, it and I
In restless sympathy here lie.

To a Waterbed

No Frog Prince ever had a pond
So faithful, murmurous, and fond.
Amniotically it sings
Of broken dreams and hidden springs,
Automatically it laves
My mind in secondary waves
That answer motions of my own,
However mild—my amnion.
Fond underbubble, warm and deep,
I love you so much I can't sleep.

The Jolly Greene Giant

Or is it more shocking . . . to be forced to consider that he may now be the largest of living English novelists?—Greene, the ambidextrous producer of "novels" and "entertainments"?
—Reynolds Price, in *The New York Times Book Review*

"You are large, Father Graham," the young fan opined,
    "And your corpus is bulky indeed;
Yet you pen 'entertainments' as thin as a rind—
    How do you so hugely succeed?"

"In my youth," said the writer, "I fasted on bile
    With lacings of Romanish rum;
Compounded each quarter, it swells all the while—
    Permit me to offer you some."

"Do you find," said the lad, "your Gargantuan girth
    Has impaired your professional finesse?
An author must calibrate Heaven and Earth
    To an eighth of an inch, I would guess."

"It is true," said the sage, "that my typing is rough,
    Though each key is as wide as a platter;
But the swattable critics hum wonderful stuff,
    And that is the heart of the matter!"

News from the Underworld

*(After Blinking One's Way Through "The Detection of
Neutral Weak Currents," in* Scientific American)

They haven't found the W
wee particle for carrying
the so-called "weak force" yet, but you
can bet they'll find some odder thing.

Neutrinos make a muon when
a proton, comin' through the rye,
hits in a burst of hadrons; then
eureka! γ splits from π

and scintillation counters say
that here a neutral lepton swerved.
Though parity has had its day,
the thing called "strangeness" is preserved.

Authors' Residences

(After Visiting Hartford)

Mark Twain's opinion was, he was entitled
  To live in style; his domicile entailed
Some seven servants, nineteen rooms, unbridled
    Fantasies by Tiffany
    That furnished hospitality
  With tons of stuff, until the funding failed.

The poet Wallace Stevens, less flamboyant,
  Resided in a whiter Hartford home,

As solid as his neighbors', slated, *voyant*
  For all its screening shrubs; from here
  He strolled to work, his life's plain beer
Topped up with Fancy's iridescent foam.

And I, I live (as if you care) in chambers
  That number two—in one I sleep, alone
Most nights, and in the other drudge; my labors
  Have brought me to a little space
  In Boston. Writers, know your place
Before it gets too modest to be known.

Sin City, D.C.

(As of Our Bicentennial Summer)

  Hays Says Ray Lies;
  Gravel Denies
  Gray Houseboat Orgy Tale;
  Gardner Claims Being Male
  No Safeguard Against
  Congressional Concupiscence;
  Ray Parlays Hays Lay
  Into Paperback Runaway.

Shaving Mirror

Among the Brobdingnagians Gulliver
complained of the pores, the follicles,
"with a mole here and there as broad as a trencher,
and hairs hanging from it thicker than pack-threads."

Swift hated everything's being so relative,
"so varified with spots, pimples, and freckles
that nothing could appear more nauseous";
but, hell, here we are, bad clay.

In this polished concavity mute enlargement
hovers on my skin like a flea-sized plane
surveying another earth, some solemn planet
hung long in space unknown, a furtive star.

Draw closer, visitor. These teeth
trumpet their craters; my lips are shores,
my eyes bloody lakes, the lashes alarming,
my whiskers like leafless trees—there is life!

"But the most hateful sight of all was the lice
crawling on their clothes"—an image echoed
by the king, who pronounces that men must "be
the most pernicious race of little odious

vermin that nature ever suffered to crawl
upon the surface of the earth." Hard words
from above. I say, the more there is
of me, the more there is to love.

Beyond all reproach, beyond readjustment,
among the corruptible heavenly bodies
I swim, eluding my measure, "my complexion
made up of several colors altogether disagreeable."

Self-Service

Always I wanted to do it myself
and envied the oily-handed boy
paid by the station to lift
the gun from its tall tin holster
and squeeze. That was power,
hi-octane or lo-, and now no-lead.

What feminism has done for some sisters
self-service has done for me.
The pulsing hose is mine, the numbers
race—the cents, the liquid tenths—
according to my pressure, mine!
I squeeze. This is power:

transparent horsepower, blood
of the sands, bane of the dollar,
soul-stuff; the nozzle might jump
from my grip, it appears to tremble
through its fumes. Myself,
I pinch off my share, and pay.

The Visions of Mackenzie King

*(Based, More Closely Than You Might Think, Upon
Articles in the Toronto* Globe and Mail)

I, William Lyon Mackenzie King,
age seventy-three in 1948,
Prime Minister of Canada for twenty-two years,
had visions, and as such recorded them,
though merer men might call them dreams.

In one I saw Hitler
sewing buttons on a bed quilt.
My interpretation: "a lesson in patience."

In another, Franklin Roosevelt
and I were in the home of a wealthy man,
unnamed. As we speculated
upon the means (suspect, somehow)
whereby our host had acquired his fortune,
I had to sit awkwardly upon the floor.
The meaning was clear: I should return
to "some simpler life."

In yet another, the then Princess
Juliana of the Netherlands
and her charming consort, Prince Bernhard,
came up to me ceremoniously;
I looked down and discovered
I was wearing an old-fashioned nightgown!
And, later in the dream, lacked trousers.
But no interpretation
was confided to my journal.

Mr. and Mrs. Winston Churchill
were at Laurier House, my guests; in my unease
I felt things amiss, and hastened
to offer the great man a drink and a cigar.
He had already helped himself to both.
My valet took a swig from the decanter
and in my rage I hit the presuming fellow
with a felt hat that had appeared in my hand.

I climbed a tower. There was room at the top.
But my valet, Nicol, informed me
a "private woman's club" had occupied the premises

and there could be no admission for me.
My conclusion: the summit of my calling
had been reached, but once there
I would not find the society of women
nor "what I had striven for most."

I, W. L. Mackenzie King,
recorded these visions now released
some thirty years later, as a species
of Canadian history. Now,
as then, I am embarrassed. Among
French dignitaries, my nose began to bleed.
My handkerchief was stained with blood!
"I tried to keep it discreetly out of sight."
Next, in a shadowy warehouse setting,
"furies" endeavored to assassinate me.
When I awoke at last, Gandhi was dead.

The world's blood pursued me. The great
ignored my *gaffes*. But truth will out.
The newspapers titter that I was insecure.
Shaving soap spoke to me, of Mother and dogs,
in those decades of demons of whom I was one.

Energy: A Villanelle

The logs give back, in burning, solar fire
  green leaves imbibed and processed one by one;
nothing is lost but, still, the cost grows higher.

The ocean's tons of tide, to turn, require
  no more than time and moon; it's cosmic fun.
The logs give back, in burning, solar fire.

All microörganisms must expire
  and quite a few became petroleum;
nothing is lost but, still, the cost grows higher.

The oil rigs in Bahrain imply a buyer
  who counts no cost, when all is said and done.
The logs give back, in burning, solar fire

but Good Gulf gives it faster; every tire
  is by the fiery heavens lightly spun.
Nothing is lost but, still, the cost grows higher.

So, guzzle gas!—the leaden night draws nigher
  when cinders mark where stood the blazing sun.
The logs give back, in burning, solar fire;
nothing is lost but, still, the cost grows higher.

On the Recently Minted
Hundred-Cent Piece

What have they done to our dollar, darling,
    And who is this Susan B.
Anthony in her tight collar, darling,
    Instead of Miss Liberty?

Why seems it the size of a quarter, dearie,
    Why is it infernally small?
To fit in the palm of a porter, dearie,
    As tip, though he mutter, "That's all?"

Who shrank it, our greenback and buck, beloved,
    And made it a plaything of tin?
Father Time, Uncle Sam, Lady Luck, beloved,
    Have done done our doll dollar in.

Typical Optical

In the days of my youth
   'Mid many a caper
I drew with my nose
   A mere inch from the paper;
But now that I'm older
   And of the elite
I find I can't focus
   Inside of two feet.

First pill-bottle labels
   And telephone books
Began to go under
   To my dirty looks;
Then want ads and box scores
   Succumbed to the plague
Of the bafflingly quite
   Unresolvably vague.

Old novels and poems
   By Proust and John Donne
Recede from my ken in
   Their eight-point Granjon;
Long, long in the lens
   My old eyeballs enfold
No print any finer
   Than sans-serif **bold.**

The Rockettes

Now when those girls, all thirty-six, go
to make their silky line, they do it slow,

so slow and with a smile—they know
we love it, we the audience. Our
breaths suck in with a gasp you hear
as their legs in casual unison
wave this way then, and that, and their top
hats tilt in one direction,
and their sharp feet twinkle like a starry row
as the pace picks up, and the lazy legs
(thirty-six, thirty-six, what a sex
to be limber and white and slender
and fat all at once, all at once!)
that seemed so calm go higher, higher
in the wonderful kicks, like the teeth
of a beast we have dreamed and are dreaming,
like the feathers all velvet together
of a violent contracting that pulls us in,
then lets us go, that pulls us in,
then lets us go; they smile because
they know we know they know we know.

Food

It is always there,
Man's *real* best friend.
It never bites back;
it is already dead.
It never tells us we are lousy lovers
or asks us for an interview.
It simply begs, *Take me;*
it cries out, *I'm yours.*
Mush me all up, it says;
Whatever is you, is pure.

The Sometime Sportsman
Greets the Spring

When winter's glaze is lifted from the greens,
And cups are freshly cut, and birdies sing,
Triumphantly the stifled golfer preens
In cleats and slacks once more, and checks his swing.

This year, he vows, his head will steady be,
His weight-shift smooth, his grip and stance ideal;
And so they are, until upon the tee
Befall the old contortions of the real.

So, too, the tennis-player, torpid from
Hibernal months of television sports,
Perfects his serve and feels his knees become
Sheer muscle in their unaccustomed shorts.

Right arm relaxed, the left controls the toss,
Which shall be high, so that the racket face
Shall at a certain angle sweep across
The floated sphere with gutty strings—an ace!

The mind's eye sees it all until upon
The courts of life the faulty way we played
In other summers rolls back with the sun.
Hope springs eternally, but spring hopes fade.

ZIP Code Ode

*To These Newly Abbreviated States, Including Puerto Rico,
the Virgin Islands, and the District of Columbia*

aMERICA, you caTNip bIN,
   OR DEn of iNJury,
iNVest your HINDMOst FLimfLAMS in
   PAID fARes to ALbaNY.

aCT COcKY, bUT beWAIL the trIAls
   of crAZed, uNHappy MAn.
diSDain arMTwisting; tricKS and WIles
   uNMAKe a GAMIng plan.

OH, shoWY land of SChemes NEwborn
(huMDinger uNCle, be adVIsed),
   i very VAguely want
to hyMN your harDCore, PRessurized,
loWValue rows of OK corn
   from TX to VT.

Déjà, Indeed

I sometimes fear that I shall never view
A French film lacking Gérard Depardieu.

Two Limericks for the Elderly

I.

A touchy old gent from Cohasset
Declared human contact no asset.
    Said he, "When I say
    'Noli tangere,' me
Is implicit but not, I hope, tacit!"

II.

There was an old poop from Poughkeepsie
Who tended at night to be tipsy.
    Said he, "My last steps
    Aren't propelled by just Schweppes!"—
That peppy old poop from Poughkeepsie.

Mites

A house-dust mite *(Dermatophagoides farinae)*
is not a house-mouse mite *(Liponyssoides sanguineus)*
any more than speaking Portuguese is speaking Manx
or an elephant is a hyrax, though both are ungulates.

To be a mite at all! To be so small
you can rest as in a bunk bed beneath a flea's scales,
or expend a lifetime in a single chicken feather
or the mite-pouch (acarinarium) of a carpenter bee!

To dwell happy in the mouth of a long-nosed bat,
like one species of Macronyssidae's protonymph,
causing tissue destruction and loss of teeth,
or beneath the skin of a mammal, creating mange!

Think how Nature slaved over these arrangements!
Thirty thousand species of acarines,
fifty from the Antarctic alone, and some found
five miles up Everest, or a mile down in the sea!

Itch mites, cheese mites, monkey-lung mites, each
making its way through the several larval stages
to an awkward copulation (discounting
parthenogenetic ticks) and easy death—

what fresh perspectives! Specks of our shed skin
delicious boulders, our human pores
lubricious dish-shaped living rooms, and particles
our largeness elides palpable to mites, who loom

in the scanning electron microscope's gray light
as many-tentacled, with chelicerae—
as hobbled as stegosaurs by their quaint
equipment, as endearing as baffled bears,

these mini-spiders characterized by
lack of a waist, lateral eyes, and tininess.
We marvel; we pity; we loathe; we try to forget
perspectives from which *we* are smaller yet.

An Open Letter to Voyager II

Dear Voyager:
            This is to thank you for
The last twelve years, and wishing you, what's more,
Well in your new career in vacant space.
When you next brush a star, the human race
Will be a layer of old sediment,
A wrinkle of the primates, a misspent

Youth of some zoömorphs. But you, your frail
Insectoid form, will skim the sparkling vale
Of the void practically forever. As
The frictionless light-years and -epochs pass,
The rigid constellations Earth admires
Will shift and rearrange their twinkling fires.
No tipped antenna-dish will strain to hear
Your whispered news, nor poet call you dear.

Ere then, let me assure you you've been grand.
A little shaky at the outset, and
Arthritic in the swivel-joints, antique
In circuitry, virtually deaf, and weak
As a refrigerator bulb, you kept
Those picture postcards coming. Signals crept
To Pasadena; there they were enhanced
Until those planets clear as daylight danced.
The stripes and swirls of Jupiter's slow boil,
Its crazy moons—one cracked, one fried in oil,
One glazed with ice, and one too raw to eat,
Still bubbling with the juice of inner heat—
Arrived on our astonished monitors.
Then, following a station break of years,
Fat Saturn rode your feeble beam, and lo!—
Not corny as we feared, but Art Deco—
The hard-edge, Technicolor rings; they spin
At different speeds, are merely meters thin,
And cast a flash-bulb's shadows. Planet three
Was Uranus (accented solemnly,
By anchormen, on the first syllable,
Lest viewers think the "your" too personal):
A glassy globe of gas upon its side,
Its nine faint braided rings at last descried,
Its corkscrew-shaped magnetic passions bared,
Its pocked attendants digitized and aired.
Last loomed, against the Oort Cloud, blue Neptune,

Its counterrevolutionary moon,
Its wispy arcs of rings and whitish streaks
Of unpredicted tempests—thermal freaks,
As if an unused backyard swimming pool,
Remote from stirring sunlight, dark and cool
(Sub-sub-sub-freezing), chose to make a splash.
Displays of splendid waste, of rounded trash!
Your looping miles of guided drift brought home
How fruitless cosmic space would be to roam.
One awful ball succeeds another, none
Fit for a shred or breath of life. Our lone
Delightful, verdant orb was primed to cede
The H_2O and O and N we need.
Your survey, in its scrupulous depiction,
Purged from the solar system science fiction—
No more Uranians or Io-ites,
Just Earthlings dreaming through their dewy nights.

You saw where we could not, and dared to go
Where we would be destroyed; you showed
A kind of metal courage, and faithfulness.
Your cryptic, ciphered, graven messages
Are for ourselves, designed to boomerang
Back like a prayer from where the angels sang,
That shining ancient blank encirclement.
Your voyage now outsoars mundane intent
And joins blind matter's motions. *Au revoir*,
You rickety free-falling man-made star!
Machines, like songs, belong to all. A man
Aloft is Russian or American,
But you aloft were simply sent by Man
At large.
              Sincerely yours,
                        A fan.

Classical Optical

The gray Graeae—
Deino, Enyo, Pemphredo—
shared one eye,
but boasted two
"ae"s—ae ae.
If ae's could see
those three Graeae
need not have grieved.

But ancient Greece
was heavily into
fate and tragedy,
not therapy;
even Tiresias's
sex-change operation was
permitted to
stall halfway through.

Neoteny

According to Webster's, "the condition
of having the period of immaturity indefinitely prolonged,
as in the axolotl." The axolotl?
Who invited this Mexican salamander
to the party? According to *The New York Times Magazine*,
neoteny is what we human beings share
with sheep and dogs, housecats and cattle—
the retention, that is, of childish trust and openness,
of "expectation of care and feeding,"
which drew us all together in domestication's epoch,
at the messy end of the Pleistocene—

all those glaciers, retreating and advancing
rather impetuously, as geology goes.

In that unsettled era, evolution favored
the late-developing, the infantile-tentative,
the experimentally wandering, the young-at-heart
neotenates, their characteristics not stodgily locked in.
Welcome, we said, in our ramshackle settlements,
to the waggle-tailed dog, all overeager helpfulness,
and the violet-eyed sheep, with no thought in its head
but *Feed me,* and the cow, thinking *Milk me*
and *Please fence me in.* Came the cunning kitty-cat,
mewing, only superficially aloof, not above it all
at all, but slyly grateful for a bed
of warm straw (the grasses and grains themselves
clamoring to be domesticated) in exchange for the catch
of an odd mouse or two, the mice themselves
in from the fields for a crash pad and a crumb.

Neotenates bumble about, mounting ewes not in heat
or even of their own species—this trait, too,
conducing to one big family, chomping as one, huddling,
shivering at the thought of the glaciers coming back.
In the horse's wide jelly of an eye, his rider
is just another horse, of another color.
O paradise of babes! The saber-toothed tiger, mature
to a fault, has joined the voluptuously hairy mammoth
in time's tarpit, while we, saying *goo-goo,*
saying *bow-wow* and *baa,* saying *moo* and *meow,*
go flocking down the chutes and corrals of the future,
all woolly and cozy and docile, ever trusting,
our trustingness vindicated, our populations exploding
while the untameable rhino runs vainly for cover
and the axolotl ("esteemed for food in Mexico,"
says Webster's) covets our loveableness.

Notes

4. **Ex–Basketball Player.** My only oft-anthologized poem. The second stanza receives footnotes in some textbooks, to explain that once upon a time a gasoline station might offer a variety of brands of gasoline, with the trade names identified on glass heads above the pumps, and that ESSO, predecessor of EXXON, was one of the brands. The crowdlike candies are behind the luncheonette counter, beyond reach.

7. **March: A Birthday Poem.** The child, in the event, came late: Elizabeth Pennington Updike was born in Oxford, England, early in the morning of April 1, 1955, the joke being on me. In the United States, it was still the last hours of March.

10. **Tao in the Yankee Stadium Bleachers.** I had taken along to the ball game a paperback copy of Arthur Waley's *Three Ways of Thought in Ancient China,* and peeked into it between innings.

14. **Mobile of Birds.** Perhaps the same mobile evoked in the short story "Toward Evening," which was brought home by the young New Yorker, Rafe, to his wife and infant daughter: "The mobile was not a success. Alice had expected a genuine Calder, made of beautiful polished woods, instead of seven rubber birds with celluloid wings, hung from a piece of coarse wire. Elizabeth wanted to put the birds in her mouth and showed no interest in, perhaps did not even see, their abstract swinging, quite unlike the rapt infant shown on the box."

15. **Shillington.** Written for the semicentennial celebration of my home town's incorporation in 1908, at the request of the late Charles J. Hemmig. Mr. Hemmig was a remarkable man, a loyal Shillingtonian for ninety years, who loomed large to our household, for as the supervising principal of the Shillington public schools he had considerable power over my schoolteacher father. My mother always thought that Mr. Hemmig, then a young principal, could have done more to ease her own initiation, in the mid-Twenties, into the world of teaching; she walked out of the classroom after a few hours, with lasting reverberations and self-recriminations. On the other hand, Mr. Hemmig sold my

grandfather the only shares of stock that held their value after the Crash, and he wrote a generous and shrewd letter, which my mother preserved, supporting my family's wild idea of sending me to Harvard. One of my earliest starts at a novel had Mr. Hemmig shadowily in mind, as the man in whose "interpretation everything was very relative"—a quote from Kierkegaard that I later attached to the historical figure of James Buchanan. I was pleased that he asked me.

Lines 14–16. Sizable spheres of artificial stone were ornaments quite common on the retaining walls of towns in eastern Pennsylvania.

15. **Suburban Madrigal.** Sitting in the first house I (et ux.) owned, 26 East Street, Ipswich, Massachusetts, waxing lyrical as I survey my domain.

16. **Telephone Poles,** lines 21–22. Based on my understanding that many telephone conversations are simultaneously transmitted over the wires and unscrambled at the end.

17. **Mosquito.** A number of correspondents informed me that only female mosquitoes "bite"; they need the sip of protein-rich blood to mature their eggs. Yet to make the pronoun "she" or "it" (I have tried it both ways) diminishes the music of the lines and falsifies the subjective experience. The mosquito felt, to the male poet as he lay there, like a male antagonist in the ominous bedroom dark. "It" ticks. "She" rather brutally sexualizes the encounter, and overloads the metaphor of "lover." I would omit the poem as hopelessly marred but for losing the last two, gender-free stanzas.

18. **Trees Eat Sunshine.** Cf. "Fever," page 28. A religious vision abetted, as is not infrequently the case, by illness.

18. **Winter Ocean.** Flavored by a translation I did soon after college, combining avian allusions in two Anglo-Saxon poems, "The Wanderer" and "The Seafarer":

> . . . Again the wretch wakens
> to sight dead-leaflike waves before him;
> sleet, frost, and hail, confused, fall;
> the sea-fowls bathe, broaden their feathers.
>
> Now in my heart-mood circles my thought,
> out of the breastlock, swings with the flood;
> over the whale-land widely it turns.
> Back to me comes my solitary soarer

greedy and screaming, urging the whale-path,
my heart irresistibly to the lakes of the sea.

19. **Seagulls.** My distinct memory is that I was pondering gulls while
lying on Crane Beach in Ipswich when the first stanza came over me
in a spasm of inspiration. Penless and paperless, I ran to the the site of
a recent beach fire and wrote in charcoal on a large piece of unburned
driftwood. Then I cumbersomely carried my improvised tablet home.
It must have been late in the beach season, and my final stanzas slow
to ripen, for the poem's completion is dated early December.

20. **Seven Stanzas at Easter.** Composed for a religious arts festival
sponsored by the Clifton Lutheran Church, of Marblehead, Massachusetts, which I sometimes attended. Norman Kretzmann was pastor.
Gratifyingly, the poem won first prize and has figured in a number of
neo-orthodox sermons.

22. **B.W.I.** Composed on the island of Anguilla, while lying on a dark
Edwardian sofa, where I wrote during our weeks of tropical sabbatical.
A brother effort, "Tropical Beetles," with its bouncier metrics, is con-
signed to Light Verse (page 308).

24. **Summer: West Side.** The 1960 date on this surprised me, the poem
so savors of my months of living at 126 Riverside Drive, just below
Eighty-fifth Street, late in 1955.

27. **The Solitary Pond.** "Route 11" in real life was Route 10, connect-
ing Morgantown and Reading. The memory was painful, and the poem
slow to find its way into print.

29. **Earthworm.** *The New Yorker* resisted the last stanza, though it held
the kernel of my philosophy. I acceded, reluctantly, to its omission,
while remaining greatly grateful for the encouragement, advice, and
checks received from Katharine S. White, Howard Moss, and Alice
Quinn, the magazine's poetry editors, all these years. One hundred
thirty-five times they said yes, by my calculations.

29–31. **Old-Fashioned Lightning Rod, Sunshine on Sandstone, The
Stunt Flier.** The three were jotted down in one brief June visit to my
parents in Pennsylvania, typed up on my mother's typewriter, mailed
off to *The New Yorker,* and—two out of the three—swiftly accepted.
Those were the days! And yet, the poetic evidence indicates, I was full
of aches and pains and unease. The past is paradise, but not when it is
the present.

31. **Calendar,** line 12. "Jay" used, not quite correctly, to mean most any

bird. Blue jays, of course, don't generally migrate. The genus is called *Garrulus*, and the English word may come from the same root as the French *gai*.

32. **The Short Days.** Light in form, but for me it holds, along with "Wash" and "Telephone Poles," a place and a time—the workaday East Street neighborhood where I lived with my growing family for thirteen years. As with "Summer: West Side," I thought it composed earlier than it evidently was.

33. **Movie House.** Written with the Strand Movie Theatre in Ipswich in mind, and with no premonition that, unlike the pyramids, it would be torn down—in 1985, to make way for a bank's expansion.

34–35. **Vibration/The Blessing.** This pairing, generated unforcedly by the chronology, makes in my mind a fragile pair of wings mirroring the duet "Flirt"/"Fever" of over two years before. Though I wasn't counting lines in those *vers-libre* days, they have thirteen lines each, one more than the earlier pair.

38–39. **Azores,** lines 9–16. "Shrilly" modifies "hail" and "pretty" modifies "hillsides." *Harper's*, in the January 1964 issue, printed the poem with a "the" inserted before "hillsides," which made havoc of the syntax but had made momentary sense to a tired copy editor.

40. **Erotic Epigrams.** Tristan and Iseult were much on my mind in this period; cf. the short story "Four Sides of One Story" in *The Music School* and "More Love in the Western World" in *Assorted Prose*.

44. **Nuda Natens,** first word. Originally "Marie."

Last word. The terminal "a" is not, as I once thought, a feminine ending but the plural of the singular *pudendum,* a neutral noun derived from *pudēre,* "to be ashamed," and usually plural, like the English term "genitals."

45. **Postcards from Soviet Cities,** Moscow, line 6. GUM: the great emporium on Red Square, an acronym for "Gosudarstvyenni Universalni Magazin" (State Universal Department Store).

48. **Camera.** The first quality camera I ever owned, it was, strange to say, Russian—called a Zenit and purchased with some of my excess rubles. The photographs it took had a romantic tint, a warm Slavic humanity, no Nikon since has matched.

50. **Décor.** The bar, with its Southern resonances, was, I believe, in Washington, D.C.

50. **Poem for a Far Land.** The susceptible poet homesick for the Soviet Union, in which he had spent a month, being made much of.

51. **Dog's Death.** The dog's name was Polly; she didn't live with us on East Street very long. Sometimes it seems the whole purpose of pets is to bring death into the house.

56. **Seal in Nature.** Seen off Martha's Vineyard in 1966, in one of our months of summer rental.

59. **Bath After Sailing.** Late in the next summer, with Professor Manfred Karnovsky staunch at the helm of his twenty-foot sloop, we sailed from Menemsha Harbor to a boatyard beyond Falmouth on a day that got stormier and stormier. There I was, pumping the bilge while trying not to fall off of what seemed a vertical deck; mountainous waves around us were mocked by the calm, towering apparition of the Martha's Vineyard ferry, serenely plying its route while we fought for our lives.

64–101. **Midpoint,** Canto I, line 155: ". . . the Hill of Life?" My mother saved the drawing; here it is:

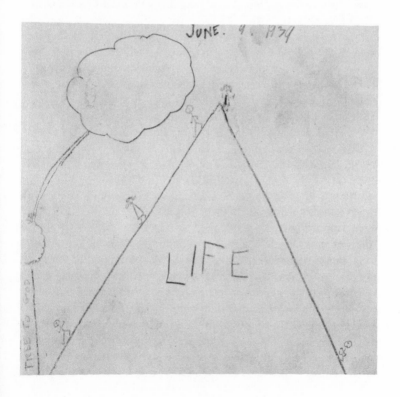

Line 174: ". . . still alive." My father died in April 1972, at the age of seventy-two; my mother in October 1989, at the age of eighty-five.

Line 181, "From *Time*'s grim cover . . ." Issue of April 26, 1968.

Canto II, page 75. The two fine-grained portraits appeared, top, in *The Register* for Harvard's freshman class and, bottom, four years later, in the yearbook for the graduating class. See "Apologies to Harvard," lines 34–38: ". . . And spit me out, by God, a gentleman."

Canto II, page 76, bottom. Two pictures of the same baby, the subject of "March: A Birthday Poem."

Canto III was closely based upon the September 1987 issue of *Scientific American*, devoted to "Materials."

In Canto IV, almost all of the quotations are from Walt Whitman's "Song of Myself." The prose "his eyes shut . . . eye in it" is from the last chapter of James Joyce's *Ulysses:* not Bloom (no foreskin) but Lieutenant Mulvey, on the rock of Gibraltar. The marginal quotation, "the ant's . . . world," is from Ezra Pound's *Cantos,* Canto LXXXI.

103. **Living with a Wife.** Composed, evidently, the year we lived in London, at 59 Cumberland Terrace, though the imagery is all-American—except, possibly, for the bathtub. My wife did much of our wash in it, the washing machine having never worked, though we were paying a princely rent.

110. **On an Island.** Tortola, in the British Virgins.

111. **Marching Through a Novel.** *Rabbit Redux,* in 1970.

112. **Night Flight, over Ocean.** The Pacific.

113. **Phenomena,** line 1. We had moved to 50 Labor-in-Vain Road, on a tidal inlet called Labor-in-Vain Creek.

116. **The House Growing.** The same ancestral Pennsylvania house as in "Sunshine on Sandstone" and "Old-Fashioned Lightning Rod," and the site of the pear tree in "Query."

116–20. **Cunts.** A strange poem to follow the lines on my father's death, but written eight months after, on the inspiration of the lewd flier amply quoted, and of the general sexual pressure of the times. *New York Quarterly* was good sport enough to publish it, and Frank Hallman was enthusiastic enough to bring it out in a limited edition (276 signed copies, 1974)—a handsome thin brown book, wider than it is tall, that has become by now, I believe, my highest-priced collector's item. Two friends have complained to me that their copies have been stolen from their shelves. No doubt it's the title people are stealing, and not the content, whose firmly moral inspiration is announced in the opening line.

120–5. **Apologies to Harvard.** Composed under the clear influence of L. E. Sissman, whose outburst of autobiographical verse, mostly blank, powered by the nearness of his death and a prodigious festive way with the English language, was to me the most impressive event in poetry in the 1960s. Ed's own Phi Beta Kappa poem, the beautiful "Temporary Measures," had been delivered two years earlier.

128–9. **Heading for Nandi.** When this appeared in *The New Yorker*, several letters protested that that place was called Nadi. But it was identified as Nandi in the Honolulu airport, and if it had been called Nadi I wouldn't have written the poem.

Line 22. Fayaway is Melville's lovely native companion in *Typee:* "the beauteous nymph Fayaway, who was my peculiar favourite. Her free pliant figure was the very perfection of female grace and beauty. Her complexion was a rich and mantling olive, and when watching the glow upon her cheeks I could almost swear that beneath the transparent medium there lurked the blushes of a faint vermilion. The face of this girl was a rounded oval, and each feature as perfectly formed as the heart or imagination of man could desire. Her full lips, when parted with a smile, disclosed teeth of a dazzling whiteness; and when her rosy mouth opened with a burst of merriment, they looked like the milk-white seeds of the 'arta,' a fruit of the valley, which, when cleft in twain, shows them reposing in rows on either side, embedded in the red and juicy pulp."

130–1. **Note to the Previous Tenants.** By the new tenant at 151 Beacon Street, where I lived for twenty months in the mid-1970s.

Line 18. There is some connection, it may be, between the "ideal woman" and the "deal" hoped for in the last line of the preceding poem, written three months before.

135. **Sunday in Boston,** line 9. A large equestrian statue of George Washington in the Public Garden, now restored to the brown tint of fresh bronze, was in those years weathered to a patina of pistachio-green.

Line 11. The spectacular Hancock Tower, presenting one of its broad glass sides in this direction, was credited to the architectural firm of I. M. Pei; Henry N. Cobb was its actual designer and—when its giant panes began to fall out—its defender against civic calls for a radical redesign.

135–6. **Raining in Magens Bay.** On the island of St. Thomas.

137–41. **Leaving Church Early,** lines 48–49. My dear grandmother, Katie Hoyer, in her seventies at this time, suffered from Parkinson's disease and often could not get her speech organs working. My mother called this poem "harsh," and now I see what she meant; an adolescent harshness is part of the picture.

Lines 98–99. The "incongruous painting," by Alice W. Davis in 1933, of the Provincetown dunes, now rests on my third floor, which has a view of the "unattainable sea." I wonder if the painting, our landlocked family's most precious work of art, got me to the New England shore.

141–2. **Another Dog's Death.** Helen, a golden retriever and family pet for many years.

149. **Spanish Sonnets,** VIII, line 2. In Spanish, Juana la Loca (1479–1555): the third child of Ferdinand and Isabella, she inherited the thrones of Castile (in 1504) and Aragon (in 1516) through the deaths of the precedent heirs and the ambitions of her husband, Philip the Handsome of Habsburg. After her husband's unexpected death in 1506, her mental imbalance passed into insanity, and in 1509 she retired to Tordesillas, where she lived in squalor, under guard, with the embalmed corpse of her husband. She was the mother of the Emperor Charles V.

Line 6. The able favorite of the inept John II of Castile, de Luna was executed in 1453, after thirty years of dominating the throne and directing its prerogatives toward his own aggrandizement. According to William H. Prescott's *History of the Reign of Ferdinand and Isabella,* "As he ascended the scaffold, he surveyed the apparatus of death with composure, and calmly submitted himself to the stroke of the executioner, who, in the savage style of the executions of that day, plunged his knife into the throat of his victim, and deliberately severed his head from his body." The king, who did not long outlive his favorite, would have countermanded the execution but for the steely insistence of his queen, Isabella, the granddaughter of the monarch of Portugal and the mother of the more famous Isabella. It had been de Luna, ironically, who had arranged the marriage, against John II's own inclination to marry a French princess.

151–2. **To Ed Sissman, I,** line 5. Josèph's, long-gone, was in the Seventies the premier eating-spot in Boston. The accented second syllable was part of its panache.

Line 14. Most of Sissman's witty and genial poetry was produced while he was struggling with Hodgkin's disease, which eventually killed him, in 1976, at the age of forty-eight.

156–8. **An Oddly Lovely Day Alone**, line 28. *The Coup* was up for it, as I remember. The calm day was typical of six years' worth spent at 58 West Main Street, Georgetown, Massachusetts—a red clapboard house that reminded me, in its long shape and comforting proximity to a busy street, of the first house of my life, 117 Philadelphia Avenue, in Shillington.

165–9. **The Moons of Jupiter.** Should this be classed as light verse, along with "Cosmic Gall," "The High-Hearts," "The Naked Ape," "Skyey Developments," and the not dissimilar "Open Letter to Voyager II"? Like these, "The Moons of Jupiter" derives from, to quote my own criterion, "the man-made world of information." But the poem also derives from the real, and brings back things seen and felt—the unjust parental slap, the sneering note passed hand to hand in a classroom, the punch given back to the ribs of the opposing body, the love of excrement, and the cosmic acrophobia of the last stanza.

Line 106, "enormity." Used in its preferred sense of, as Webster says, "a grave offense against order, right, or decency," with a pun upon its secondary, semi-literate, and increasingly common sense of "enormousness."

169. **Upon the Last Day of His Forty-Ninth Year.** That is, I was about to turn forty-nine and enter my fiftieth year. My fiftieth birthday was hedged with so much ceremony as to muffle the terror.

174–5. **Small-City People.** Inspired by Lawrence, Massachusetts, a city my occasional visits to have supplied urban furniture for the short story "More Stately Mansions" and the novel *Memories of the Ford Administration*. The poem "July" came to me in the stately park there. Lawrence reminds me of Reading, Pennsylvania, a city where I always feel excited and childlike.

182–3. **Aerie.** No sooner had this poem appeared in print, than the enchanted barbershop on a top floor of Massachusetts General Hospital vanished—one more amenity down the drain.

184–5. **The Code**, lines 19–24. Cf. "English Train Compartment," lines 12–21; "Sunday," lines 6–12; and "São Paulo," lines 14–15.

191–204. **Seven Odes to Seven Natural Processes,** *Ode to Rot,* lines 18–19. Richard Eberhardt's most celebrated poem, "The Groundhog."

Among its noble lines: "And in intellectual chains / I lost both love and loathing, / Mured up in the wall of wisdom."

To Evaporation, lines 9–10. From the article "Kinetic Theory of Matter" in the *Encyclopaedia Britannica,* 1969 edition.

Ode to Growth, line 35. From the article on "Growth" in the same invaluable source.

To Fragmentation, lines 40–41. Habakkuk 3:6.

Line 45. *Hamlet,* I.ii. Some editors have offered "sullied" as the word Shakespeare intended.

Ode to Entropy, line 33. William Philip Arthur Louis, son of Prince Charles and Princess Diana of the United Kingdom, born June 21, 1982. After Charles, he stands next in line to the British throne.

Lines 43–45. In *Deliverance to the Captives* (Harper & Brothers, 1961), page 41: "But to believe, to accept, to let it be true for us, to begin to live with this truth, to believe it not only with our minds and with our lips, but also with our hearts and with all our life . . . no human being has ever prayed for this in vain."

To Crystallization, lines 35–37. *Stendhal: On Love* (Anchor edition, 1957), page 324.

Ode to Healing, line 31. *Hamlet,* II.ii.

207–8. From Above. A distillation, this poem, of several poems composed high above the earth, gazing out of airplane windows at a level of global reality unseen until this century.

208–9. Somewhere. Actually, in the Malá Strana section of Prague, while sitting in a guest suite of the Petschek "palace," which since 1946 has been the American Ambassador's Residence. William Luers, who had previously sheltered me on State Department–related trips to the Soviet Union and Venezuela, was my host.

210. Klimt and Schiele Confront the Cunt. After viewing the Vienna Show at the Centre Georges Pompidou in Paris in 1986, a show that included some meticulous watercolors by Adolf Hitler.

211–2. Returning Native, line 13. Greenbrier (genus *Smilax*) is also called catbrier, for its anxious small claws. Cf. "The Solitary Pond," lines 7 and 12.

213. Goodbye, Göteborg, line 7. In this civilized country, a bell dings when the light is green, signalling to the blind that it is safe to cross.

220–1. In Memoriam Felis Felis, line 37. A bit of poetic license: "spice" conceived as the plural of "spouse."

Line 38. Not "alcoholic angels," as the editor made it when this poem appeared in *Grand Street:* the sense is "alcoholics [whom] angels copulating," etc.

224. **Seattle Uplift,** line 7. An irrational fear, of course. See "The Moons of Jupiter," lines 104–8.

Lines 12–14. For the frustrated satisfactions, see "In Memoriam Felis Felis," lines 11–14, 42–48.

231. **Generic College,** line 2. The epaulettes offer a clue to the specific college; few such institutions save Washington and Lee could claim a military man as a "founder"—though Lee might be better described as a resuscitator.

243–4. **Fly.** Written in the winter of 1991, during the heavy-bombing phase of the Gulf War.

245–6. **July,** lines 4–12. Perhaps these lines make full sense only to those few of us who remember the summer baseball games at the Shillington playground field in the Thirties and Forties, with soft drinks being sold for a nickel from a zinc-lined cooler there in the shade of the wild cherry trees. The trees were not shapely and Japanese but tall and scraggly; children climbed them. The bolder they were, the higher they went, the girls rewarding timid boys on the ground with a glimpse of their underpants.

248. **Literary Dublin,** lines 3–4. An invented name, unlike the others.

Light Verse

257. **Mountain Impasse.** Composed in college. Included at the urging of Rodney Dennis, who claimed to like the poem above all others of mine. Heaven forbid that anyone buying this book would not find in it a favorite.

258. **Duet, with Muffled Brake Drums.** From this poem's acceptance by *The New Yorker* in June of 1954 I date my life as a professional writer. The concluding triple rhyme and final hexameter are devices I had noticed in Dryden.

259. **Player Piano.** To the tune of "The Isle of Capri." The rhythm came over me compulsively, I remember, on Star Island, off the New Hampshire coast.

263. **Shipbored.** An allusion to the writing of this poem can be found in my short story "The Blessed Man of Boston, My Grandmother's Thimble, and Fanning Island" *(Pigeon Feathers,* 1962).

264. **The Clan.** Celebrities all, as of 1954. The end-of-the-line punctuation has been adjusted repeatedly.

264. **Youth's Progress.** Epigraph from the overseas *Life*, which, to a young American in England, brimmed with native magic.

265. **Humanities Course.** Professor Varder is the personification of Harvard College, I suppose. I resented the way that humanistic knowledge nibbled away at my Christian faith, but, then, did not knowledge—in the form, first, of the high regard in which the Middle Ages were held in the academic fashions of the early Fifties—help me to keep my faith, as well? I used to go to the Lutheran church just down the street from Lowell House, and successfully courted a Unitarian minister's daughter.

270–1. **Superman.** Written before Super Bowls (on Super Sundays) existed, or superdelegates.

271–3. **An Ode.** The editorial appeared in the issue of September 12, 1955. The first quotation is considerably abridged, from the florid following: ". . . unparalleled prosperity. It has gone further than any other society in the history of man toward creating a truly classless society. Yet it is still producing a literature which sounds sometimes as if it were written by an unemployed homosexual living in a packing-box shanty on the city dump while awaiting admission to the county poorhouse."

274–5. **A Bitter Life**, lines 6–14. *Hap*: Apis, the bull-god of Egypt, a reincarnation of Osiris. *Garuda*: a man-bird, the steed of Vishnu; Hindu. *Italapas*: coyote, one of chief Chinook Indian deities. *Seb*: otherwise Geb, Keb, or Qeb, a divine goose; Egyptian. *Hua-hu Tiao*: a protean creature, snake or white rat, with the power to assume the shape of a man-eating winged elephant, etc.; Chinese. *Gulltopr*: also Goldropf; in Teutonic legend, Heimdall's horse. *Quetzalcoatl*: the name means "serpent dressed with green feathers," though he was, of course, an anthropomorphic Aztec god. *Kukulkan*: another feathered serpent, Maya this time. *Onniont*: a monster snake worshipped by the Huron Indians. Audhumbla: a cow who nourished Ymir, the first giant; both sprang from the mist, in Norse legend. *Ix*: one of the four Bacabs, who stood at the four corners of the world and held it up; Maya. *Geryon*: the son of Chrysaor and Callirrhoë, he lived on Erytheia and possessed three heads, three bodies, and enormous wings; Greek. *666*: the beast of Revelation 13. *The ox Ahura Mazda made*: a raging, senseless creature; the first creative effort in the animal line formed by the

Persian Lord of Wisdom. *Fomors*: hideous misshapen monsters representing the kingdom of darkness; Celtic. *Deevs*: Persian evil spirits, huge and ugly, sporting long horns and fangs. *Graeae*: sisters to the Gorgons, they had only one tooth and one eye among them; Greek (see "Classical Optical," page 356).

275. **A Wooden Darning Egg.** The first line of this quaint poem contributed the title of my first collection; it was my first book, and never since have I struggled so for a title. I found among my papers of the time one inscribed CELERY HEARTS, above this quotation: ". . . the pleasure given me as a child by that dainty white tree in the heart of the celery, tender and moist, that must grow first, before the necessities of growth force the plant to put up coarse and stringy shields; seemingly infrangible, until one bites the leafy top, and discovers in the trunk an intricacy of interlocking moons." Never quite satisfied with *The Carpentered Hen*, I asked that the British edition, by Victor Gollancz, be titled *Hoping for a Hoopoe*.

276–7. **Publius Vergilius Maro, the Madison Avenue Hick.** After Edgar Lee Guest's once-celebrated poem "Home," whose most famous line is remembered as "It takes a heap o' living to make a house a home." Actually, it runs, "It takes a heap o' livin' in a house t' make it home," and is followed by, "A heap o' sun an' shadder, an' ye sometimes have t' roam / Afore ye really 'preciate the things ye lef' behind, / An' hunger fer 'em somehow, with 'em allus on yer mind."

279–80. **Room 28.** Though the manuscript is firmly dated nine months after my return from England, I must have taken notes on the contents of this exhibition room, as of 1955. It has long since been rearranged.

286. **Popular Revivals 1956,** line 16. That is, *The Last Hunt*, with Stewart Granger, Robert Taylor, Debra Paget, and Lloyd Nolan (M-G-M, Eastmancolor CinemaScope).

The second pair of lines in the second stanza represent, I suppose, a crest of verbal ingenuity from which I could only decline.

288–9. **A Rack of Paperbacks.** When they were a novelty, fresh as spring flowers in the bookstores of Harvard Square and Greenwich Village. Those first charming Anchors, with their covers all by Edward Gorey! Everyman's for the Silent Generation!

292. **Planting a Mailbox.** This poem signals the move, in early April of 1957, from 153 West Thirteenth Street, New York City, to Ipswich, Massachusetts. The box was planted at the corner of Essex and Heartbreak Roads.

295–6. **The Menagerie at Versailles in 1775.** A "found" poem; this passage may be located, in prose and punctuated a bit differently, on pages 555–56 of the Modern Library Giant edition of Boswell's *Life of Samuel Johnson*.

301. **Deities and Beasts.** All rockets and missiles, in the Cold-War springtide of the late Fifties.

309. **Agatha Christie and Beatrix Potter,** line 13. Originally read, "God bless you, girls," which has become very politically incorrect, though at the time it seemed harmless.

316. **Upon Learning That a Town Exists in Virginia Called Upperville.** The humor of it considerably depended upon my name following the final line, in staid *New Yorker* fashion.

317–8. **I Missed His Book, but I Read His Name.** Written as if the name were pronounced iambically, *Anantanarayanan.* An Indian in an audience before which I had read these verses came up afterwards and very politely told me that it is pronounced A*nan*tana*ra*yanan, dactylically, the last syllable scarcely audible and certainly unfit to bear all my thumping rhymes. I will never read the poem aloud again, but here it is, as an offering for the eye.

324–5. **Exposure.** A souvenir of my one academic stint. In the summer of 1962, the office of the English Department at Harvard, in Warren House, had acquired a brand-new IBM Selectric, with its magical twirling alphabet ball. Testing my prerogatives as a summer-school teacher of creative writing, I sat down at the department's marvellous new machine and typed this poem on it. The poem had come into my head while I was driving into Cambridge, and I had scrawled it on the back of a tune-up receipt. The presence of "Aunt Flo" consigns it to the light-verse category.

339. **Insomnia the Gem of the Ocean** and **To a Waterbed.** The waterbed inspiration, intended for one poem, split, like a watery amoeba, into two.

342. **Authors' Residences,** lines 14–17. See "Note to the Previous Tenants": same place, the only place, strange to say, where I have ever lived alone, without progenitors, roommates, spouses, dependents, or pets. The high point of my tenancy was reached the winter night when I forgot my key and, with the compliance of the two bachelor girls in the apartment above, climbed out on the dizzyingly rickety fire escape

and—while other tenants of the building, mistaking me for a cat burglar, screamed with alarm behind their locked windows—crept along and down to my own window, which was unlocked. The sublime moment of dropping like an intruder into the welcoming space of one's own habitual existence: it's enough to make one believe in the transmigration of souls.

342. **Sin City, D.C.** Scorn not as contemptibly trivial these verses' crystallized inkling that some valuable secret lurks beneath a confluence of headline names. Other men look for a mysterious pattern in prime numbers or the extended digits of pi. At the height of our national discontent in 1968, I wrote:

> Poor people's march, Rustin quit it;
> In Boston, Raskin was acquitted.
> In Washington, Rusk took the rostrum
> To swear that Rostow has the nostrum;
> Reston writes about it all—
> > Black Power,
> > the Resistance,
> > the Red Menace.
> Ruskin wrote *The Stones of Venice.*

344. **Self-Service.** Marking the late-Seventies moment, long dissolved in history's shimmering vapors, when self-service gasoline pumps were a novelty.

346–7. **Energy: A Villanelle.** More gasoline. We were obsessed with it, evidently, back in the Carter era.

347. **On the Recently Minted Hundred-Cent Piece.** Our "doll dollar" was issued only in 1979, done in by public repudiation. The silver half-dollar, another vanished coin, used to be roundly called a "fifty-cent piece."

350. **The Sometime Sportsman Greets the Spring.** Like "Island Sun," written because *The New York Times* asked me for a seasonal poem. Not the best reason to write a poem, but not the worst, either.

351. **ZIP Code Ode.** My own idea, strangely. I am still waiting for a sign of gratitude from the Postmaster General.

351. **Déjà, Indeed,** line 2. Or, one could say, *Un film français sans Gérard Depardieu.* An earlier version went on,

And if by happy chance I do, I swear
The screen will swell with Isabelle Huppert.

But I felt less strongly, finally, about her *ubiquité*.

352. **Two Limericks for the Elderly.** Elicited by *The New York Times Book Review*, in honor of Edward Lear's one-hundred-sixty-fifth birthday. The second one, in repeating the first line for the fifth, is more classically Learesque. The best limericks, for this celebration, came from X. J. Kennedy, I must admit.

353–5. **An Open Letter to Voyager II.** This time, *Life* asked. The Voyager duo and their photographs had already figured in my poetry; lines 24–28 here were prefigured by "The Moons of Jupiter."

Appendix A:

Poems in Previous Collections Omitted

Bestiary (7/21/60, *TP*)
Cheerful Alphabet of Pleasant Objects, A (8/21/57, *CH*)
Head of a Girl, at the Met (4/1/84, *FN*)
Lament of Abrashka Tertz, The (1/66, *FN*)
Light-Headed in Sweden (11/77, *FN*)
Love Sonnet (1969?, *M*)
Ode III.ii: Horace (4?/54, *CH*)
Poetess (*p.* 9/53, *CH*)
Population of Argentina, The (*p.* 2/53, *CH*)
Pussy (10/16/75, *T&T*)
Recitative for Sorely Tested Products (11/11/54, *CH*)

Appendix B:

Poems Published in The New Yorker *Omitted*

Jack (*p.* 10/19/57)
Old Copy Desk Editor (*p.* 7/20/57)
O Leo Leddi (*p.* 6/1/57)
Quilt: A Patriotic Lullaby [Quilt] (*p.* 11/16/57)
Reflection [Mirror] (*p.* 11/30/57)
Solid Comfort [Easy Chair] (*p.* 2/18/56)
Title (*p.* 1/31/59)

Index of Titles

Each title is followed by its date of composition. An exact date generally indicates the day of dispatch, when the poem was thought fit to be sent off to a magazine for submission, as duly noted in the upper right corner of my retained copy. Later revisions do not change this notation. In the absence of clues provided by manuscript, memory, or editorial communication, the periodical publication date is given, signified by *p*. I thank Elizabeth Falsey and Deborah Garrison for helping my search. Previous collections are abbreviated as follows:

CH = *The Carpentered Hen and Other Tame Creatures* (Harper and Brothers, 1958; reissued, with some revisions, by Alfred A. Knopf in 1982)
TP = *Telephone Poles and Other Poems* (Knopf, 1963)
M = *Midpoint and Other Poems* (Knopf, 1969)
T&T = *Tossing and Turning: Poems* (Knopf, 1977)
FN = *Facing Nature: Poems* (Knopf, 1985)
U = previously uncollected

A Note About the Author

John Updike was born in 1932, in Shillington, Pennsylvania, in the home of his maternal grandparents. His father was a high-school mathematics teacher. Graduated from Harvard College in 1954, Updike spent a year in England on the Knox Fellowship, at the Ruskin School of Drawing and Fine Art in Oxford. From 1955 to 1957, he was a member of the staff of *The New Yorker,* to which he has contributed poems, short stories, and book reviews. Since 1957, he has lived in Massachusetts. He is the father of four children, grandfather of three boys, and the author of fifteen novels, along with twenty-some other titles, including five previous collections of poetry.

A Note on the Type

The text of this book was set in a digitized version of Janson, a typeface long thought to have been made by the Dutchman Anton Janson, who was a practicing type founder in Leipzig during the years 1668–1687. However, it has been conclusively demonstrated that these types are actually the work of Nicholas Kis (1650–1702), a Hungarian, who most probably learned his trade from the master Dutch type founder Dirk Voskens. The type is an excellent example of the influential and sturdy Dutch types that prevailed in England up to the time William Caslon developed his own incomparable designs from them.

Composed, printed, and bound by
The Haddon Craftsmen, Inc.,
Scranton, Pennsylvania